VOID

Library of
Davidson College

The Character of Beauty in the Victorian Novel

Nineteenth-Century Studies

Juliet McMaster, Series Editor
University Professor
University of Alberta

Consulting Editor:

James Kincaid
Professor of English
University of Colorado, Boulder

Other Titles in This Series

Tennyson and Personification: *The Rhetoric of "Tithonus"*	Daniel A. Harris
A Pre-Raphaelite Friendship: *The Correspondence of William Holman Hunt and John Lucas Tupper*	James H. Coombs et al., eds.
Murder and Moral Decay in Victorian Popular Literature	Beth Kalikoff
Carlyle's Life of John Sterling: *A Study in Victorian Biography*	Robert Keith Miller
Victorian Word Painting and Narrative: *Toward a Blending of Genres*	Rhoda L. Flaxman

The Character of Beauty in the Victorian Novel

by
Lori Hope Lefkovitz

Ann Arbor, Michigan

823.09
L493c

Copyright © 1987, 1984
Lori Hope Lefkovitz
All rights reserved

Produced and distributed by
UMI Research Press
an imprint of
University Microfilms, Inc.
Ann Arbor, Michigan 48106

Library of Congress Cataloging in Publication Data

Lefkovitz, Lori Hope, 1956-
 The character of beauty in the Victorian novel.

  (Nineteenth-century studies)
  Revision of thesis (Ph.D.)—Brown University, 1984.
  Bibliography: p.
  Includes index.
  1. English fiction—19th century—History and
criticism.   2. Beauty, Personal, in literature.
3. Characters and characteristics in literature.
4. Heroes in literature.   5. Heroines in literature.
6. Values in literature.   I. Title.   II. Series:
Nineteenth-century studies (Ann Arbor, Mich.)
PR878.B4L5   1987   823'.8'09353   86-24927
ISBN 0-8357-1755-0 (alk. paper)

88-9647

*For my parents,
Rudy and Lola Lefkovitz,
with love*

Contents

Acknowledgments *ix*

1 Introduction: A Book by Its Cover *1*
   "The Algonquin Cinderella"

2 The Eye of the Beholder: Reader as Spectator *9*

3 The Bodies and Spirits of the Age: Competing
   Categories of Value in Nineteenth-Century England *21*
   Art and Nature
   Nature and Nurture
   Delicacy and Health: Pygmalion's Galatea and Little Nell

4 Shaping the Body to Fit the Eye: Austen's *Persuasion*
   as a Romantic Cinderella *43*

5 Charm: The Nature of Art *59*
   Beginning with the Beginning of *Middlemarch*
   Mothers and Harlots, Bedrooms and Battlefields: Hebrew
      Scriptures and Midrash
   Spenser's Una and Duessa; Milton's Dalila
   The Bequest of the Jewel Box: Scott's *Ivanhoe*
   Thackeray's Rebeccas
   Concluding *Middlemarch*
   Jewel Caskets after *Middlemarch*
   The Future of an Allusion

6 Grace: The Birth of Breeding *115*
   Male Beauty Contests: *Daphnis and Chloe* and
      Wuthering Heights

The Wild Boy of Aveyron: Itard's Diary and Shattuck's
  The Forbidden Experiment
Coats and Tales: Joseph in Hebrew Scriptures, Midrash, and Koran
Joseph and Daphis: Fielding's *Joseph Andrews*
Beauty in the Beast: *Wuthering Heights*
Wild in the Third Story: *Jane Eyre*
Foundling of Low Birth: *Great Expectations*

7 Delicacy: The Flower of Health   157
   Delicate Beauty Goes Out: George Eliot's *Adam Bede*
   Lilies Exposed: Dinah and Susanna in Hebrew Scriptures,
     Apocrypha, and Midrash
   Crimson Rose: Hetty Sorrel
   Scarlet Rose: Hester Prynne
   Lily is Rose: Dinah and Hetty
   The Certain Beauty of Health: Gissing's *The Odd Women*
   The Delicacy of Health: Hardy's *Jude the Obscure*

8 Conclusions: Beauty beyond Description   201
   Beast in the Beauty: *The Picture of Dorian Gray*
   Arrowy Nose in Short Tense Flight, Eyes like Drenched
     Violets: Woolf's *Orlando*

Notes   217

Bibliography   233

Index   241

Acknowledgments

First thanks are due to Robert Scholes, Roger B. Henkle, and Mark Spilka, each of whom commented generously and instrumentally on drafts of this manuscript, making it more correct and informed than it would otherwise have been. Among their distinctive responses I was able to locate my subject. As directors of my graduate education, Roger Henkle and Robert Scholes provided me with invaluable training, encouragement, and friendship.

I also wish to thank my teachers, colleagues, and students at Brown University and Queens College, CUNY for being willing and challenging audiences. The friends with whom I discussed my subject in classrooms and living rooms far and wide are too numerous to name, but I am especially grateful to Nancy Comley, Susan Katz, George P. Landow, Thais Morgan, Freddie Rokem, and Claire Rosenfield for significant help at various stages of my work. Although they are free of direct connection to this project, I remain sensible to the early influences on my thinking of Philip Fisher, Allen Grossman, Karen Milk Klein, and Theodore Harris. I warmly appreciate James Kincaid's advice and enthusiasm, and for such assistance as made this book materialize.

More personally, my parents and my husband's parents have lent extraordinary support to me and this project. Memories of my grandparents, Samuel and Mala Weinstein, and their interest in the progress of this work often provided essential motivation.

Marcy Rachel Lefkovitz kept improving my text as she labored with the repeated critical attention that one rarely devotes to the work of another. I thank her for her sustaining cheer and intelligence.

Finally, Leonard Gordon pursued his own scholarship with beauty on his mind. Each of these pages contains fruit of that loyalty. I thank him too for the unfailing criticism, the lively conversations, the added perspectives, and the many and various comforts that make all the difference but that I have long learned to take for granted.

1

Introduction: A Book by Its Cover

Victorian fiction is rich in physical description, and heroes and heroines, who are usually the most fully described characters in a novel, invariably develop into standards of beauty.[1] This book considers how physical description functions as a strategy of characterization in the realist novel and how descriptions of beauty translate the essential values of a text into a visual aesthetic. Important social implications emerge: in the descriptions of heroes and heroines, novelists promote those cultural values that the idealized figures embody, and description is a significant way in which sexual difference is encoded in literature and enforced by society. Because the rhetoric of description refers the reader to earlier ideals in the literary tradition, my analyses of Victorian texts rest upon analyses of earlier literature, demonstrating how the novelist's rhetorical choices reflect prevailing attitudes towards the past.

Readers have not suspected these powers of description because we have actually been trained to ignore descriptions of beauty; accordingly, we rarely interpret them as vehicles for meaning or as aspects of characterization. From Aristotle's dictum that "character is action" through contemporary critical theory, character has consistently been defined with respect to plot. Although we may speak of "acting out of character," action has been thought to constitute the human subject. Rhetorical studies associate characterization with verbs rather than adjectives. By these emphases we have learned to regard description as one of the excesses of realism, important for its literal rather than its figurative meaning. Even as literary theory calls mimesis into question and "the representation of reality" yields to "the-effect-of-the-real," description is still thought of as a kind of textual "static" that fills up the narrative world but does not contribute to that world's meaning.[2] Often subconsciously produced, descriptive language has thus been presumed innocent and has been allowed to operate on the level of the reader's subconscious. Nothing that operates on the level of the subconscious should be presumed innocent.

The implications of a hierarchy that subordinates description to action have begun to be examined in recent theories of description, and art historians are now reassessing the position of non-narrative visual art.[3] While few explore how descriptive imagery may codify (or create) not only realism but reality itself, in *Word and Image: French Painting of the Ancien Régime,* Norman Bryson does call "optical truth" into question. He writes: "It is clear that the term 'realism' cannot draw its validity from any absolute conception of 'the real', because that conception cannot account for the historical and changing character of 'the real' within differing cultures and periods."[4] Bryson demonstrates that when we study realistic images in visual art, what we can discover is how a culture imagines its own reality, what *it recognizes* as the real. My work begins from Bryson's premise but is equally predicated on the differences between visual and verbal description. Significantly, physical descriptions of beautiful characters often will *not* visualize.

Ideals of beauty, which so obviously change to accommodate the values particular to a time and place, also show us how a culture imagines its own reality, but the language of such descriptions shows us reality in all of its contradiction. Descriptions of beauty often will not translate into visual images because beauty's ineffable character is expressed through subtle contradiction. Unlike other appearances that literature describes, beauty is especially elusive, as descriptions of beauty, like the workings of a dream, are overdetermined.

Beauty, as a subject of investigation, has been comparably elusive. Because ideals of beauty do change, aesthetics, the traditional science of beauty, has had to proclaim everything and its opposite. We will see that while aesthetics has futilely looked for the natural, unchanging laws of the naturally beautiful, beauty is culturally determined and culturally variable.[5] Beauty is always a matter of culture, though it masquerades as nature. The following chapters elaborate upon this claim and explore its various consequences for reading literature, theorizing about texts, and seeing women and men in the world.

The cliché has it that "beauty is in the eye of the beholder," a truism that suggests our belief in the subjective character of aesthetic appreciation. Beauty is indeed in the eye of the beholder, but the beholder is a controlled subject. Physical description participates in that control by training the eyes of the spectator. In description we find values and the self that fiction would mold us into becoming. It is a divided self.

"The Algonquin Cinderella"

To introduce this consideration of beauty in fiction, I reprint a special version of an old and familiar plot. Idries Shah prefaces "The Algonquin Cinderella" by remarking upon the extraordinary number of "Cinderella-type" stories found all over the globe.⁶ This narrative paradigm offers satisfying reversals that correct injustice, and the story's cultural ubiquity testifies to its responsiveness to basic human situations. As such, the Cinderella plot has often been subjected to analysis.

I want to look at it too, but with an eye towards characterization rather than plot, paying attention to this version's treatment of beauty. We will discover that where plot offers comforting stability and closure, the character of beauty and the beauty of character remain tantalizingly open. I will subject this story to some considerable analysis of my own because I am treating it as an allegory of my own larger subject, the elusive character of beauty.

* * *

There was once a large village of the MicMac Indians of the Eastern Algonquins, built beside a lake. At the far end of the settlement stood a lodge, and in it lived a being who was always invisible. He had a sister who looked after him, and everyone knew that any girl who could see him might marry him. For that reason there were very few girls who did not try, but it was very long before anyone succeeded.

This is the way in which the test of sight was carried out: at evening-time, when the Invisible One was due to be returning home, his sister would walk with any girl who might come down to the lakeshore. She, of course, could see her brother, since he was always visible to her. As soon as she saw him, she would say to the girls:

"Do you see my brother?"

"Yes," they would generally reply—though some of them did say "No."

To those who said that they could indeed see him, the sister would say:

"Of what is his shoulder strap made?" Some people say that she would enquire:

"What is his moose-runner's haul?" or "With what does he draw his sled?"

And they would answer:

"A strip of rawhide" or "a green flexible branch," or something of that kind.

Then she, knowing that they had not told the truth, would say:

"Very well, let us return to the wigwam!"

When they had gone in, she would tell them not to sit in a certain place, because it belonged to the Invisible One. Then, after they had helped to cook the supper, they would wait with great curiosity, to see him eat. They could be sure that he was a real person, for when he took off his moccasins they became visible, and his sister hung them up. But beyond this they saw

---

"The Algonquin Cinderella," from *World Tales* by Idries Shah, copyright © 1979 by Technographia, S.A. and Harcourt Brace Jovanovich, Inc. Reproduced by permission of Harcourt Brace Jovanovich, Inc.

nothing of him, not even when they stayed in the place all the night, as many of them did.

Now there lived in the village an old man who was a widower, and his three daughters. The youngest girl was very small, weak and often ill; and yet her sisters, especially the elder, treated her cruelly. The second daughter was kinder, and sometimes took her side; but the wicked sister would burn her hands and feet with hot cinders, and she was covered with scars from this treatment. She was so marked that people called her *Oochigeaskw*, the Rough-Faced-Girl.

When her father came home and asked why she had such burns, the bad sister would at once say that it was her own fault, for she had disobeyed orders and gone near the fire and fallen into it.

These two elder sisters decided one day to try their luck at seeing the Invisible One. So they dressed themselves in their finest clothes, and tried to look their prettiest. They found the Invisible One's sister and took the usual walk by the water.

When he came, and when they were asked if they could see him, they answered: "Of course." And when asked about the shoulder strap or sled cord, they answered: "A piece of rawhide."

But of course they were lying like the others, and they got nothing for their pains.

The next afternoon, when the father returned home, he brought with him many of the pretty little shells from which wampum was made, and they set to work to string them.

That day, poor little Oochigeaskw, who had always gone barefoot, got a pair of her father's moccasins, old ones, and put them into water to soften them so that she could wear them. Then she begged her sisters for a few wampum shells. The elder called her a "little pest," but the younger one gave her some. Now, with no other clothes than her usual rags, the poor little thing went into the woods and got herself some sheets of birch bark, from which she made a dress, and put marks on it for decoration, in the style of long ago. She made a petticoat and a loose gown, a cap, leggings and a handkerchief. She put on her father's large old moccasins, which were far too big for her, and went forth to try her luck. She would try, she thought, to discover whether she could see the Invisible One.

She did not begin very well. As she set off, her sisters shouted and hooted, hissed and yelled, and tried to make her stay. And the loafers around the village, seeing the strange little creature, called out "Shame!"

The poor little girl in her strange clothes, with her face all scarred, was an awful sight, but she was kindly received by the sister of the Invisible One. And this was, of course, because this noble lady understood more about things than simply the mere outside which all the rest of the world knows. As the brown of the evening sky turned black, the lady took her down to the lake.

"Do you see him?" the Invisible One's sister asked.

"I do, indeed—and he is wonderful!" said Oochigeaskw.

The sister asked:
"And what is his sled-string?"
The girl said:
"It is the Rainbow."
"And, my sister, what is his bow-string?"
"It is The Spirit's Road—the Milky Way."
"So you *have* seen him," said his sister. She took the girl home with her and bathed her. As she did so, all the scars disappeared from her body. Her hair grew again, as it was combed, long, like a blackbird's wing. Her eyes were now like the stars: in all the world there was no other such beauty. Then, from her treasures, the lady gave her a wedding garment, and adorned her.

Then she told Oochigeaskw to take the *wife's* seat in the wigwam: the one next to where the Invisible One sat, beside the entrance. And when he came in, terrible and beautiful, he smiled and said:
"So we are found out!"
"Yes," said his sister. And so Oochigeaskw became his wife.

* * *

The characters in this folktale are presented to the reader both in terms of their beauty and in terms of their ability to see beauty. Because people in the story are not what they seem to be, the characters' main task is to discover the right relationship between appearances and reality. At the heart of the narrative lie questions about beauty's visibility, about the cosmic sanction of beauty, and about the correct equation of the body's beauty and the soul's beauty. Yet these are the very questions that remain unsettled by the story's conclusion (the invisible becomes visible, the ugly beautiful), though the reader derives clear lessons about virtue, truth, and justice. We pass through the door of beauty to arrive at truth only to discover that, if we glance back, the door itself has moved or, perhaps, disappeared.

The only named characters are the hero and heroine, and their names, being Indian names, are essential, that is, the name is supposed to correspond to the character's main attribute. Thus, Oochigeaskw, the Rough-Faced-Girl, is marked by her marked face as disadvantaged and undesirable, just as the Invisible One is special and desirable because he cannot be seen. At the same time, the principal condition of the story is that the Invisible One will marry the girl who *does* see him and who thereby proves that he is not essentially invisible but only apparently so.

The reader and the villagers understand, by implication, that the girl who passes the test of sight must be an exceptional character herself, and Oochigeaskw's sisters "dressed themselves in their finest clothing and tried to look their prettiest" to be as exceptional as they could be. Assuming that the best will win the hero, the sisters try to be pretty when they set out for the lakeshore because they associate best with beauty. As soon as we recognize that it is Oochigeaskw who will be the second-sighted heroine, we therefore expect that she cannot be essentially ugly. Beneath her rough face must be a character worthy of so splendid a reward. Like the villagers, the reader equates beauty and worth, and because magic is a convention of this genre, we are not in the least surprised by Oochigeaskw's transformation. Thus, the most important fact about the hero is that he *is* and *is not* invisible, just as the most significant fact about Oochigeaskw is that she *is* and *is not* unlovely.

Although fairy-tale heroes and heroines are typically beautiful, the Invisible One and Oochigeaskw are initially defined by the very absence of beauty; the former cannot be seen at all, and the latter is manifestly unattractive. At the same time, the reader supposes, long before we are expressly told, that the Invisible One and Oochigeaskw are beautiful. Not only has our experience with narrative taught us to assume that heroes and heroines are beautiful, but when we read narrative, we expect beauty of the body to correspond to beauty of the soul. We understand that physical description is a system of codification: because the Invisible One is desirable and invisible—that is, because his presence is evident in spite of his apparent absence—the reader recognizes a feature of divinity and assigns other divine attributes to him; similarly, Oochigeaskw is familiar to us as a type: the victimized but virtuous character who emerges as a beauty when she is discovered by he who has the wisdom to appreciate her and the power to reveal her.

This folktale matches the quest for divine truth with the service of cosmic justice. Each village girl tries and fails to discover the Invisible One and each day the sister—a kind of priestess who mediates between the Invisible One and the world—sets out to discover her brother's true bride. In spite of Oochigeaskw's scars, apparent poverty, ridiculous attire, and "awful" appearance, the sister treats her kindly because, as the narrator tells us, "the noble lady understood far more about things than simply the outside which all the world knows." Paradoxically, it is only the "noble lady" who has the understanding to see potential nobility in the youngest and least well-endowed daughter of an anonymous villager.

The sister knows that appearance and money are meaningless, but when Oochigeaskw proves that she too has the nobility and the inner vision to see beyond appearances, the sister not only transfigures Oochigeaskw's body, but she also adorns her in treasures. Divine compensation for the mistreatment that Oochigeaskw endured is meted out in the forms of beauty, marriage, and money. These are the rewards that the story values. But the narrative pretends to scorn these values because Oochigeaskw earns her rewards in spite of (or because of) her frailty, scars, and cheap clothes; the best husband is won without the aid of superficial beauty. Of course when the Invisible One comes home that evening, he smiles at a bride who is superficially magnificent as he declares, "So we are found out!" The beauty of both the ugly and the invisible can now be seen. The discoveries have all been made; the gods are righteous, and truth has triumphed over appearance.

The lesson of the story seems to be that "the mere outside of things which all the world knows" lies and that the world is easily deceived. A person who seems poor, unsightly, and undeserving on the surface may be beautiful on the inside: she may be the gods' favorite. Don't judge a book by its cover. But this is the very message that the story undercuts when it assures us that the hero and heroine are the most beautiful people in the world; the just gods do reward virtue and faith with love, wealth, and beauty. We are given two contradictory messages: the poor, simple, unloved, and unlovely may be worthy, but the worthy are rich, wise, beloved, and beautiful.

When we look more closely at the hero's and heroine's beauty, the distinction between the literal and the figurative blurs. Literal as invisibility and ugliness are in the story, the beauty of Oochigeaskw and the Invisible One may be merely figurative after all. Although the reader is told that they are beautiful, what they look like is left almost entirely up to our imagination. Once beautiful, they are described through figures or metaphors, and transfiguration is a symbolic, rather than a realistic, operation. Thus, while Oochigeaskw is described in precise detail before her transfiguration, her beauty is described only in abstract and metaphorical language. Why she is regarded as ugly is clear: we know not only that she is small, weak, sickly, and scarred, but we also know the size of her ill-fitting moccasins, the other particulars of her makeshift attire, and that she is so "strange" that even the loafers cry out "Shame!" Once she is bathed and combed, however, the narrator's style of description changes. Beauty is defined as the absence of features of ugliness: we learn that the "scars disappeared." Beauty is expressed through catachresis: her hair grew long "like a blackbird's wing," and her eyes "were now like the stars." The Invisible One's "terrible beauty" is also conveyed through images that must have exemplified, for the MicMac Indians, nature's most beautiful and awesome phenomena: of his beauty, we learn only that it is "wonderful," that he draws a sled-string which is "the Rainbow" and that he carries a bow-string that is "the Milky Way." Beauty cannot be specifically or literally articulated.

The story also works as a parable about reading. Because the common girls can only imagine common beauty (sled-strings of rawhide), their expectations restrict their vision. The Invisible One, his sister, and Oochigeaskw distinguish themselves as characters because their physical uniqueness is matched by singular powers of perception. They are gifted with the ability to see the significance of one another's surfaces. A character's beauty, like his or her heroism, derives from the ability to transcend the limitations of convention. But the narrative itself cannot transcend convention (in the real world there is nothing else) and resorts to hyperbole in its own descriptions of unique beauty: "In all the world there was no other such beauty" as that of the Rough-Faced-Girl. The natural and divine beauty of this hero and heroine must be accepted by the reader on faith, and the story is, above all, about faith.

This folktale encourages us to suspect appearances and be wary of our own faulty perceptions. Beauty is in the eye of the beholder. People see differently, but only the second-sighted recognize true beauty when they are in its presence. Yet for all of the narrator's efforts to teach us that human perception is subjective, that divine justice works mysteriously, and that the inner eye must penetrate false surfaces, the only way that the narrative can effectively persuade us of the hero's and heroine's exceptional characters is to insist upon their exceptional beauty, a beauty so exceptional that it cannot be described; it can only be repeated, and it can only be compared to the cosmos that authorizes it. Beauty, as a feature belonging to heroes and heroines, is an essential but slippery quality of character. By the end of the story, we do not know if beauty is significant or insignificant, real or an illusion. The narrative insists upon having it both ways. Such is the character of beauty.

2

The Eye of the Beholder: Reader as Spectator

In "The Algonquin Cinderella," appearance is linked to essence, but the characters' appearances cannot be fixed by the reader. Even in so simple a genre as the folktale, the characters' beauty complicates the reading process. In realist fiction, as in the folktale, characters who are beautiful derive much of their interest and meaning from the fact of their beauty. More importantly, in "The Algonquin Cinderella," beauty's unstable character enables the transmission of mutually exclusive social messages. The reader is at once encouraged to and discouraged from associating worth with such apparent rewards as beauty and wealth. In the realist novel, where physical description is more elaborate and more weighted with connotations, beauty points to still more meanings that cannot be reconciled. The reader interprets this excess as complexity of character. Because the surface of the beautiful body is a playground for multiple shifting significances, beautiful characters, heroes and heroines, are left open to the possibility of endless rereadings.

Although the language that describes a fictional character's beauty produces multiple and varied meanings, readers comfortably perceive valuable complexity for several reasons. First, such language can appeal simultaneously and ambiguously to different, even competing, codes ("female blossom" may positively connote blooming health or the fragility of a flower). Second, such language can point simultaneously inside and outside, unobtrusively challenging the opposition between literal and figurative. Finally, we understand what is meant by a beautiful character, even though "beauty" and "character" are often felt to be contradictory concepts. Experimentation in the visual arts shows that blankness of expression is most often perceived as beauty but that disturbing that blankness by varying proportions is required to animate the human form; the classic form acquires individuation or character as beauty is destabilized.

"The character of beauty," like "the subject of beauty," is a pun. Characters have character as does beauty, and subjects (topics) can be subjects (people) who can, in turn, act as subjects and be subjugated. Language confuses the abstract and the concrete, the literal and the figurative, the inside and the outside. The language of physical description is weighted language, such that adjectives move easily from the surface of the body to the depths of being: bright eyes may point to a bright mind or intelligence. Apparently neutral phrases denoting physical features often refer to larger cultural contexts, as dark hair and eyes may be an appeal to either the realm of exoticism or of demonism until the work fixes its readers' choices. But neither option needs be realized. In the case of this example, nineteenth-century literature often conflated the exotic (which has positive connotations) with the demonic (which has negative connotations) and produced the ambivalent "supernatural."

Although the language surrounding the human body often points inside and outside simultaneously, I do not mean that Victorian writers subscribe to the science of physiognomy. Physiognomy has the appearance of a science precisely because it articulates what we all already believe, that an honest face hides an honest heart. While some readers have invoked the science of physiognomy in their analyses of eighteenth- and nineteenth-century fiction, I would argue instead that we all practice physiognomy unawares and that the displacement of the literal with the figurative is a fact of language that disturbs our convictions about the ways in which we interpret character.[1]

On the surface of the body, where beauty is said to reside, literal and figurative, appearance and reality, matter and spirit continually displace each other. Our uses of the word "figure" are illustrative. "Figure" (symbol) gives us figural and figurative, but "figure" is also face (as in the French) and body ("an hourglass figure"). Moreover, "figure" refers to social stature: "a great figure in parliament." In the language of literary study, the opposition between literal and figurative is fundamental, and the act of interpretation is an act of penetration: we move beneath the surfaces of texts and characters to discover meaning in their depths. But as we penetrate clear blue eyes we discover clarity of vision—the outside and inside appear inside out. Disfiguring, in fiction, thus becomes a symbolic act (as in the smallpox contracted by the formerly dangerous beauty Madame de Merteuil at the conclusion of Laclos' *Les Liaisons Dangereuses* or equally unrealistically, the sweet Esther Summerson's recovery from the effects of the same disease in Dickens' *Bleak House*); superficial disfigurements are read as judgments because marks created by a punitive author/God penetrate deeply. From "figure," we also get "configuration," and in the chapters which follow, I use the word "configuration" to refer to cultural ideals of beauty, linguistic constructs in which features of appearance correspond to qualities of character.

Aesthetic principles are often contradictory precisely because external perfection can index imperfection within. Beauty has classically been defined both by its perfect regularity and by its subtle irregularity. Francis Bacon's view that "there is no excellent beauty that has not some strangeness in the proportion,"[2] thus contrasts with Thomas Aquinas' assertion that "beauty consists in proper proportion."[3] That it is *character* which disturbs what would otherwise be the blankness of proper proportion is a nineteenth-century discovery in the field of spectator psychology. Character expresses itself in the space between what the nineteenth-century Swiss humorist Rudolphe Toepffer first called "permanent and impermanent traits."

The conscious experimentation of visual artists provides insights into the unconscious workings of novelists who use physical description to animate characters. In *Art and Illusion,* E.H. Gombrich explains the process of manipulating conventional features to animate the face, but he finds his own conclusions anticipated in Toepffer's 1845 pamphlet on physiognomics:

> Thus a little experimentation with noses or mouths will teach us the elementary symptoms, and from here we can proceed, simply by doodling to create characters. Toepffer maintains that the heroes of his stories thus arose out of his pen-plays. Only one more step is needed for the picture story. We must learn to distinguish between what Toepffer calls the "permanent traits" indicating character and the "impermanent ones" indicating emotion. As to the permanent ones, Toepffer makes fun of the phrenologists of his time who sought the root of character in isolated signs.... Toepffer looks for what psychologists would call the "minimum clues" of expression to which we respond whether we meet them in reality or in art. In trying to find out what happens, not to the doodle but to himself, when clues are systematically varied, Toepffer uses them as a tool to probe into the secrets of physiognomic perception.[4]

Exploring the history of caricature, Gombrich looks at the work of the eighteenth-century painter, Alexander Cozens to demonstrate that it is difficult to create character out of beauty's blank expressions:

> In an interesting series of prints Cozens presents a standard head of classical beauty and that blankness of expression that often goes with it. By systematically varying the proportions, he attempts to investigate the creation of what he calls "character" through deviations from the canon. His attempt misfired because it was too subtle. It is hard to see much difference between the various types of beauty because he tried to remain within the laws of decorum. But the principle he advocated proved useful in the robust hands of a humorous artist.

Gombrich's point is clear when he compares Cozens' preliminary experiments with the more developed experiments of Francis Grose, an Englishman who published *Rules for Drawing Caricatures* in 1788. Gombrich goes on to discuss Grose's discoveries:

> The academic standard of the face, which corresponds to the standard of Greek art, is experienced as beautiful, he says, precisely because it lacks proportion. Try varying the proportions as drastically as you like, and watch what happens. You will soon be equipped with a repertory of funny faces that will be useful in drawing humorous pictures.[5]

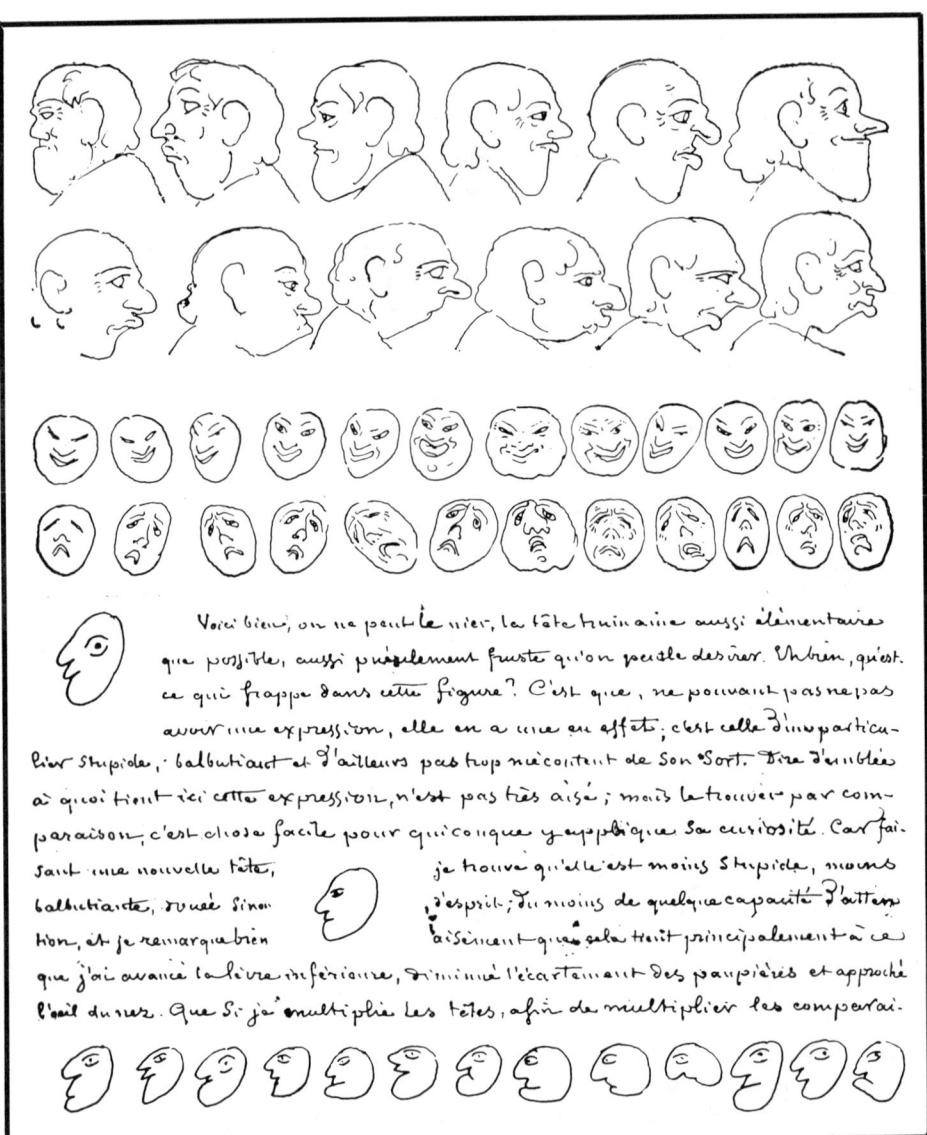

Figure 1. Combinations of Expressions in Various Facial Elements
(Rudolphe Toepffer, "Essay du physiognomie," 1845)

That the price of beauty is loss of character is a perception that has had unequal consequences for the sexes. To say that a man has character is to admire what is unconventional about him; to say the same of a woman is to imply that she lacks beauty.

The nearest verbal equivalent to caricature is parody, and the humorous characters of parody or satire are rarely presented or experienced as beauties. (Here *poesis* has an advantage over *pictura* because appearance expressed in a verbal construct can seem specific without being so.) The movement from Cozens to Grose functions on a continuum that corresponds to the usual distinction in literary studies between flat and round characters. In myth, fairy tale, and allegory, we expect characters of absolute virtue to be absolutely beautiful. Because it is not difficult to discover what constitutes either virtue or beauty in these genres, their characters are more or less closed to interpretation. Of fiction's heroes we make the demand that they be "true to nature" (lifelike) as well as "true to art" (transcending the mundane). This paradox opens characters to interpretation because it is the illusion of truth that is the mastery of fiction; art is valued as natural when it most artfully falsifies nature.

We avow a preference for round characters, but we allow Dickens, and sometimes Thackeray, relatively flat characters because comedy and satire achieve their pointed aims, as E. M. Forster hints in *Aspects of the Novel,* at the expense of roundness. By contrast, we appreciate George Eliot for the complexity of her characterizations and accordingly classify her novels among other "novels of character." From myth, romance, fairy tale, and allegory to realist fiction and finally away from the conventions of realism, it is tempting to argue that the march of the tradition is from clarity to complexity; the absolute beauty of Spenser's virtuous allegorical figures provides the skeletal basis for Thackeray's creations who, in turn, are subjected to Eliot's refining hand. This formula does not, in fact, apply well, and it is flat characters and stick figures which can instruct us in the politics and psychology of realistic portraiture.

Much of Gombrich's work in art history is devoted to the discovery of this psychology. Gombrich arrives at seventeenth-century portraiture via studies of the sketchbook and caricature. In both *The Story of Art* and *Art and Illusion: A Study in the Psychology of Pictorial Representation,* he exposes realism as a conditioned response in the viewer. Gombrich finds in Baroque portraiture the studied spontaneity that we often consider to be the later legacy of Romantic poetry. He writes that Frans Hals (1580–1666), whose work brought so little income to the painter, seizes a fleeting impression of his sitter "in a characteristic movement and mood" that "could never have been achieved without a very calculated effort." Gombrich politely warns us against assuming that Hals was read the same way in his own time as he is in

14 *The Eye of the Beholder*

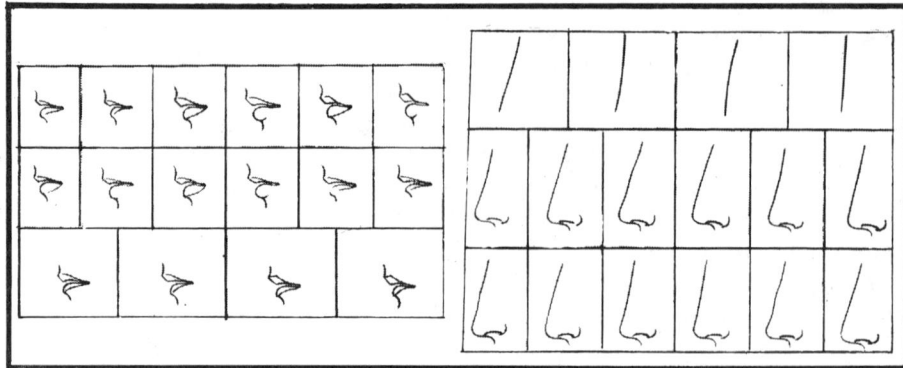

Figure 2. Physical Elements of Beauty
(Alexander Cozens, "Principles of Beauty Relative to the Human Head")

ours: "It is difficult to imagine how bold and unconventional these paintings must have looked to the public."[6] What is convincing and natural for us took some getting used to in the seventeenth century.

"The Experiment in Caricature," a chapter in *Art and Illusion,* asks how seventeenth-century caricature succeeds in convincing without being realistic. This question motivates Gombrich's later essay, "The Mask and the Face: The Perception of Physiognomic Likeness in Life and in Art," in which Gombrich again uses caricature as an approach to the question of achieving natural-looking likenesses. The analogy between pictorial and verbal portraiture is dangerous, but parody and allegory share enough with caricature that we may cautiously apply some of Gombrich's insights here. As impressed as we often are with parody's ability to capture a person's essence in brief, so are we taken with the genius of the painter who scribbles for a few minutes and presents us with a souvenir of ourselves. Gombrich disillusions us:

> We enjoy this game and rightly admire the painter or the caricaturist who can, as the saying goes, conjure up a likeness with a few bold strokes, by reducing it to essentials. But the portrait painter knows that the real trouble starts when you have to proceed in the opposite direction. However skillful he may have been with his first rough outline, he must not spoil the sketch on his way to the finished portrait because the more elements he has to handle, the harder to preserve the likeness.[7]

Caricature is effective because its very simplicity allows the viewer to supply whatever information may be missing, and one is not likely to quarrel with one's own imagination or memory. In allegory too, a description that

The Eye of the Beholder 15

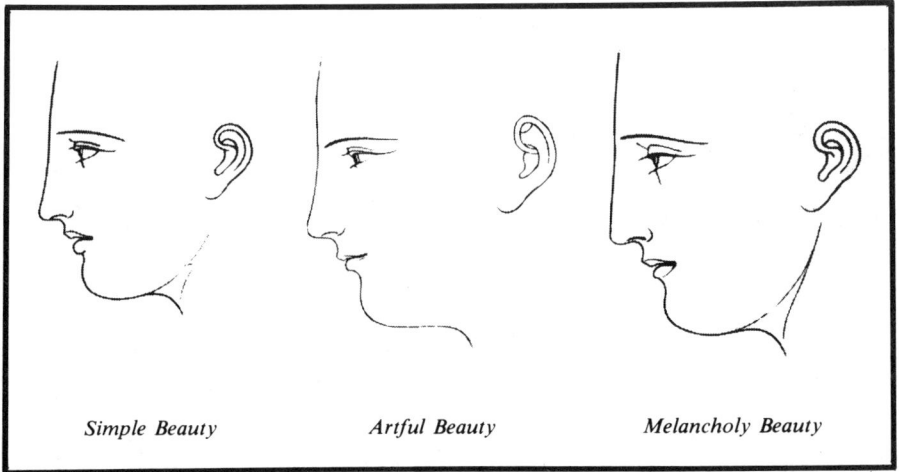

Simple Beauty   Artful Beauty   Melancholy Beauty

includes white skin and chaste beauty is enough for the reader to flesh out an emblem of beauty perfectly familiar to us from painting and lore. The only restriction is that no two pieces of suggestive detail contradict one another. Each bit of information must appeal to the same code. Gombrich spells out the advantages of this procedure:

> The best safeguard against the "unnatural look" or the frozen mask has always been found in the suppression rather than the employment of any contradictions that might impede our projection.

There is no smooth transition from caricature or likeness to a character who is also a work of art. We must take a philosophical and technical leap to our most valued portraits which, be they graphic or verbal, are filled with details that contradict and are in tension with one another. Gombrich explains that the perfectly consistent portrait is unable to hold our attention. Taking an engaging example of eighteenth-century art, of Quentin de la Tour's portrait of Mlle Fel, he writes:

> The very combination of slightly contradictory features, of a serious gaze with a shadow of a smile results in a subtle instability, an expression hovering between the pensive and the mocking that both intrigues and fascinates.[8]

Moreover, the portraitist "must exploit the ambiguities of the arrested face that the multiplicities of possible readings result in the semblance of life" (p. 17). The beauty of perfection, simply asserted and developed with a few

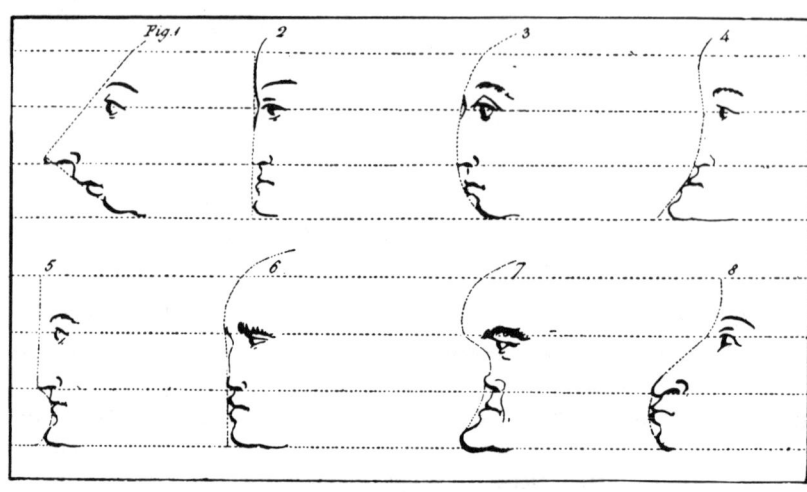

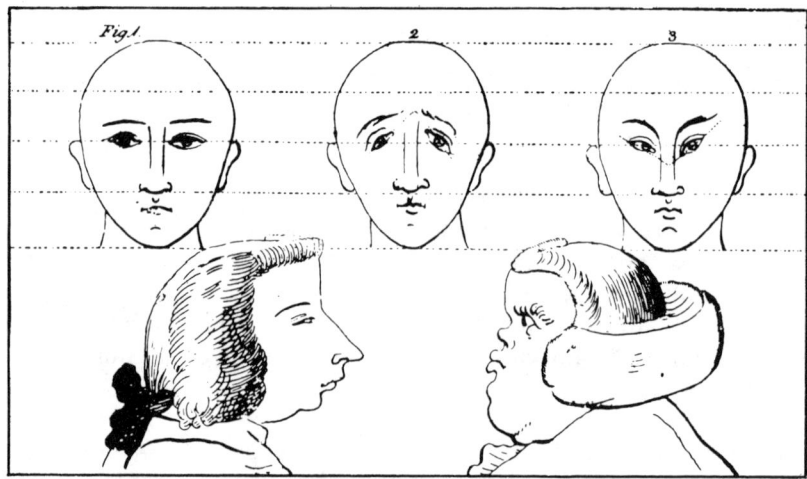

Figure 3. Physical Elements of Caricature
(Francis Grose, Rules for Drawing Caricature, *1788)*

significant details, is the beauty of allegorical or fairy-tale heroines. Realistic heroes are lifelike because the perfection of the work of art is animated by incoherent details that serve to keep the figure dynamic.

In *Ways of Seeing,* John Berger makes an analogous distinction between the nude and the beauty of the naked body on canvas and draws out its social implications. Nudity is emblematic; nakedness is dynamic. Nudity is for the voyeur, conventionalized, clear, and generalized, while nakedness is individualized, personal, and human. The nude exploits, while the naked body on canvas is a celebration. How is a rare image of nakedness achieved? Why, asks Berger, does Rubens' portrait of Hélène Fourment confront us as a painter's experience?

> The profound reason is a formal one.... Beneath the fur coat that she holds across herself, the upper part of her body and her legs never meet. There is a displacement sideways of about nine inches: her thighs, in order to join on to her hips, are at least nine inches too far to the left.
>
> Rubens probably did not plan this: the spectator may not consciously notice it. In itself it is unimportant. What matters is what it permits. It permits the body to be impossibly dynamic. Its coherence is no longer within itself but within the experience of the painter.[9]

All kinds of characters, more or less fully developed, populate stories. We take flatness and roundness to be a simple matter of quantity of description and relative predictability of behavior when in fact the distinction is fraught with political, psychological, and artistic consequences. The description of Rosamund Vincy's education at Mrs. Lemon's in *Middlemarch,* for example, is as close to parody and caricature as George Eliot ever allows herself to get. When Rosamund is treated thus glibly, we are discouraged from taking her seriously, just as the nude fails to enlist our sympathy. Thackeray's animation of his puppets shows that he has learned the lesson of allegory well. Standing on the line between writing uni-dimensional figures, emblems of truth, and complex characters with multiple values at war within them, Thackeray keeps his readers off balance, in and out of sympathy with his characters.

Before Roland Barthes wrote that characters are proper nouns to which adjectives adhere,[10] E.M. Forster had already spoken of characters as word masses. Forster qualifies this sobering observation, adding that when a novelist writes about people, "a new emphasis enters his voice: an emphasis upon value."[11] Forster sensed, but could not quite pinpoint, why flat characters are more closely associated with value than round ones. Just as Gombrich comes to realism from the sketchbook, so Forster identifies flat characters with types or caricatures "constructed round a single idea or quality" (p. 67). The advantage of flat characters is that they are easily recognized and easily remembered. But Forster, who "must admit that flat people are not in themselves as big achievements as round ones," confesses himself at something of a loss in the face of Dickens:

> Those who dislike Dickens have an excellent case. He ought to be bad. He is actually one of our big writers, and his immense success with types suggests that there is more in flatness than the severer critics admit. (pp. 71–73)

And there is more to flatness than severer critics admit. Flat characters display their meanings to the world not only memorably and recognizably, but with the strength of conviction that convention affords. Like the nude, the flat character's beauty is an offering: a repeated formula, a ritual of desire or repudiation. The readability of allegory's figures instructs us in the difficult readability of fiction's characters who possess an elusive beauty that expresses slippery truths.

The female body is objectified by its beauty, and the reader, always masculinized as spectator by the text, is made to wish to possess the woman who is beautiful.[12] Physical descriptions, of beauty in particular, enforce the power of male spectatorship. And because the perception of beauty has psychologically been coded as the opposite of animation, we are encouraged to appreciate Pygmalion's statue as more beautiful than "real women" precisely because it lacks the vices associated with character and animation. In their appeals to traditional values, descriptions of beauty are quietly but powerfully conservative.

Because beauty is a cultural construct, writers can only create beauty by appeal to the authority of pre-existing ideals. The rhetoric of description used to convey beauty derives, therefore, from the literary tradition. Because literature translates art's images of beauty into verbal structures, the history of the debate on the principle of *ut pictura poesis* has been most vexing.[13] Ultimately, it is prior art and literature that authorizes beauty, and since each beauty refers to something before itself, the original model for a beautiful figure is endlessly deferred. This is what I understand Roland Barthes to mean when he writes in *S/Z* both that beauty is empty and that it always refers to well-established cultural codes:

> The young girl's beauty is referred to a cultural code, in this instance literary (it can elsewhere be pictorial or sculptural). This is a vast commonplace of literature: the Woman copies the Book. In other words, every body is a citation: of the "already-written." The origin of desire is the statue, the painting, the book....
> Beauty (unlike ugliness) cannot really be explained: in each part of the body it stands out, repeats itself, but it does not describe itself. Like a god (and as empty), it can only say: I am what I am. The discourse, then, can do no more than assert the perfection of each detail and refer "the remainder" to the code underlying all beauty: Art. In other words, beauty cannot assert itself save in the form of a citation...; it derives from its Model not only beauty but also language; left on its own, deprived of any anterior code, beauty would be mute. Every predicate is denied it; the only feasible predicates are either tautology (a perfectly oval face) or simile (lovely as a Raphael Madonna, like a dream in stone, etc.): thus beauty is referred to an infinity of codes: lovely as Venus? But Venus as lovely as what? As herself? As Marianina?[14]

Barthes does not, however, tell the whole story. He neglects *the story* itself, the fact that Adonis, or Venus, or the Madonna each sports a beauty that acquires its meaning from narrative contexts; each is as beautiful as his or her characteristic qualities. Venus is as lovely as the qualities that we associate with her (chastity or power, for example). Ironically, Barthes neglects the importance of coding, to which he habitually directs our attention. When a character is described as being as lovely as a Raphael Madonna, the analogy carries with it all that the figure of the Madonna means to us. Once such a figure is also established as a work's heroine, the Madonna (an image complete with a constellation of associations) is privileged over her potential rivals in beauty: for example, the childlike beauty or the wealthy and experienced *femme fatale*. Thus, the tradition—that interaction among texts that combines to form a consensus—works as a conservative force in the depiction of heroes and heroines. At the same time, innovations in the idealization of appearance thus directly challenge tradition's authority over those values associated with human character.

Ultimately, describing beauty is all about literary convention and departures from convention. The writer of realist fiction invites us to imagine beauty by appealing to our preconditioned desires. By overcoding beauty and by referring to traditional and popular images of beauty, room is left for the reader to imagine the face and figure of the hero and heroine. We are often given a set of details with which to work, and then we draw upon the ideals of beauty that we remember from art and advertisements. The textual exchange illustrated in the following chapters functions according to this economy. Because physical features have a spiritual worth, new characters capitalize on the feature-values supplied by the tradition. Thus, in the economy of character production, each text not only carries the backing of the system but also contributes to the value of the currency. Characters are produced economically because a text need supply only enough linguistic material for the reader to recognize that these are familiar products. The rest of the labor comes from the unsuspecting reader. "The reader's share," to adapt Gombrich's useful concept, "the beholder's share," is the knowledge, meanings, and associations that the reader brings to—but assumes that he or she has found in—the work.[15]

Our own desire as readers is enforced by our placement in the society of the novel. Beauty is created not only through the evocations of description but also through the provocations of desire: beauty is produced within a structure of desire. That which is beautiful is loved and that which is loved appears beautiful. Heroes and heroines are desired by at least two other characters (usually desirable themselves) who form the minimal triangle by means of which desire generates the perception of beauty.[16] Because the hero or heroine also embodies desired virtues, beauty is further reinforced as the ultimate symptom of virtue. The body becomes a repository for those values which characters and readers want to possess.

Keats's Grecian Urn, speaking for art, prescribes the limits of earthly knowledge when it affirms that "Beauty is truth, truth Beauty." In myth, fairy tales, romance, and allegory we find a correspondence between beauty and truth. But, unaltering monument that it is, the urn is less fickle than we, who are ever-changing in our perceptions of both beauty and truth. For this reason it behooves us to investigate the novelist's motives in, and methods of, refusing allegory's seeming simplicity. Realism suspects allegory of didacticism in its renderings of transparent characters; we identify transparency with effacement because we think a legible face to be no face at all, a mask instead. If uncomplicated meanings are untrue to the complexities and ambiguities of people, as writers and critics of fiction always imply, then we must discover of what stuff fiction's complex characters are made and how fiction succeeds in asserting the truth of its beauties and the beauty of its truths.

3

The Bodies and Spirits of the Age: Competing Categories of Value in Nineteenth-Century England

> ... *almost all philosophers have confused ideas of things, and speak of material things in spiritual terms, and of spiritual things in material terms.*
>
> Blaise Pascal
>
> *For God has equipped both soul and body with such great wisdom and workmanship that, through the original constitution and essence of each, everything which happens in one corresponds perfectly and automatically to whatever happens in the other....*
>
> Gottfried Wilhelm Leibniz

The ambiguous relation of body and spirit signals a paradox that underlies most discussions of beauty. In William Hogarth's 1753 treatise, *Analysis of Beauty,* he first invokes the authority of one "old adage," "the face is the index of the mind," and then replaces it with another, *fronti nulla fides.*[1] Readers and writers of nineteenth-century literature also oscillate unself-consciously between these two convictions. The ambiguous relation of the material to the symbolic has consequences for aesthetics: the appreciation of beauty is, we are convinced, subjective, so that in defining the beautiful writers manipulate readers into a position of shared subjectivity; yet we also believe that beauty carries aesthetic and ethical value. These truths are mutually exclusive: beauty is subjective and not rule-governed, but aesthetic sense is a matter of taste and education.

Because we know that there exists a consensus about what is beautiful even as we are taught that such tastes are up to the individual, criteria for value find expression in a vocabulary that recurs in apparently value-free contexts.

Figure 4. James Scott, *Queen Victoria*
Fashionable women grew larger and stronger with the queen.
Paris, Louvre.
(©*Giraudon; Photo courtesy Art Resource*)

One such context is the language of physical description. The language that describes competing idealizations of nineteenth-century heroes and heroines resonates with the language in which incompatible but simultaneously held social beliefs were debated. Conversely, the language of philosophical debates and public controversy echoes in descriptions of heroes and heroines. It is that language which we will attend to here.

Unaffected simplicity characterized one variety of beauty, adorned stylishness another. Nineteenth-century English literature and culture idealized a wide variety of beauties, from the Quakerish Jane Eyre to the classical Gwendolyn Harleth, from the Romantic ideal of feminine weakness to the dark exuberant sensuality of Catherine Earnshaw. Such Byronic heroes as Rochester or Heathcliff, in spite of their creators' ambivalent presentation of their features, both physical and spiritual, were sufficiently recognized as beauties to have been worthy of emulation by fashionable men.[2] But the wild Heathcliff is a far cry from Eliot's artistic Will Ladislaw, and the attractions of Anne Elliot, the blooming twenty-seven-year-old heroine of Austen's *Persuasion,* are quite different from those of Dickens' and Lewis Carroll's innocent child heroines. In Gaskell's *North and South,* Margaret Hale is the preferred beauty precisely because she is, as her name suggests, heartier and more mature than her beautiful but childlike cousin Edith, while in Hardy's *Jude the Obscure,* the delicate Sue passes close inspection better than her robust rival Arabella.

Although these ideals flourished more or less concurrently, several rationales could be made to account for changing fashions of beauty. For example, heroes and heroines became more fully fleshed out in descriptions as the novel form developed, and they became literally more fully fleshed as the bourgeois reading public acquired greater prominence and needed to admire characters of strength. While several novelists, especially women, introduced older, larger-bodied heroines, other writers persisted in the idealization of innocent childlike femininity. One might also argue that the novel, which is a distinctively middle-class genre, developed idealizations that moderated stereotypical images of the aristocratic and peasant classes. Mediating between extremes reflects the middle-class faith in democracy and capitalism. That twentieth-century avant-garde writers may have abandoned that faith is reflected in the absence or absurdity of description in experimental literature; formally and substantively, a portion of today's fiction refuses to idealize.

These generalizations are problematic. First, texts deliberately reverse themselves on matters of aesthetic judgment: Jane Eyre is and is not plain; Adam Bede presumably prefers Hetty's type of beauty to that of Dinah until he acquires better judgment; Jude prefers Sue but is inevitably seduced by Arabella. Second, the middle class in the nineteenth century did not generate its positive self-images simply by defining itself in negative relation to the class it wished to displace on the one hand and the class it wished to keep in place (and not fall back into) on the other. Images of both the aristocracy and the peasantry existed in positive and negative variations. Enterprising members of the middle class wanted to be less spoiled looking than the stereotypical simpering aristocrat clad in frills, but as handsome as the idealized lord, the well-dressed picture of competence; they wanted none of the peasant's coarseness, but they admired the laborer's brawn and the rustic's health. No middle-class woman wanted to be either as haggard as the stereotypical assembly line worker or as weak and useless as the humorous caricature of the aristocratic wife, a mere over-adorned fixture. But she might fancy herself as beautiful as an idealized vision out of pastoral romance, as lithe and energetic as an independent woman, or as pretty as a princess. These contradictory icons could be called forth as the occasion required: middle-class ideas of beauty straddled class boundaries as these images and the qualities they signified underwent reassessment.

Rather than look for the meaning of trends in changing ideals of beauty over the course of the century, we discover more about the era's earnest self-criticism and blind spots by focusing on how these trends incorporate self-contradiction. A character who apparently champions one set of values might have underlying and *redeeming* features that caution the reader against over-investing in those values. This ambivalence is a factor in the middle-class tendency to emulate both upper and lower-class characteristics, an ambivalence often expressed in physical or sexual renderings of the middle class as an "imposter class," one without "real" social power, yet assertive and virile. Thus, adjectives are mixed and matched such that the look of experience is tempered by marks of innocence or the appearance of strength is qualified by signs of delicate sensitivities. Using another strategy, writers enforce and criticize new values by drawing beauty as a composite of widely opposed traditional ideals. For example, when modern outlooks threatened religious convictions, compromises were drawn: Dorothea Brooke, we are told at different times, looks like Antigone and Theresa: a free-thinking pagan, who is, after all, a saint; a saint who is a free thinker.

Each figure of beauty uniquely combines a variety of meaningful traits, and the descriptive possibilities of combining adjectives and references are many. To see an individual character as exemplary of some nineteenth-century ideal, it is therefore necessary to place characters within a classification system that enables us to generalize. We can find such a system of classification in the discourses that we have inherited from the nineteenth century. Since ideals of beauty were described in the same language as that which characterized discussions of social issues, this coincidence can be used to map nineteenth-century concerns. In particular, debates such as those about art versus nature, nature versus nurture, delicacy versus strength, or innocence versus experience were sufficiently important to nineteenth-century philosophizing that they informed people's organizing ideas about the world. Every figure of beauty will thus contain and betray these tensions. Reminding ourselves of nineteenth-century ideas about art, grace, health, and the like better prepares us to hear some of the special resonances that nineteenth-century transformations of traditional ideals would have had for nineteenth-century readers.

In my literary analyses I will focus on each of three ambiguous features of beauty (charm, grace, and delicacy), showing how beauty expresses tensions between binary oppositions. The oppositions considered here are art and nature, nature and nurture, and delicacy and health. While these features of beauty and these oppositions were selected from a broad field, I justify my choices in the pages that follow by demonstrating that they were much on the minds of Victorians. In the case of each of these vexed oppositions, we will see that the nineteenth century inherited mixed values from the past and developed paradoxical beliefs to accommodate competing claims to truth; Victorian thought had to reconcile the claims of nature with those of art, those of birth with those of breeding, and the claims of those theories that celebrated human animalism with those that honored human divinity.

Art and Nature

Ideals of beauty and art change materially as a society's issues change. For example, we will see that for Austen a woman's "charm" must come naturally; in *Persuasion,* Anne Elliot's appearance must improve without makeup, and Wentworth distinguishes himself from Mr. Elliot because Wentworth is not "too polished." Makeup in Austen's fiction means vanity, and the impulse to take the body into one's own hands and order it into beauty must be checked. For all Cinderellas, the cosmos—God or nature—endows beauty. Such is not always the prevailing view as ordering one's appearance is also treated as a human expression of divinity. "Cosmos" derives from the Greek word meaning "to order" or "to adorn," and from "cosmos" derives our word "cosmetics." This argument between art and nature is an old one. And the oldest of the decorative arts, Gombrich writes, were those which were practiced on the human body:

> Needless to say, the dressmaker's power to conjure with the figure and thus to contradict biblical authority, which tells us that we cannot add a cubit to our stature, is only one of many ways in which the body can be manipulated in its appearance. Even body-painting or tattooing, which may be the oldest form of decorative art, must have been practiced with this aim consciously or unconsciously in mind. Perceptual and emotional reaction naturally cannot be separated in this wide field of expressive and erotic emphasis, which we do not propose to enter. The more meaningful a part of a body may be in these terms, the more

sensitive it is likely to be to perceptual modification. We all know how the look of the eye can be transformed by make-up—as in the case of Greta Garbo—and what a difference a change in hair-style may make to the appearance of the face. The framing shapes transform the meaning of the objects they enclose.[3]

Transforming the body into an object of art is a way of making it meaningful. And it is unavoidable. Cosmetics, charms, jewels, may be chosen or rejected, but even natural charm *supplements* nature; acting, behaving well, seeming like a lady or a gentleman, requires a mask. The nineteenth century worried deeply over the distinction between art and nature, and the proper domain of each, though in the Baroque Era or in the Elizabethan age of drama, people had little trouble understanding art *as* nature. Today we may still value being natural, but as Gombrich points out, modern sociologists often remind us that we are our personae, that all behavior is acting or "masking":

> The art which experiments with the mask is of course the art of disguise, of acting. The whole point of the actor's skill is precisely this: to compel us to see him or her as different people according to different roles. The great actor does not even need make-up to enforce this transformation....
> Sociologists have increasingly reminded us of the truth that we are all actors, we all obediently play one of the roles which our society offers us—even the "hippies" do. In the society with which we are familiar we are extremely sensitive to the outward signs of these roles and much of our categorisation proceeds along these lines. We have learned to distinguish the types with which our actors and satirists keep us in touch....
> We model ourselves so much on the expectations of others that we assume the mask... and we grow into our type till it moulds all our behavior down to our gait and facial expression. It seems that there is nothing to exceed the plasticity of man except, of course, the plasticity of woman. Women work more consciously on their type and image than most men do, and often they try by means of make-up and hair style to shape themselves into the image of some fashionable idol of the screen or of the stage.[4]

Phrased in this way, human plasticity is unavoidable, and women have the advantage over men. Like many in the nineteenth century, however, we are capable of regarding the conscientious practice of such artistry as a producer of "false" beauty, signifying the vice of deception. The place of art, charms, any ordering of or supplement to nature to create the appearance of beauty was a matter of moral and philosophical importance that found articulation in critical discourses in a language that was easily transferred to literature's descriptions of beautiful characters: artful and charming characters, both good and evil, carry the baggage of these debates.

When science and religion came into conflict, aesthetic questions arose which carried the art/nature debate forward in new terms. Given a new, mechanistic conception of the universe, the "honesty" of beauty could be less well trusted. Shaftesbury phrases one premise of philosophers of aesthetics:

"the most natural beauty in the world is honesty and moral truth. For all beauty is truth. True features make the beauty of a face...."[5] For Shaftesbury's moralists, the issue becomes where one locates "true" features, and his Theocles suggests that the "beautiful, the fair, the comely, were never in the matter, but in the art and design; never in body itself, but in the form or forming power." Philocles then resolves to resist the splendor of "metals and stones, however precious and dazzling... when they pretend to set off human beauty and are officiously brought to the aid of the fair" (*The Moralists,* Part III, Section II), but ultimately the argument resolves such art into Nature, on the understanding that the world itself is a "powerful charm" of nature's making.

The German idealists worked under this influence, but Kant, in his discussion of taste, divorces "charms" and "emotions" from forms: "That taste is always barbaric which needs a mixture of charms and emotions.... Nevertheless charms are often not only taken account of in the case of beauty (which properly speaking ought merely to be concerned with form),... but they are passed off as in themselves beauties."[6] On the other hand, echoing Ovid, Kant writes that "Nature is beautiful if we are conscious of it as art while it yet looks like nature" (p. 314).

Hegel prefaces his discussion of beauty with respect to art and nature by discounting Nature's beauty as an uninteresting subject since, "in the case of natural beauty we are too keenly conscious that we are dealing with an indefinite subject-matter destitute of any real criterion."[7] Hegel argues against the position that human art "is of subordinate rank to the works of Nature," because art originates in the human soul: "And for this reason the work of art is of higher rank than any product of Nature.... Everything which partakes of spirit is better than anything begotten of mere Nature" (pp. 398–99). Here, with art on the side of spirit, art acquires superiority over nature.

These debates among German Romantic philosophers were extended in the literary theories of the English Romantic poets early in the nineteenth century. Wordsworth's aim was, of course, to create a more "natural" poetry (in the senses of "spontaneous," "ordinary" and about "the natural world") than that of eighteenth-century Neoclassicism. He subscribed to the art/nature dichotomy and championed nature. Coleridge took issue with this distinction and distinguished instead between the natural and the supernatural; for *The Lyrical Ballads,* Wordsworth was "to give the charm of novelty to things every day," while Coleridge undertook the task of articulating "the dramatic truth of such situations" as those with "supernatural agents and incidents."[8]

In *The Mirror and the Lamp,* M. H. Abrams finds that the fundamental difference between Wordsworth and Coleridge is that Coleridge had to collapse the art/nature distinction in order to validate art's nature. Abrams writes that "Coleridge's elaborate dialectic is designed... to show that this opposition cannot be sustained."⁹ Abrams explains that Coleridge's critique begins by exposing the rhythms of Wordsworth's "natural language" as "a matter not of nature, but of artifice and convention." Yet Abrams also points out that the main lines of Coleridge's argument resemble "the theories of artful poetic ornament he was attacking," particularly when he accounts for meter as a "'charm' which is 'superadded' to natural language." For Wordsworth meter is "merely a supernumerary charm"; Coleridge, "in the tradition of neo-classic criticism, establishes the making of poems to be a deliberate art, rather than the spontaneous overflow of feeling." For Coleridge, Wordworth's "nature" cannot be "the criterion of highest poetic value," because, explains Abrams, Coleridge views the greatest poetry as "the reconciliation of nature and art," blending and harmonizing "the natural and artificial." Poetry is natural and artful, and "the paradox that what is natural in poetry includes art... is attested by the creative poets of all ages."

While we regard "the return to nature" as a Romantic legacy (meaning by "nature" such things as clouds, water, and trees), the Romantic return to nature was rather a return to the essence (nature) of things. Carl Woodring follows the complex roads that the ideas of Nature and Art took in the nineteenth century, beginning with the Romantic definition of Nature as a "unitary principle" from which derive our expressions "human nature," "second nature," and "better nature."¹⁰ Nature, for Austen, Schiller, Wordsworth, Lamartine, and Pirsig is in *us,* not in the seas. Woodring then refers to Coleridge's use of Schelling's doctrine that art is the best way of imagining nature and calls this process "an epistemological merry-go-round, with the mind hot for nature but chasing only itself." Woodring further argues that "it is a historically disabling mistake to say... that the English Romantics despaired because they could no longer believe in a divinely ordered universe." Instead, aesthetics shifted to an appreciation of both nature and mind as "willful, energetic, and dynamic." What Darwin upset was not so much Augustinian Christianity as the conviction that "whatever is is right." Only by the century's end did all of the arts join hands in proclaiming their independence from nature. Woodring writes:

> With the arts taking in each other's laundry, attention turned to artificiality in general: to masks, cosmetics, actors, the Harlequinade, dancers and the dance, form, design, style, and on to the over-elaboration of style to which Symons assigned the name Decadence. Painted ladies were now a thing to paint. In "A Defense of Cosmetics," for *The Yellow Book,* Max Beerbohm praised his age for separating once more the surface of the face from the soul.

Beerbohm, by implying a return to an older and antithetical authority of beauty, calls us back to the Elizabethan age when Shakespeare's Lear would balance his attack on cosmetics ("God hath given you one face, and you make yourselves another") with a statement that nature often needs some supplement. Woodring summarizes this ideology: "if you allow humanity only the bare necessities of external nature, then human life, and human nature, will be bestial. And that, for man, would be unnatural."

The novelist characterizing "an honest beauty" needed to mediate among this array of claims on behalf of nature and art. The problem of producing an artless beauty plagued women readers in their lives. Lois Banner writes that "in trying to be beautiful, women have been prey to unattractive qualities of narcissism and consumerism. Early in the nineteenth century, a Cinderella mythology became for women the counterpart of the self-made man mythology for men." Banner goes on to explain that this mythology, which enforced consumerism (artfulness), did not subside: "By the late nineteenth century an elaborate system of symbols, rules, and rewards had arisen to reinforce the Cinderella mythology."[11] Still those rules which encouraged artifice did so for the sake of bringing one's natural beauty to the surface.

Nature and Nurture

While the premises in one realm of discourse, that belonging to philosophers of aesthetics, artists, and art critics, were based upon the distinction between art and nature and sometimes on the distinction between the natural and the supernatural, other realms of discourse focused on the distinction between the human and the bestial. When art saved man from being "unnaturally bestial," art became more valuable than nature because man was presumably a better thing than an animal. Political philosophy, in the tradition of Hobbes, thus reenforced the valorization of art by presuming that nature required controlling. Art is man's nature, Hobbes writes in the beginning of *The Leviathan:* "Nature, the art whereby God hath made and governs the world, is the art of man, as in many other things, so in this also imitated, that it can make an artificial animal...."

While art and the supernatural apparently increased in prestige over the course of the nineteenth century, paradoxically, political philosophy was challenging the tradition of Hobbes that provided the ultimate rationale for art's value as a beautifier. Coleridge's argument that the natural was continuous with the supernatural was less an innovation than a reversion to and revision of the tenets of medieval theology, which had equated the monstrous with the supernatural.[12] In one version of this schema, beast and monster were metaphors for one another, and both were evil in contrast with man and the divine. From Rousseau's new definition and assessment of the state of nature through Darwin's theory of evolution, beauty came to be discovered in that nature which was wild, animal, and beastly.

Just as artful or charming women and ideas were alternately regarded as the embodiment and the antithesis of the beautiful so too the wild man and nature's wildness underwent continual reassessment. In *The Pursuit of the Millennium*, Norman Cohn reproduces a 1545 image of the Pope/Antichrist as the Wild Man of medieval demonology. In the caption, Cohn writes that this figure "was a monster of erotic and destructive power—an earth spirit originally of the family of Pan, the fauns... but transformed into a terrifying demon."[13] Thus, from mythological images of gentle human/animal beauty arose the Wild Man as a negative force of the supernatural. Rousseau's "Noble Savage" recovered the connotations of benevolence that had formerly been associated with the wild, though Rousseau's image of man in nature resembled the demon Wild Man more closely than it did Pan.

The nineteenth-century assessment of untamed nature as a standard of beauty partially functioned to justify the mythology that Banner opposes to the Cinderella mythology, the valorization of the self-made man. But another paradox thereby asserted itself. If one was no longer born into privilege (in a state of nature, we are equally noble because we are equally savage), one acquired privilege by working and training oneself; wildness may be natural, but it became one's duty and goal to tame oneself. Untamed nature provided the standard of beauty, but the new elite distinguished itself because it was self-made, self-cultivated, well-bred, well-educated, and upwardly mobile.

The Wild Man Within, edited by Dudley and Novak, traces the history and function of this myth from the Renaissance to Romanticism, and in his introduction Haydn White points out that from the Bible to the Wild Woman and Man of medievalism, these creatures were, above all, ugly, the wild woman both hideous and a monster of sexuality.[14] With time, this representation went from being an ugly creature in supernatural space to being a psychological category, the ugly and sexual in ourselves. This tradition informs most readings of the mad woman in Brontë's *Jane Eyre* and other wild figures in Gothic romance.[15]

Even as the idea of the Wild Man was then associated with beauty in the natural world (stormy seas and children in a state of nature), it also developed antithetically into a metaphor for human ugliness. Barbarism became a category of anthropology which, as White points out, implies a distinction between "'natural' humanity on the one side and 'artificial' humanity on the other." The nineteenth-century's transfigurations of the Wild Man spawned beautiful and ugly variations depending upon the realm of discourse which adopted them: political philosophy, on the one hand, or the newly created fields of psychology and anthropology on the other. It should not surprise us then that Victorian literature's characters of beauty had to be both natural and well-bred, avoiding the Scylla of savagery (madness, over-sexuality, or barbarism) and the Charybdis of aristocratic over-breeding (the ugly opposite of the healthy Noble Savage).

The other area in which the same vocabulary was reassessed was in discussions of plant and animal life.[16] Keith Thomas, in *Man and the Natural World,* explains that agriculture, through a displacement of adjectives, was once a sign of civilization: "uncultivated land meant uncultivated men."[17] In the seventeenth century, domesticating animals was regarded as a moral act; "it civilized them." Eastern cultures which respected animal life were regarded as godless because God's first act was to give man dominion over nature. On the other hand, "the Judeo-Christian inheritance was deeply ambivalent. Side by side with the emphasis on man's right to exploit the inferior species went a distinctive doctrine of human stewardship and responsibility for God's creatures" (p. 24).

Thomas goes on to explain that from Aristotle and the Bible we inherited the particular notion that "man ... was more beautiful, more perfectly formed than any of the other animals" (p. 31). Man was represented as an animal until grace regenerated him into a human spirit. At the same time, "all the bodily functions had undesirable animal associations," so that for some modesty more than reason was the mark of humanity (and thus of beauty). Lust and long hair were synonymous with brutishness and ugliness. Thomas observes that it "was a comment on human nature that the concept of 'animality' was devised. As S. T. Coleridge would remark, to call human vices 'bestial' was to libel the animals" (p. 41). Coleridge's comment signals a reversal as it demonstrates that the nineteenth century both inherited and criticized this division between man and beast, allowing beast a potential advantage.

The opposite of the beast in the natural world was the flower, an exemplar of beauty. Between the sixteenth and nineteenth centuries, there was a spectacular growth in domestic flower cultivation (Thomas, p. 223). Moreover, the code of flowers was elaborate and "flowers followed fashions as much as clothes" (p. 231). Flowers were valued for their beauty, their usefulness, and their moral virtue: "in the 1860s the love of flowers and the taste for gardening was seriously suggested as a means of reducing the high rate of illegitimacy in Cumbria" (p. 234). Flowers enjoyed their widest appeal in England.

While one might assume that this plant/animal dichotomy placed femininity on the side of flowers and masculinity on the side of animals, such was not the case. Infants and small children were regarded as nearest the animal state ("unbridled colts," like the young Heathcliff); women came next ("breeders"), and finally the poor ("brutes in understanding"). "Most beastlike of all," writes Thomas, "were those on the margins of human society: the mad ... and the vagrants.... Once perceived as beasts, people were liable to be treated accordingly." While the nineteenth century persisted in these beliefs, it also reassessed the beauty of plants and animals in the wild. The seventeenth-century conviction that beauty is geometrical and "clipped" was abandoned in favor of that irregular wildness which became subject to "the highest aesthetic admiration." "The wilder the scene, the better its power to inspire emotion" (Thomas, p. 259). At the same time that the wild in man had to be contained and tamed and at the same time that art was valorized as the divine force in man which improves upon his animal nature, God was thought to make Himself manifest in natural "wildness"; for the Romantics, "nature improved was nature destroyed."

Yet another paradox generated out of these revisions in various areas of thought was that wildness became a standard of value during a Utilitarian Age, when "the classical ideal of beauty and utility seemed unattainable" (Thomas, p. 235). Labor, money and energy were increasingly spent on that which was said to produce "the disfiguring effects of new buildings, roads, canals, tourism and industry" (p. 286). Thomas wryly comments: "the irony was that the educated tastes of the aesthetes had themselves been paid for by the developments which they affected to deplore" (p. 287). Thomas' work, subtitled "A History of the Modern Sensibility," takes his reader on the path from the abuse of animals and land to current environmentalism; this path appears to have been a less-than-straight one.

According to John Berger, the decisive change in man's relation to the natural world came in the nineteenth century: "The nineteenth century, in western Europe and North America, saw the beginning of a process... by which every tradition which had previously mediated between man and nature was broken."[18] Berger refers neither to the rediscovery of beauty in wild nature as heralded by Rousseau nor to the identification of man and wild beast (on the basis of shared beauty or ugliness), but rather to the transformation of the animal itself in the human imagination. Man and animal once led parallel lives; man's metaphors were animal metaphors. In the nineteenth century, anthropomorphism began to make people feel uneasy because "animals... gradually disappeared." For Berger, "the decisive theoretical break came with Descartes," because "Descartes internalised, within man, the dualism implicit in the human relation to animals" (p. 9).

Berger discusses the effects of this loss of animals for representation; the ways in which literature, drawing, comics, and the other arts depicted animals—or people as animals—changed. More importantly, people saw animals differently, and animals and people ceased to be able to look at each other. Now the animal was trained to look humanly expressive. Thus, the nineteenth century saw the beginning of two new institutions: the zoo and the household pet. The former testified to conquests over the foreign and the wild, and the latter testified to the destruction of a separate life for animals; both phenomena attest to the marginalization of animals and the extinguishing of "the look between animal and man."

Berger's analysis, striking in itself, points up yet another challenge to Victorian categories. While the wild man or woman, who had previously been regarded as beastly in a negative sense, was being naturalized and was acquiring beauty, real beasts were disappearing from human life. In marginal space, in the zoo, looking at animals never satisfies, and out of this dissatisfaction came the representation of beautiful beasts (the Byronic hero). At the same time, one ideal of female beauty became the "pet," the domesticated kitten (such as George Eliot's Rosamund Vincy or Hetty Sorrel). The adorable beloved animal became a metaphor for wily beauty.

With the valorization of the most fit animal as the most beautiful man, an axiom of social Darwinism, health and vitality became criteria for beauty. Spiritedness seemed to supercede passivity; vitality became as admirable as well-restrained behavior; the wild were more lovely than the mild. But with the recovery of art as a value, the most beautiful person was he or she who most resembled an objet d'art; moreover, the healthy woman was an ugly beast of sexuality. At one extreme, beauty was represented as the epitome of health; at another extreme, beauty was ultimate passivity on the model of the marble statue.

The word "spirit" itself contains these competing values. Spirit is not material; it is the "breath" of life in us, and the word "spiritual," therefore has connotations of divinity, passivity, and serenity. "Spirit" refers as well, however, to imps (spirits) and to vital fluids (semen and liquor), so that "spirited"—a word that most often modifies young girls or horses—has precisely the opposite connotations of "spiritual." Among the contradictory values that true beauty embodied, beauty had to be both spirited (lively) and spiritual (serene).

Delicacy and Health: Pygmalion's Galatea and Little Nell

Consider the Pygmalion myth: "One man, Pygmalion, who had seen these women/ Leading their shameful lives, shocked at the vices/ Nature has given the female disposition/ Only too often, chose to live alone,/ To have no woman in his bed."[19] It takes a statue of his own fashioning, an ivory girl "with greater beauty than any girl could have" to change Pygmalion's resolve. But while the artist shares his bed with a statue, without a human spirit, she proves less than fully satisfying.

Venus, the trickster goddess of love and beauty, acts in character when she is moved to answer Pygmalion's prayer. One wonders, however, if she is rewarding Pygmalion for his labors or punishing him for his hubris. Could it be that Pygmalion got more than he bargained for? A spirited girl, as the myth assumes, has the shameful "vices Nature has given the female disposition all too often." For a spiritual girl Pygmalion might have prayed to Venus' archrival in beauty, Psyche, goddess of the soul and wife of Eros. It is possible, however, that the abstemious Pygmalion secretly desires a woman with Natural vices when "he loves the body he has fashioned... pays her compliments, and brings her presents such as girls love... decks her limbs with dresses, and her fingers" with rings, all of which "become her," though she "seems more lovely naked." It is to a physical not a spiritual being that Pygmalion "plays lover again, and over and over touches her body with his hand," ultimately discovering that "the lips he kisses are real indeed, the ivory girl can feel them and blushes and responds." Galatea's appeal is also her deficiency; as a beautiful lifeless body, she is a rare woman without vice, without vice because she is without life.

Approaching the limit of perfection, "the image seemed that of a virgin, truly almost willing, save that modesty prevented, to take on movement"; the ivory girl was poised on the brink of animation. Hers was the beauty of potential waiting to be realized, tension before release, the beauty of the figures and landscapes on Keats' Grecian Urn. At the instant when she took her first breath, when modesty ceased to prevent her from turning in her creator's bed, she must have been impossibly beautiful, a woman, as the myth tells us, "with greater beauty than any girl could have," a woman as beautiful as a work of art. One wonders if Galatea's blush and response did not signal the beginning of the end. The statue moves with a will of her own, and her color changes from white to red. Did she become a spirited and troublesome girl as Shaw's Eliza Doolittle does in the modern "Pygmalion"? Did her skin begin to wrinkle and did life's trials and frustrations begin to leave their imprints on her body?

Beauty, because it is defined out of oppositions, approaches fantastic limits as it approaches perfection: statue, beast, wild woman, death. Samuel Richardson's heroines became prototypes for this contradiction. In *Pamela's Daughters,* Utter and Bridges write that,

> To the twentieth century reader, Pamela seems grovelingly submissive. This places her in the larger of the two classes of women in literature, the submissive and the imperious, those who obey and those who command, the Penelopes and the Clytemnestras, the Griseldas and the Cleopatras.[20]

Whether or not they are right about Pamela herself, Utter and Bridges are right about the paradox of delicacy: "physical delicacy is her salvation; her weakness is her strength" (p. 13). But they write later that "the Helpless Female was shaped by the forces that were shaping civilization," and that the configuration of the delicate woman was an impossible one because:

> Delicacy, physical, mental and moral, becomes so essentially female that it develops into feebleness in all categories. Mental delicacy points to spelling and punctuation as intellectual achievement and dictates the concealment of any higher powers if they exist.

> Moral delicacy prevents a girl from receiving money if she has transgressed so far as to earn it. With this powerful equipment of feebleness she must defend her priceless chastity.... if the villain pursues her, she must not show either speed or endurance in her flight. Delicacy holds her helpless; chastity must be defended. It is an unfailing dilemma. (p. 41)

Out of the paradox of this ideal of beauty came descriptions of beautiful corpses. Dickens' Little Nell, like Clarissa Harlowe, is most beautiful when lifeless:

> She was dead. No sleep so beautiful and calm, so free from trace of pain, so fair to look upon. She seemed a creature fresh from the hand of God, and waiting for the breath of life; not one who had lived and suffered death....
>
> Where were the traces of her early cares, her sufferings, and fatigues? All gone. Sorrow was dead in her, but peace and perfect happiness were born; imaged in her tranquil beauty and profound repose.
>
> And still her former self lay there, unaltered in this change. Yes. The old fireside had smiled upon that same sweet face; it had passed like a dream through haunts of misery and care; at the door of the poor schoolmaster on the summer evening, before the furnace fires upon the cold wet night, at the still bedside of the dying boy, there had been the same mild lovely look. So shall we know the angels in their majesty, after death.[21]

On the body of Nell, origin and end meet as they are figured in the traces that are now "all gone." Birth and death are twice exchanged for one another: first, Nell is pictured as a creature who had never lived, so pure in her beauty that she apparently waits for God to breathe life into her body, rather than as one who has lived and died; second, we are told that this death is a birth, that while sorrow and all that is negative have died, peace and perfect happiness are born. The Pygmalion myth is reversed as Nell is pictured at her death as unspotted as the ivory girl had been before life. Perfect beauty, vulnerable and mutable, exists only as potential or memory. Thus, Dickens magically removes the "traces of her early cares, her sufferings and fatigues."

At the same time, Dickens insists that Nell is unchanged: "Her former self lay there, unaltered in this change." The narrator recognizes and emphasizes the paradox by isolating an affirmation: "Yes" stands alone as a sentence. Life's signs are removed, but the narrator implies that Nell never had displayed any signs of life. The phrase, "the same" is twice reiterated: "the same sweet face" and "the same mild lovely look." Thus, Nell is at once dramatically transfigured and unaltered by death. She who had always been an angel becomes an angel.

The difficulty of this passage comes, in part, from Dickens' effort to reconcile two contradictory social messages. The first is that spiritual beauty—feminine weakness—is a liability in this cruel world, and that such a woman is ever threatened with death. The second is that spiritual beauty signifies those qualities of soul that are invulnerable and eternal; it is the only beauty, the beauty of absolute goodness, that survives through death. Thus, the very qualities that destroy Nell preserve her, preserve the face that "passed like a dream through haunts of misery and care." The bodily Nell had been more dream than reality. Because the body's beauty manifests the soul's beauty, the body is immaterial. Consequently, Nell's death deserves to be lamented and celebrated.

Romantic beauty is "fair," a word that means both "pale" and "beautiful" and as an adjective indicates woman, the "fair sex." Like the word "faint," which describes things on the verge of disappearance, this kind of Romantic beauty is, by definition, ready to evaporate. Romantic heroines faint and die; the French word *mourante* captures all of these senses: "dying, languishing, expiring, fainting, fading." The Romantic obsession with mutability encouraged a preference for fair, faint, and dying beauty. Such spiritual females, divested of the power of energy, reverse the other type of Romantic heroine, the woman of art, whose disproportionate powers belong to the Medusa, the fatal woman, the *femme fatale*. While the one beauty dies, the other kills. As such, we can understand Pygmalion's bind, a man who could love no woman but a lifeless one and yet desired of her the sexual responses that might have, for all we know, killed him with pleasure. As unrealized sexuality, Dickens' Nell must die.

As early as when Lovelace describes Clarissa's corpse, he refers to the beauty of his "charmer," thus conflating the *femme fatale* and the *femme mourante*. Yet this exchange of opposites is not only typical in nineteenth-century literature, but it is frequently found in criticism of Victorian ideals of beauty. For example, Nina Auerbach writes:

> Victorian culture abounds in icons of beautiful corpse-like women and in women—such as Dickens' Little Nell Trent . . . —who are transfigured in trance, sleep, lifelike death, or embalmed life. . . . Life and death, the transcendent and the inorganic, the timelessness of myth and the contemporaneity of technology, converge in the embodiment of womanhood whose supine stillness contains the powers of her age. . . . The Sleeping Beauty's meaning lies in her destined awakening and her attendant power to awake her world. True, only the Prince can wake her, but his power, like that of Svengali, Dracula, and Freud in his mythic projection of himself is a limited catalyst for her broader and more disruptive powers: she alone can galvanize an entire society of which, like Ayesha, Lilith, and Eve, she is both the mesmerizing and the animating spirit. Embodying victim who consecrates herself into a queen, the Sleeping Beauty who fascinated the age was a troubled and revolutionary intimation of her own power when awake.[22]

This analysis, because it uncovers the repressed fear of female power that justifies idealizations of weakness, misleadingly suggests that dying women really were powerfully fatal. Instead, ideals of feminine weakness, dying beauties, betray male fear of women's potential strength. Hence women are imagined to be beautiful when they are weakest.

Auerbach writes in the tradition of Mario Praz who, in *The Romantic Agony*, begins his chapter on the beauty of the Medusa by discussing not women who kill, but women who die:

> But there is no end to the examples which might be quoted from the Romantic and Decadent writers on the subject of the indissoluble union of the beautiful and the sad, on the supine beauty of that beauty which is accursed....
>
> In fact, to such an extent were Beauty and Death looked upon as sisters by the Romantics that they became fused into a sort of two-faced herm, filled with corruption and melancholy and fatal in its beauty—a beauty of which, the more bitter the taste the more abundant the enjoyment.[23]

Praz regards the Fatal Woman, often localized in exotic places, as providing an opportunity for writers to indulge in "unbridled desires" and the "cruellest fantasies" (p. 207). From being a model of delicacy and languorous weakness, she becomes at once "La Belle Dame," the punishing beauty, and the woman of beauty who is punished herself. Both the *femme fatale* and the *femme mourante* risk being exemplars of ugliness as well as beauty. For Shelley, the Medusa of his poem has fatal beauty, and Freud in his essay on "Medusa's Head" takes the sting out of even that exemplar of feminine power. Freud reasons that the snakes on the head actually "mitigate against the horror of castration." They multiply the phallus, and the spectator's stiffening consoles him, reassuring him of his own potency. [24]

The "Belle Dame" and the Sleeping Beauty, the Medusa and the corpse of Nell, Cleopatra and Clarissa, the female sadist and masochist cease to be antitheses in a body of literature that proffers each type, in many variations, as an object of beauty and erotic fantasy. Shelley (in his poem "Medusa") and Dickens alike direct the gaze of the reader to an impossibly powerful and impossibly self-destructive ideal of womanhood. Rachel M. Brownstein perceives Clarissa, whom Richardson proposes as an "Exemplar to her sex," in this light:

> What Richardson means by an Exemplar is the feminine ideal of his time. She is a young woman, perfectly chaste, dutiful, obedient, religious, useful, orderly, charitable, thrifty and kind. She acts and requires others to act according to a firm ethical standard. But her essence is aesthetic. In effect the bourgeois Christian Exemplar is an adaptation of the cliché that a woman is a goddess, a convention of courtship, literature and polite society that, as Richardson knew and Mary Wollstonecraft was soon to say, has long served to enslave women. An Exemplar is too good for the real goods of the real world. She is not born but made;... she is not human but perfect.... her secondary task is to be a didactic work of art, to exist in a form sufficiently clear and attractive so as to inspire other girls to be like her and thus keep the world pleasant and safe for its owners.[25]

Dorothy Van Ghent, in her reading of the "Clarissa-symbol," finds Clarissa a paradox of the pure and debilitated love-goddess created through a strategy of voyeurism.[26] The death scenes in both *Clarissa* and *The Old Curiosity Shop* are ultimately voyeuristic.

Because they reject Clarissa as a prototype for "the immaculate heroine of the Gothic novels of the turn of the century," Elizabeth MacAndrew and Susan Gorsky argue in "Why Do They Faint and Die?—The Birth of the Delicate Heroine" that such heroines persist in Victorian literature as models of "good nature."[27] Even Clarissa Harlowe is, according to this view, too spirited to have functioned as a model for pale Victorian heroines. Although Clarissa "faints under stress and dies of a broken heart... she also has a fine arrogance, a sharp tongue, the ability to take matters into her own hands.... Her death itself is a triumph, not a defeat." Instead, they argue that the "afflicted heroine... migrated from the sentimental novel" to lift the reader "out of his humdrum self through the sublime." The Gothic heroine is not a realistic figure; instead she is meant to be a receptacle for values "suited to 'raise our affections.'" "Exquisite, delicate, and passive," the heroine represents "human nature, the human potential we must try to realize." By forcing the reader to watch the villain's cruel treatment of the heroine, these fictions elevate our sympathies for idealized and passive virtue.

According to this reading, as in the analyses of Praz and Auerbach, the Delicate Heroine is a model of strength. But even as debility was a sign of beauty, the absence of spirit was unlovely. Victorians stressed the importance of health and legislated to ensure sanitation. The Latin word *sanus*, from which both "sane" and "sanitary" derive, suggests the internal wholeness that Victorians called "nature."[28] One wanted, as Herbert Spencer wrote, "a nation of good animals" (Haley, p. 22). But that good health and spirit that came to characterize one kind of beauty was suspect as well. Given the power of the image of the debilitated woman, it is not surprising that, as Haley observes, "in Eliot's novels those unacquainted with infirmity... tend to have short memories and little imagination" (p. 196).

An examination of the medical literature and scientific assumptions of the late nineteenth century reveals that women were exempt from the Darwinian revolution. While male beauty could be regarded as healthy animalism, female beauty remained angelic or demonic, as the ideal woman continued to be defined by her relative constitutional weakness. Sarah Stage writes:

> Goaded on by exhortations of a culture that placed a premium on such catchwords as "rugged individualism" and "survival of the fittest," men labored under a staggering set of internalized demands epitomized in the concept of the "self-made man." Where men were weighted down with demands, women became weighted down with restrictions. Determined to be all strength, men saw in women all weakness....
>
> The bifurcation of human attributes that became evident in the nineteenth century, in which manhood became synonymous with strength and womanhood with weakness, did not mark a new departure so much as it exaggerated an ancient perception.... Early arguments on women's inferiority drew support from the Bible. By the middle of the

nineteenth century, the Bible began to lose its hold as a source of social wisdom. Science, the new faith of the century, provided the framework within which the social questions of the day were examined.... The odd assortment of beliefs which paraded as "scientific fact" was particularly apparent in the popular medical literature....

The constriction of women's sphere apparent on the social level was paralleled in medical writing by a constriction in the field of vision which led doctors to focus, with obsessive concern, on women's organs of reproduction. Michelet's characterization of the nineteenth century as the age of the womb, taken literally, ... enabled men to view women as a creature apart. The distinguished British physician Henry Maudsley concluded a discussion of women's sexual organs in 1870 with the observation that "the forms and habits of mutilated men approach those of women."

Stage explains that viewing woman as a "mutilated man" provided the scientific justification for social restrictions at the same time that "her reproductive system came to be seen as a sacred trust.... As one doctor put it, it was as if 'the Almighty, in creating the female sex, had taken the uterus and built a woman around it.'" Stage quotes Hippocrates' famous aphorism: "What is woman? Disease," and she remarks that nineteenth-century doctors thought no differently. Quoting Michelet, Stage explains that menstruation was understood as "love's eternal wound," "a morbid state," a sign of invalidism, "romanticized into an infirmity." At the same time, weak women acquired strength through intercourse because of the ancient and still widely held belief that the emission of semen "enfeebles the body." The woman, "as sperm-absorber not only sapped his powers but grew stronger in the process."[29]

Thus, while man was regarded as an animal, woman could retain her status as a domestic angel, beautiful in her natural invalidism. At the same time, any unnatural desire for strength, any sexual or social desire, was understood literally as a threat to the health of the male of the species. The Victorians accordingly stressed the hazards of syphilis and childbed fever, the actual diseases that stood behind these medical myths. Given these tenets of medicine, it is small wonder that the *femme fatale* saps her victim of strength by provoking him to lust.

Strong women were not only threatening, but they were "unnatural"; science demonstrated that weakness was a woman's natural condition, and women, therefore, aspired to the ideal of beauty that fashion and medicine alike promoted. Alison Lurie explains how fashion cemented the relationship between social and medical truth:

> Early nineteenth-century fashions were designed to give a look of fragile immaturity. They emphasized weakness of both structure and substance through the use of pale colors and delicate, easily damaged materials. More ominously, these clothes ensured the charming ill-health of their wearers by putting them into thin-soled slippers and short-sleeved, low-necked dresses of semitransparent muslin. When worn in the drafty ballrooms and along the icy, muddy lanes of a British or North American winter, such clothes were almost a guarantee of the feverish colds and sore throats that are so common in the novels of Jane Austen and the Brontës....

> By the 1830s, female fashions offered somewhat more protection from the climate, but they continued to suggest—and to promote—physical frailty. Early Victorian costume not only made women *look* weak and helpless, it made them weak and helpless. The main agent of this debility, as many writers have pointed out, was the corset, which at the time was thought of as not a mere fashion but as a medical necessity. Ladies' "frames," it was believed, were extremely delicate; their muscles could not hold them up without assistance. Like many such beliefs, this one was self-fulfilling. Well brought-up little girls, from the best motives, were laced.... By the time they reached late adolescence... their back muscles had often atrophied to the point where they could not sit or stand for long unsupported. The corset also deformed the inner organs and made it impossible to draw a deep breath. As a result the fashionably dressed lady blushed and fainted easily, suffered from lack of appetite and from digestive complaints, and felt weak and exhausted after any strenuous exertion....
>
> ...[M]ore important than the medical justification of the corset was its social justification. Women were considered the frailer sex not only physically but morally: their minds and their wills as well as their backs were weak.... Purity and innocence could be preserved only by constant vigilance. Therefore she must not attend a university or follow a profession... and she must not see any play or read any book that might inflame her imagination.

Lurie argues that the early Victorian woman needed to be supported and confined in her clothing for the same reason that she was excluded from professional life. Wondering why women submitted to these uncomfortable fashions, Lurie writes that not only did women know that they would be admired as "beautiful, charming and elegant," only if they were so attired, but that they also believed the propaganda that confining and deforming clothing was a medical and moral necessity: "Tight lacing was associated in the popular imagination with virtue: a well-dressed woman whose stays were loose... was probably a loose woman."[30]

In the Victorian imagination, female beauty, like female sexuality, was defined in terms of an irreconcilable opposition, though each model contained its own contradiction: the pure woman worried about her "unnatural" urges and the impure woman was "naturally" pure. Peter T. Cominos, in his important study of "femina sensualis," summarizes this ideology:

> Women were classified into polar extremes. They were either sexless ministering angels or sensuously oversexed temptresses of the devil; they were either aids to continence or incontinence.... Although apart, these polarities shared an attitude of disguised masculine hostility toward women. It was a fragment of that anti-feminine ideology that represented at the level of consciousness those corresponding relations of domination and dependent submission that characterized family existence.

Thus,

> Victorian society and the family spawned two kinds of women, the womanly woman and her negation, the whorely whore: the pure and the impure.... The pure woman was

innocent, inviolate, inspirational and indulged; the impure woman (less than a woman) was doubtful, detestable and destroyed. No dialectic could join the two; a great impassable gulf divided them.[31]

Each of these types existed, as well, as a model of beauty. The former, a *femme mourante,* was charmingly infirm, angelic or divine, fragile as a "flower," gentle as a kitten, naturally graceful; the latter, a *femme fatale,* seemed beautiful but was, in reality, artful as a witch, a monster of sexuality, a lustful beast, and supernaturally strong.

Nineteenth-century discourse in such fields as philosophy, sociology, agriculture and medicine reveals a variety of bodies and spirits of the age that may be reduced to opposing types. Each type, however, implied and contained the features of that to which it was opposed. The best of mothers in Victorian England faced a double bind: to ensure their daughters' beauty (and the power of beauty) they had to make them suffer and restrain them. In an 1895 version of the Cinderella story, the violence of amputation (the stepmother in the version of the brothers Grimm chops away at her daughters' feet to make them fit the slipper) is replaced by what the Victorians regarded as a less distasteful gesture: the stepsisters tighten their bodices.[32]

Bodies are shaped to fit the spirits of the age, and those "spirits" manifest themselves in language. In *Illness as Metaphor,* Susan Sontag characterizes the differences between our century and the nineteenth century in terms of their different treatment of illness in language and, therefore, in life.[33] TB, a romantic disease in the nineteenth century, was imagined to beautify its victims, whereas cancer, our century's terrifying disease, is described in metaphors that lead us to be repelled by cancer sufferers. In *The Unfashionable Human Body,* Bernard Rudofsky catalogues many of the ways in which different cultures deform the body in the name of beauty. Elaine Scarry in *The Body in Pain* relates the body's situation in language to its situation in torture and war.[34] Cultural categories vary: to us it seems bizarre that women in certain tribes take pleasure in molding their children's skulls to ensure their eventual desirability. Because we may not know the meanings assigned to this ideal of beauty—how the head is described in language, and what history stands behind it—the act seems cruel and the result does not look to us like beauty. Out of the dichotomies of art and nature, nature and nurture, and delicacy and health, however, derive sets of criteria for beauty in nineteenth-century England that seem to us today more or less "natural." But even as we identify the features of natural beauty, we find nature redefined or we find ourselves being asked to prefer new qualities which oppose and supercede nature: the charm of artistry, the grace of cultivation, the strength of superman, the divinity of debility.

4

Shaping the Body to Fit the Eye: Austen's *Persuasion* as a Romantic Cinderella

Beauty deeply concerns all of the characters in Jane Austen's *Persuasion* (1816), though one of the novel's basic messages is that "beauty is in the eye of the beholder." Of course Austen gives this popular message her usual discriminating twist: one can find the best beauty in the most worthy characters if only one knows what to look for. Establishing the morally correct standard of value becomes the novel's preoccupation, and as this is Austen's last full novel, the task is accomplished with the powers of subtlety for which her craft, at its best, is famous. While this novel is carefully nuanced, beauty is described sparsely and redundantly, as is typical in early nineteenth-century novels. The characters of beauty in this novel thus provide us with clear examples because they are both early and late representations, having been born late in the career of one of the century's earliest classic novelists.

The heroine of *Persuasion* seems to possess those qualities most valued by the novel in which she figures. Anne Elliot is more mature, more cultured, more delicate, more artless, and more humble than her rivals in beauty. At the same time, for much of the story, this heroine is represented as being less beautiful than those with whom she competes for affection. It is precisely that which Anne Elliot lacks that the novel establishes as the essential criteria for beauty: youth, stature, bloom, vitality, charm, and self-assertiveness. It seems that by the novel's end, however, either Anne Elliot has been transfigured or the reader's standard of value has changed such that Anne emerges from the shadows, Cinderella-like, fully deserving of Captain Wentworth, her prince. Both processes are at work, and they conceal each other and they work against each other: the heroine's appearance undergoes dramatic reversals, and the reader becomes educated by the fiction to admire qualities that were always Anne Elliot's. By the novel's end, Anne Elliot and Captain Wentworth meet two standards of beauty, each of which precludes the other. The other characters of beauty seem one-dimensional and lacking by comparison with the hero and heroine.

In this respect, Anne Elliot and Captain Wentworth are not unlike the hero and heroine of "The Algonquin Cinderella." The heroine is both the least beautiful and the most beautiful marriageable woman in the society of the fiction, and the hero's universally admired beauty proves to be matched by a perfect character only when he selects the right bride. But the magical transformations of fairy tale are rendered realistic by the strategies of a complex narrative that particularizes the hero's and heroine's qualities. While we are simply assured of Oochigeaskw's and the Invisible One's beauty, Austen tells us precisely what constitutes the value of her characters; thus, the characters' development and the reader's developing sensibilities make this fantasy plausible. Our interest here is to discern the categories within which Austen articulates beauty without looking far beyond the novel itself.

Persuaded by her well-meaning friend Lady Russell and her less than well-intentioned family, Anne Elliot had turned down a marriage proposal from the man she loved, Frederick Wentworth. The novel's plot turns, of course, on the question of who will marry whom now that Anne and Captain Wentworth find themselves in each other's company after an eight-year separation. The plot's complications derive from the competition presented by the other men and women in the society of the novel. These characters are presented in terms of their qualities of beauty and in terms of their evaluation of beauty; each character's physical appeal corresponds directly to character traits, and the underlying moral fabric of the novel is composed of threads of description woven into a pattern out of which one ideal woman and one ideal man will emerge. Several questions guide the reader who is guessing about who will marry whom: Are the particular features of Captain Wentworth's beauty and character such that he still suits Anne Elliot? If not, who then will be the new hero, the man whose qualities make him deserving of the heroine? On the other side, has Anne Elliot been so transformed by the years that she can no longer attract her handsome sailor? If so, which woman will win him now?

After all is said and done, Anne Elliot becomes engaged to Frederick Wentworth, and when they renew their alliance, Frederick compliments her on her beauty by reporting a conversation that he recently had with his brother:

> "... He enquired after you very particularly; asked even if you were personally altered, little suspecting that to my eye you could never alter."
>
> Anne smiled, and let it pass. It was too pleasing a blunder for reproach. It is something for a woman to be assured, in her eight-and-twentieth year, that she has not lost one charm of her earlier youth: but the value of such homage was inexpressibly increased to Anne, by comparing it with former words, and feeling it to be the result, not the cause of a revival of his warm attachment.[1]

Wentworth's pleasing blunder, the implication that Anne must have altered to other eyes if not to his, leaves Anne assured that "she has not lost one charm of her earlier youth." Does the narrator mean that she has lost none of the charms of her earlier youth or that she merely retains the one charm still useful for captivating the hero? This, the novel's last reflection on Anne's beauty, summarizes her appeal: Anne, in spite of all, has charmed and secured the most handsome man in the novel. His warm attachment, now revived, results from whatever are those charms that belong to Anne alone.

The former words, remembered now, were spoken after Frederick Wentworth had seen Anne again for the first time, and they were reported to her by her sister Mary:

> "... Henrietta asked him what he thought of you, when they went away; and he said, 'You were so altered he should not have known you again.'"
> ... "Altered beyond his knowledge!"... Doubtless it was so; and she could take no revenge, for he was not altered, or not for the worse.... No; the years which had destroyed her youth and bloom had only given him a more glowing and manly look, in no respect lessening his personal advantages....
> He had thought her wretchedly altered, and, in the first moment of appeal, had spoken as he felt. He had not forgiven Anne Elliot. She had used him ill; deserted and disappointed him; and worse, she had shewn a feebleness in character in doing so, which his own decided, confident temper could not endure. She had given him up to oblige others. It had been the effect of overpersuasion. It had been weakness and timidity.
> He had been most warmly attached to her, and had never seen a woman since whom he thought her equal; but.... Her power with him was gone forever.
> It was now his object to marry. (pp. 51–52)

It is "power" over her man that Anne has lost, a power that derives, as the passage clearly suggests, from being perceived of as beautiful. Wentworth retains his charm because she "had seen the same" man, *the same* man *altered* by years at sea which had given him a "glowing open look." The narrator, close to Anne's own consciousness, suggests that Anne's self-perception is that she has indeed been wretchedly altered by loss of "youth and bloom." At the same time, the narrator supplies Anne with an interpretation of Captain Wentworth's words that has nothing at all to do with how she actually looks. He sees no beauty in Anne because he sees bad character there: weakness and timidity. The narrator implies that Anne herself thinks both that she is altered and that if she had been forgiven for past "weakness," she would not have been found so unlovely.

The established tension is that Anne still loves a man who apparently no longer loves her, but though his object is to marry someone else, neither person has found anyone equal to the other in all of the intervening years. This chapter ends with the threat that Captain Wentworth may now be charmed into marriage by either Henrietta or Louisa Musgrove. Having said that "it was his object to marry," the narrator adds that "he was rich," and

> fully intended to settle as soon as he could be properly tempted.... He had a heart for either of the Miss Musgroves, if they could catch it; a heart, in short, for any pleasing young woman who came in his way, excepting Anne Elliot....

Wentworth tells his sister Sophia (her name connotes wisdom, just as his suggests that his having "went" was "worth" it) that,

> "a little beauty, and a few smiles, and a few compliments to the navy, and I am a lost man...."
> He said it, she knew, to be contradicted.... and Anne Elliot was not out of his thoughts, when he more seriously described the woman he should wish to meet with. "A strong mind, with sweetness of manner," made the first and last of the description. (p. 52)

The language by means of which this projected marriage scenario is described portrays women as the daughters of Eve, trappers of men. Anne has lost "power" (though later we learn that she lost not one "charm"); Frederick needs to be "properly tempted," and his heart is there for the Miss Musgroves if one of them "can catch it." In the description that he wants contradicted, Frederick conjures up the Miss Musgroves (youth, pleasantness, a little beauty, a few smiles, and readiness to compliment the navy); his serious description applies to his memory of Anne Elliot, "a strong mind, with sweetness of manner."

Although the criteria for a wife are ironically posed, eligibility to marry the hero finds its requirements in this passage in a set of adjectives that will be so often repeated in the novel that the reader must take them seriously. Anne, "with feebleness of character... timid and weak" as well as cruel ("she had used him ill; deserted and disappointed him"), is his model of strength of mind and sweetness of character. Both descriptions apply to Anne as she had been long ago, and the descriptions contradict each other: we are offered several synonyms for weakness and cruelty, and we are asked to regard Anne as unmatched for her strong mind and sweetness. The other oppositions here established complete the grid within which beauty and character are particularized; they include bloom and youth (both of which have been destroyed in Anne and both of which the Miss Musgroves have), a little beauty and happy smiles (which Anne, as opposed to her rivals, gave up when she gave up Frederick), and offering compliments to the navy. The latter is Louisa Musgrove's strongest suit, because Anne did not marry Frederick Wentworth precisely for the reason that her friends wanted her to marry a gentleman rather than a sailor. While the women are defined in terms of oppositions within a code of flowers (the ability to "charm" with youth, bloom, sweetness, gaiety), male beauty is drawn by means of an opposition between the codes of "The Gentleman" and "The Sailor."

Between the time when Frederick found Anne "altered beyond his knowledge" and the time when he tells her that to his eye "she could never alter," is the visit to Lyme during which Anne *does* alter. Both Musgrove sisters are present, though Louisa seems to have caught Frederick's heart. Present as well are two other men who single Anne Elliot out for admiration. Captain Benwick admires Anne for her kindness and intelligence, but an anonymous stranger singles Anne out on the basis of looks alone. It later turns out that this stranger is Anne's cousin, her father's heir:

> When they came to the steps, . . . a gentleman . . . politely drew back, and stopped to give them way. They ascended and passed him; and as they passed, Anne's face caught his eye, and he looked at her with a degree of earnest admiration, which she could not be insensible of. She was looking remarkably well; her very regular, very pretty features, having the bloom and freshness of youth restored by the fine wind which had been blowing on her complexion, and by the animation of eye which it had also produced. It was evident that the gentleman (completely a gentleman in manner) admired her exceedingly. Captain Wentworth looked round at her instantly in a way that showed his noticing of it. He gave her a momentary glance,—a glance of brightness, which seemed to say, "That man is struck with you,—and even I, at this moment, see something like Anne Elliot again." (p. 89)

Anne is characterized by "very regular" and "very pretty features," though she had long wanted the bloom, freshness, and animation of youth. In this passage, Anne recovers all that her beauty lacked, at the same moment that a man appears who has that which Wentworth lacked, the promise of a baronetcy. Although Anne does not yet know this crucial fact, she appreciates his gentlemanliness above all, and though she does not think him handsome, she does want to know him. The narrative insists upon this point by forcing another chance meeting:

> This second meeting, short as it was, also proved again by the gentleman's looks, that he thought hers very lovely, and by the readiness and propriety of his apologies, that he was a man of exceedingly good manners. He seemed about thirty, and, though not handsome, had an agreeable person. Anne felt that she should like to know who he was. (pp. 89-90)

By now, the elements for a complex plot are all in place. Anne's rivals, Henrietta and Louisa, fast resolve into one serious rival, Louisa, and Wentworth soon finds that it is Mr. Elliot and not Benwick who will pursue Anne. But the hero's and heroine's attractions are not only defined in relation to their competitors for each other's affections but also in relation to the rest of the novel's characters. We see Wentworth compared to the Miss Musgroves' brother (who, now married to Anne's sister Mary, had been turned down by Anne), and we see him compared to his brother naval officers. Similarly, Anne is set in relation to her two sisters, Elizabeth and Mary, and to two unlovely women (Mrs. Clay and Mrs. Smith). Anne's beauty is also defined in relation to that of both of her parents, and most importantly, both the hero and the heroine are seen in relation to themselves as they had been eight years before.

While it first appears as if Anne alone has none of the personal advantages most praised by the narrator, as we learn to fully appreciate the subtleties of her character, we come to realize that she alone has all of the contradictory prerequisites for beauty in properly muted form. Each character, save Anne and Captain Wentworth, is reduced to a type; a leisurely look at the descriptions of the other men and women of the novel reveals that no character of beauty is beautiful without qualification; each woman is excessively herself: too hearty or too delicate; too wild or too mild; too artful or too simple; too stately or too slight. Likewise, each man becomes a caricature of himself: too frail or too hale; too large or too small; too polished or too natural. Frederick wins his competition because, like Anne, he possesses each quality in the right measure. The hero and heroine alone cannot be captured in a phrase. Austen handles everyone else with irony.

The narrative's descriptive passages are punctuated with information that the reader needs to interpret description. What I have called the "code of flowers" finds much elaboration in the novel and would have been familiar to the reader who remembered Richardson's Clarissa as a "wilted lily"; today's reader knows as well that the metaphor of woman as flower would hold the Victorian imagination: Hawthorne's Hester Prynne is identified with the red rose; the graves of little girls were often adorned with sculptures that literalized Ruskin's definition of girls as "flowers to be plucked"; George Eliot's Hetty is a rose, while Dinah has the face of a lily. *Persuasion* makes early use of this code. The types of flowers themselves are yet unspecified; beautiful women simply bloom, and unlovely women lack bloom.

The code of the sailor also finds much explanation in *Persuasion:* vitality and a weathered look is contrasted with the gentleman's polished grace and affectation; the former type acquires his prestige through labor, while the latter type acquires his prestige with birth. In Melville's *Billy Budd* (whose name makes him a flower), the features of the handsome sailor will be generated out of a conflation of these two codes of beauty. As Barbara Johnson observes, Billy Budd is also a self-contradiction; he is the gentle (nonviolent) man who kills.[2] As "the handsome sailor," he descends from Captain Wentworth. The background to *Persuasion* is made of the cultural associations and connotations that cling to these varieties of masculine and feminine beauty. The descriptive passages in *Persuasion* reveal that beauty is defined essentially through the oppositions of artfulness (charm, makeup, ability to acquire power) and naturalness; good breeding (earned wealth) and high birth (unearned rank); innocence (youth) and experience (maturity); and vitality (the bloom of good health) and delicacy (the flower's fragility). Out of a complete mixture of these categories emerge a heroine and hero.

Anne Elliot is positioned as a kind of Cinderella in her household. The mother who would have appreciated her is dead, and her father and sisters take her labors for granted and have no sympathy for her own pain. For much of the story even the maternally affectionate but misguided godmother, Lady Russell, sees little beauty left in a faded Anne Elliot. The handsomest of the sisters is Elizabeth, who physically resembles her father and who therefore shares his character flaws as well. The beauty of father and daughter is inextricably bound up with their social pretensions. Of the sisters, Elizabeth alone blooms, though her bloom is made mockery of because she is well beyond her first "spring," and at twenty-nine, risks becoming a type that would later be fixed in the Victorian novel: the spinster. Mary, on the other hand, "even in her bloom, only reached the dignity of being a 'fine girl'" (p. 30), and she is characterized principally by her physical weakness: she is a caricature of the current Romantic ideal (a hypochondriac), a caricature of the domestic angel to come (an inadequate wife and mother), and a caricature of the great lady of the past (ever concerned with her place at the table). But because Elizabeth is handsome and because Mary is married, Anne is "nobody" by comparison.

We first meet the formidable presence of Sir Walter Elliot who is described with no small touch of mirth:

> Vanity was the beginning and the end of Sir Walter Elliot's character; vanity of person and of situation. He had been remarkably handsome in his youth; and at fifty-four, was still a very fine man. Few women could think more of their personal appearance than he did; nor could the valet of any new made lord be more delighted with the place he held in society. He considered the blessing of beauty as inferior only to the blessing of a baronetcy; and the Sir Walter Elliot, who united these gifts, was the constant object of his warmest respect and devotion. (p. 2)

By comparing Sir Walter to a valet, Austen suggests that Sir Walter is a poor example of a man of class. With this description of vanity, Austen makes the further point that beauty and social position are of little worth without cultivated qualities, and that as the "beginning and end of character," these accidental and inherited gifts are quite insufficient.

The reader then sees the Elliot women through their father's eyes, whose perception we have been taught to question:

> Elizabeth had succeeded, at sixteen, to all that was possible, of her mother's rights and consequence; and being very handsome, and very like himself, her influence had always been great, and they had gone on together most happily. His two other children were of very inferior value. Mary had acquired a little artificial importance, by becoming Mrs. Charles Musgrove; but Anne, with an elegance of mind and sweetness of character, which must have

> placed her high with any people of real understanding, was nobody with either her father or sister: her word had no weight; her convenience was always to give way;—she was only Anne. (p. 3)

To contrast with Sir Walter's perception, the narrator introduces nameless "people of real understanding" who would see beyond the appearances to sweetness of character and elegance of mind. These adjectives, meant here to distinguish between Anne's outer and inner qualities, will, as we have already seen, come to define Anne's physical beauty as well, her features and bearing. Elegance, in particular, serves to prove that though Anne's family regards her as its least socially estimable member, she, like Cinderella, is a "natural" aristocrat. One purpose of this novel is to restore the heroine to her birthright. Because her family is convinced that she is "nobody," this can only be accomplished if Anne were to marry a wealthy man.

While Anne, because she is not vain, appears to be the least socially ambitious Elliot, she has also been the only one prepared to live on an income that would have ensured the ultimate dignity of the family estate. And it is she who cares about that dignity. From her mother, Anne has inherited qualities of "industry and moderation," qualities more usually associated with the poor woman, qualities that were necessary to protect people of rank in precarious financial positions. To protect Anne's social position was precisely Lady Russell's motive when she stood in the way of her goddaughter's marriage eight years before:

> Anne Elliot, with all the claims of birth, beauty, and mind, to throw herself away at nineteen; involve herself... in an engagement with a young man, who had nothing but himself to recommend him, and no hope of attaining affluence, but in the chances of a most uncertain profession, and no connexions to secure even his further rise in that profession.... (p. 21)

The novel's plot does and does not justify Lady Russell's objections. On the one hand, "the young man who had nothing but himself to recommend him" does rise to rank and wealth; on the other hand, without rank and wealth, as he had been, he was less than an equal match for the heroine. Captain Wentworth at thirty-one suits Anne better than he did at twenty-three, and thus the novelist both champions the humble man who works hard and saves well, while she places ultimate value on the attainment of wealth and rank. If one has the virtues of the poor, one deserves to be rich. By taking after her mother, Anne also deserves wealth, willing as she is to live economically. Elizabeth's and Sir Walter's love of ostentatious beauty (embodied in their stately handsomeness) contrast, both superficially and profoundly, with an elegant and delicate beauty that is too subtle for them to appreciate. Like the valet to a new-made lord, they look and act nouveau riche. Wentworth, whose money *is* new, has an eye for subtler beauty.

In Anne, Lady Russell "could fancy the mother to revive again," but it is Elizabeth, having succeeded to her mother's rights, who wishes also to succeed to her mother's title. For a part of the novel the reader wonders if one of the sisters will marry their father's heir, and we half hope it will be Anne, hoping at the same time that that does not mean a repetition of Lady Elliot's mistake. "In her first bloom" Elizabeth had met Mr. Elliot and found him "extremely agreeable." The following spring, Elizabeth and Sir Walter tried and failed again to woo the heir for Elizabeth. At the time of the story, Mr. Elliot's eyes are for the more deserving heiress, Anne. From the novel's start, however, we know that Sir Walter cannot imagine such an alliance, and the narrator tells us that he never expects to record the marriage of Anne Elliot in the family book:

> A few years before, Anne Elliot had been a very pretty girl, but her bloom had vanished early; as even in its height, her father had found little to admire in her, (so totally different were her delicate features and mild dark eyes from his own); there could be nothing in them now that she was faded and thin, to excite his esteem. (p. 3)

Thus, the initial portrait of Anne is of a faded unappreciated woman. While her manner is sweet, her mind elegant, her eyes mild and dark, and her features delicate, she lacks her father's and Elizabeth's beauty. Whatever constitutes their handsomeness, however (we never learn the particulars), they lack mild dark eyes and delicacy. Anne, on the other hand, lacks only Elizabeth's "bloom":

> It sometimes happens, that a woman is handsomer at twenty-nine than she was ten years before; and generally speaking, if there has been neither ill health nor anxiety, it is a time of life at which scarcely any charm is lost. It was so with Elizabeth; still the same handsome Miss Elliot that she had begun to be thirteen years ago; and Sir Walter might be excused, therefore, in forgetting her age, or, at least, be deemed only half a fool, for thinking himself and Elizabeth as blooming as ever, amidst the wreck of good looks of everybody else; for he could plainly see how old all the rest of his family and acquaintance were growing. Anne haggard, Mary coarse, every face in the neighborhood worsting.... (p. 4)

While Elizabeth is thus described, the reader puzzles over Anne, wondering what "ill health" or "anxiety" made her "haggard" when "generally speaking" this is a time of life when "scarcely any charm need be lost." Anne, of course, lost her charm when she gave up Wentworth: "Her attachment and regrets had, for a long time, clouded every enjoyment of youth, and an early loss of bloom and spirits had been their lasting effect" (p. 22).

The description of Elizabeth as the handsomest of the sisters serves another purpose. By indicating that Elizabeth is one of those women who is handsomer at twenty-nine than she had been ten years before, the novelist treats time as no necessary destroyer of beauty. Austen gives beauty to Elizabeth and takes beauty from her with one stroke. Sir Walter, excused as only half a fool for imagining Elizabeth and himself to be unchanged, must be mistaken. That he is fool at all suggests that they are indeed changed for the worse. Mary made coarse and Anne haggard by the years, time is the ultimate destroyer of floral beauty. Time, we are given to understand, need not and yet must ruin beauty. The look of "youth," "bloom," and "spirit" are and are not affected by the years' passage.

The Musgrove sisters are the antithesis of a faded Anne:

> Henrietta and Louisa, young ladies of nineteen and twenty,... were now living to be fashionable, happy, and merry. Their dress had every advantage, their faces were rather pretty, their spirits extremely good, their manners unembarrassed and pleasant; they were of consequence at home, and favourites abroad. Anne always contemplated them as some of the happiest creatures of her acquaintance; but still... she would not have given up her own more elegant and cultivated mind for all their enjoyments. (p. 34)

Once more the reader learns that it is "elegance and cultivation" that the socially unambitious heroine most highly regards in herself. Anne, thus without envy, is first in company with Captain Wentworth at the home of the Musgroves, and the reader is envious in her place. The Miss Musgroves had earlier told Anne rapturously "how perfectly delighted they were with him, how much handsomer, how infinitely more agreeable they thought him than any individual of their male acquaintance" (p. 45), and on this night, Wentworth looks at Anne only once. Beauty's power is again referred to as "charm": "Once she felt that he was looking at herself—observing her altered features, perhaps, trying to trace in them the ruins of the face that had once charmed him" (p. 61). Austen's presentation is again ironic; she writes *as if* Anne has given into crass values by judging herself physically. But by now the reader has an investment in Anne's beauty and victory. It is we who care that she be found superior to the Musgrove sisters. The next day Anne contemplates: "Henrietta was perhaps the prettiest, Louisa had the higher spirits; she knew not now, whether the more gentle or the more lively character were most likely to attract him" (p. 63).

Wentworth places character above beauty, and it is the spirited Louisa who attracts him, though Louisa, it turns out, is too spirited and too strong-willed. Her punishment is a concussion that robs her of spirit and excellent health; the young, melancholy, handsome Benwick—whom we had imagined as a potential suitor for Anne—becomes engaged instead to the transformed Louisa. At the novel's start, it was Anne who lacked health and spirit, and Lady Russell particularly wished for her to go to Bath as it was a "change which must do her health and spirits good" (p. 11). By the novel's conclusion, Anne's spirited competitor is an invalid while her own health and spirits are fully recovered.

The novelist oscillates between antitheses in her descriptions of the men as well. Naval men are compared to gentlemen also based on criteria of health and spirit. Seamen are depicted as men whose beauty is most strong and vital and as men who are most likely to suffer loss of beauty from loss of health. When Sir Walter rents his home to Admiral Croft, Wentworth's brother-in-law, Sir Walter objects to the navy on two grounds:

> "...First, as being the means of bringing persons of obscure birth into undue distinction...and secondly, as it cuts up a man's youth and vigour most horribly; a sailor grows older sooner than any other man...." (p. 15)

Mrs. Clay responds by flattering the gentleman on whom she has set her sights, assuring him that "we are not all born to be handsome," and her father, Mr. Shephard, reassures the landlord that "Admiral Croft was a very hale, hearty, well-looking man...quite the gentleman in all his notions and behavior" (p. 17).

Wentworth stands out among all the sailors in the novel, though each has his own appeal:

> Captain Harville was a tall, dark man, with a sensible, benevolent countenance; a little lame, and from strong features, and want of health, looking much older than Captain Wentworth. Captain Benwick looked and was the youngest of the three, and, compared with either of them, a little man. He had a pleasing face and a melancholy air....
>
> Captain Harville, though not equalling Captain Wentworth in manners, was a perfect gentleman, unaffected, warm, and obliging. (p. 83)

The gentleman-sailor dichotomy collapses again in this beauty competition, and the sea is again represented as a guarantor and destroyer of that beauty which is healthy and strong. Anne, who finds "bewitching charm" in this company, can only be depressed in the knowledge that these would have been her friends, but her greatest regrets must be felt with respect to Wentworth who clearly surpasses them all.

Wentworth combines the qualities of his brother officers because he lacks their defects. The sea has neither aged him nor threatened his health as it has Harville, though like Harville, Wentworth has the strength and height to surpass Benwick; and Wentworth's manners surpass those of the "perfect gentleman."

Anne stands in a similar relation to her own sisters. Much more delicate than Elizabeth, Anne benefits from Wentworth's attention early in the novel when he perceives her fatigue and secures a place for her in Admiral Croft's carriage. Much healthier than Mary, Anne's spirit makes itself manifest when Wentworth repeats the same gesture late in the novel. This time Anne declines, preferring to walk in the rain, and she leaves with Mr. Elliot:

> As soon as they were out of sight, the ladies of Captain Wentworth's party began talking of them.
> "Mr. Elliot does not dislike his cousin, I fancy."
> "...What a very good-looking man!"...

> "She is pretty, I think; Anne Elliot; very pretty, when one comes to look at her. It is not the fashion to say so, but I confess I admire her more than her sister."
> "Oh! So do I."
> "And so do I. No comparison. But the men are all wild after Miss Elliot. Anne is too delicate for them." (p. 152)

The delicate woman acts with strength, and the novelist writes circles around Anne's beauty. Wentworth hears her praised by women who congratulate themselves for appreciating a beauty that is not apparent at first glance, a beauty that appears "when one comes to look at her." Elizabeth, early established as the more beautiful sister, now finds herself unfavorably compared with Anne by the people who make the fashions because they pride themselves on being above fashion.

Yet the same women who appreciate Anne are deceived by her cousin. They exclaim that Mr. Elliot is very good-looking, in contradiction to the narrator's earlier information that Mr. Elliot acts the part of a gentleman, though he is *not handsome.* Mr. Elliot, of course, has the worst features of a gentleman: he is too trained in the art of pleasing, too socially and financially ambitious, too polished. Anne never trusts him fully, and her suspicions are ultimately confirmed by her friend, Mrs. Smith: "Mr. Elliot is a man without heart or conscience; a designing wary cold-blooded being, who thinks only of himself.... Oh! he is black at heart; hollow and black!" (p. 171). After all of these strong words, Mrs. Smith concludes that he is "an artful man."

The art of pleasing, the ability to charm, summarizes the best and worst effects of beauty. The last word on Anne is that she has "not lost one charm"; she acquires "power" over Wentworth, just as Wentworth is described in terms of his "charming" manner and just as the sailors, in general, are "bewitching." At the same time, Mr. Elliot, condemned for "artful charm" shares this characteristic with the insinuating Mrs. Clay: "She was a clever young woman, who understood the art of pleasing" (p. 12). In Mrs. Clay, Anne sees through art's attraction as Elizabeth does not, but the descriptions of Mrs. Clay and her intentions upon Sir Walter apply, with appropriate ironic twists, to Mr. Elliot. Mrs. Clay, we are told "had freckles, and a projecting tooth, and a clumsy wrist... but she was young, and altogether well-looking, and possessed ... in pleasing manner, infinitely more dangerous attractions than any merely personal might have been." When Anne ventures to caution Elizabeth by remarking that "there is hardly any personal defect... which an agreeable manner might not gradually reconcile one to," Elizabeth argues that "an agreeable manner may set off handsome features, but can never alter plain ones" (p. 28).

Anne, upon her arrival in Bath, is vindicated and is twice compared to Mrs. Clay herself. Elizabeth whispers to Mrs. Clay that Anne is "nothing to me compared with you," and Sir Walter compliments Anne on her transformation by supposing that she has been using the same creams as those which have improved Mrs. Clay's appearance. The father remarks that he finds Anne "less thin in person, in her cheeks; her skin, her complexion, greatly improved—clearer, fresher." Anne, of course, has not been using makeup, and the vast improvement that Sir Walter finds in Mrs. Clay is purely imaginary.

Able as she is to see through Mrs. Clay's charms, Anne initially finds no fault with those of Mr. Elliot—though the narrator carefully indicates that his looks are also improved by an agreeable manner, not unlike that of Mrs. Clay:

> He was quite good-looking as he had appeared at Lyme, his countenance improved by speaking, and his manners were so exactly what they ought to be, so polished, so easy, so agreeable, that she could compare them in excellence to only one person's manners. They were not the same, but they were, perhaps, equally good. (p. 121)

The "one person," Wentworth, has natural grace, just as Anne has natural "charm." Only at one moment, however, does Anne think seriously about marrying Mr. Elliot, and it is under Lady Russell's influence. Lady Russell pleads Mr. Elliot's case, telling Anne that she is her "mother's self in countenance and disposition," and asking Anne to think of her mother's name first revived in herself. The reader must be pleased by the thought of Anne's wresting this place from Elizabeth, but Anne sobers us. At first the idea of being Lady Elliot does "bewitch" Anne's heart, but "the image of Mr. Elliot... brought Anne to composure" (p. 137). Lady Russell's motives cannot, however, be faulted. Mr. Elliot recommends himself to Lady Russell in large part because he sings Anne's praises: "'Elegance sweetness, beauty.' Oh! There was no end of Miss Elliot's charms" (p. 111). Thus, it is from Mr. Elliot that the reader finds beauty added to sweetness and elegance in the list of Anne's attractions.

This admiration was not without its benefits to Anne's actual appearance:

> But happily, either Anne was improved in plumpness and looks, or Lady Russell fancied her so; and Anne, receiving her compliments on the occasion, had the amusement of connecting them with the silent admiration of her cousin, and of hoping that she was to be blessed with a second spring of youth and beauty. (p. 104)

Lady Russell stands high in the reader's esteem because she loves Anne, but the narrator warns us early that she has one "blind spot," one fault in her vision that prevents her from properly reading beauty. Though a model of good breeding herself, Lady Russell has "aristocratic ideas" and "prejudices on the side of ancestry; she had a value for rank and consequence which blinded her a little to the faults of those who possessed them" (p. 8). This observation comes early in the novel, before the reader meets either Wentworth or Mr. Elliot, but it serves to forewarn us that Anne's best friend will be inclined to see too little good in the one man and too much good in the other. (The same aristocratic ideas make Lady Russell and all of the Elliots save Anne eager to be in the company of the aristocratic Lady Dalrymple and Miss Carteret; in these minor figures Austen debunks the aristocracy's claims to "natural" merit, and Miss Carteret is introduced into the story for no other reason than to be its plainest creature.)

After Anne accepts her lover, she draws this conclusion about Lady Russell, a conclusion about the relationship between character and appearance: "She must learn to feel that she had been mistaken with regard to both" Captain Wentworth and Mr. Elliot,

> that she had been unfairly influenced by appearances in each... that because Mr. Elliot's manners had precisely pleased her in their propriety and correctness, their general politeness and suavity, she had been too quick in receiving them as the certain result of the most well-regulated mind. (p. 216)

Appropriately enough, and ironically enough, Mr. Elliot leaves the society of the novel with the "artful woman," Mrs. Clay. The narrator hints broadly: "it is doubtful whether his cunning, or hers, may finally carry the day." Anne's engagement carries some regrets for her sisters. Elizabeth's hopes of winning Mr. Elliot are dashed, and Mary must see "Anne restored to the rights of seniority, and the mistress of a very pretty laudelette." Mary finds some consolation in the hope that Captain Wentworth might be prevented from being named a baronet (p. 217), though in the expression of this hope the reader is led to the opposite hope that Anne may yet come to be called "Lady."

Although Anne marries beneath herself in rank, Sir Walter is not unhappy with the match because he perceives that she has married above herself in beauty:

> When he saw Mr. Wentworth, saw him repeatedly by daylight and eyed him well, he was very much struck by his personal claims, and felt that his superiority of appearance might be not unfairly balanced against her superiority of rank. (p. 215)

Wentworth, who combines qualities of health and position, achieves Austen's larger purpose of invigorating the gentry. The novel ends in Austen's championing the navy. Anne "gloried in being a sailor's wife, but she must pay the tax of quick alarm for belonging to that profession which is, if possible, more distinguished in its domestic virtues than in its national importance."

From literature's Cinderellas, such as Anne Elliot, readers learn that it is as easy to mistake a beauty for a "nobody" as for a somebody. Literature's job, when it comes to beauty and characterization, is to simultaneously educate in ethics and aesthetics. In comic plots, the characters within the stories learn these lessons as well, and the unappreciated hero or heroine becomes properly appreciated. Inasmuch as readers wish to be appreciated themselves, they carry these lessons into the world, imitating the arts, as the arts imitate, realistically or unrealistically, life's controversies. Difficulties arise, however, with the realization that art's messages can contradict themselves. Every value in *Persuasion,* every character of beauty, is undercut in order to transform the least loved into the most beautiful and the least gentleman into the ideal gentleman.

Over the course of *Persuasion,* Austen has repeated one set of adjectives many times. Bloom characterized Anne at nineteen and is the distinguishing feature of female beauty. With the animation, the high-spirited character, that it signifies, the bloom of youth is a high value, yet the novel ultimately champions maturity and experience and finds the higher degree of beauty in Anne and Captain Wentworth as they are eight years older. Delicacy, which distinguishes Anne from her father and Elizabeth, is also a criterion of beauty and value, though Anne's and Wentworth's beauty is defined by health, the strength to endure life's trials and a life at sea cheerfully. Charm and the cultivated manners of good breeding are valued, but Anne and Wentworth are as comparatively artless as they are charming and well-mannered in the highest degree. The novel champions both wealth and entitlement (Anne and Wentworth now combine these virtues), though high birth only results in beauty if tempered (and it is appropriately tempered only in Anne and Wentworth) by industry and a cultivated mind. Each character's beauty is drawn out of distinctions, carefully delineated and yet always obscured, between art and nature, birth and breeding, and delicacy and strength. Out of these oppositions qualities are generated that resolve the tension between them, qualities which heroes and heroines possess. It is these dichotomies and the qualities that reconcile them that provide the structure for the chapters which follow.

5

Charm: The Nature of Art

*Yet Nature is made better by no mean
But Nature makes that mean, so over that art
Which you say adds to Nature, is an art
That Nature makes....*
Shakespeare, *The Winter's Tale* (IV. iv. 89–92)

Literature invented an origin for the arts of adornment when Adam and Eve felt ashamed for their nakedness. To beautify the body by concealing it, painting it, and ornamenting it is to continue in the spirit of that first deception. More than a symptom and reminder of lost innocence, the use of art to create beauty has been associated with witchcraft. It is associated as well with theater, artifice, and artificiality. Dressing up, making up and assuming roles are acts of bad faith: the presentation of false faces to the world, packaging to disguise the quality of the product, the masking of truth. Such is our vain attempt to supplement nature which, by definition as God's creation, cannot be improved upon. Like mating animals, people use color and smell to lure and entrap one another. Jewels and makeup conjure, create illusions, manipulate, lie; the human face and figure mock canvas and marble. Money buys the crass and superficial beauty that we call art.

In some contexts, we distrust art. In other contexts, we value art: art functions to bring natural and social disorder under control. By arranging nature's raw materials, art gives nature meaning and tames nature's excesses. Beautifying the body—a universal practice—covers indecency. Its tools are soap and water, brush and comb, clothing and gems. They are used to transform the human animal into a meaningful and valuable work of art. The art of proper carriage and deportment contributes as much to beauty as does the unalterable structure of one's bones. Adherence to codes of fashion and etiquette and observance of social laws not only enhance one's appearance but also demonstrate respect for oneself and one's fellow. As the world is but a stage, wearing one's best air is an act of good will, the presentation of one's best face to the world. Because art distinguishes people from beasts, it is more essential and natural than are our biological functions. Beautifying the body is the practice of modesty and cleanliness and the expression of a desire to be nearer humanity and God.

These opposing evaluations of art coexist in our cultural imagination and textual tradition, and the line that separates "art" in its positive sense from "art" in its negative sense cannot be drawn with a steady or confident hand. Such words as "charming," "attractive," "beguiling," and "captivating"— adjectives often used to imply a beauty of demeanor—have these contradictory connotations. The word "glamour" hides its older and ambivalent meanings: "magic, enchantment, spell" and "a magical or fictitious beauty attaching to any person or object." A verb form "to glamour" once had currency: "to affect with glamour, to charm, enchant" *(OED).* To be enchanting or charming is still to have those qualities of character and appearance that are so pleasing as to sustain attention endlessly, but the suggestion of a charm or spell leaves open the possibility that one has been charmed into captivity and out of one's better judgment. Charm remains a mixed blessing.

When art is defined in relation to nature, the value assigned nature is linked to the evaluation of art. An art that civilizes base instinct or mitigates the ferocity of tempest and wilderness implies a nature that is threatening and lacking in restraint. Art supplements the lack by curbing, or productively channeling, nature's sexual and violent excesses. Moreover, man uses art to imitate Divinity, as God's use of design is reflected in the orderliness of the universe. When our conception of art tips the balance towards connotations of disguise, craft, and deception, however, then nature is valorized. Nature is then defined as that which suffers no addition; it is prelapsarian innocence, God's work in its purest form. Art refers, therefore, to culture at its most debased in relation to nature (artifice and artificiality) and at its most elevated in relation to nature (art as the heights of human and divine expression).

Given these ambivalences, the question of whether real beauty is "natural" or controlled ("pretty as a picture") remains constantly unsettled. Although this question found early expression in the Western literary tradition, it resurfaced as a significant issue in Romantic and Victorian thought. Rousseau rediscovered the beauty of natural man at the same time that culture became a special value; the arts in particular came in for renewed appreciation as they came to be recognized as the distinctive hallmarks of a culture. Wordsworth advocated a "return to natural language" in art while Coleridge applauded the use of linguistic "charms." Major philosophical, aesthetic, and political movements of the early nineteenth century expressed ideological concerns in terms of art and nature.

In the spirit of the times, Victorian novelists grappled with the questions and contradictions of art and nature, exploring the various possibilities and

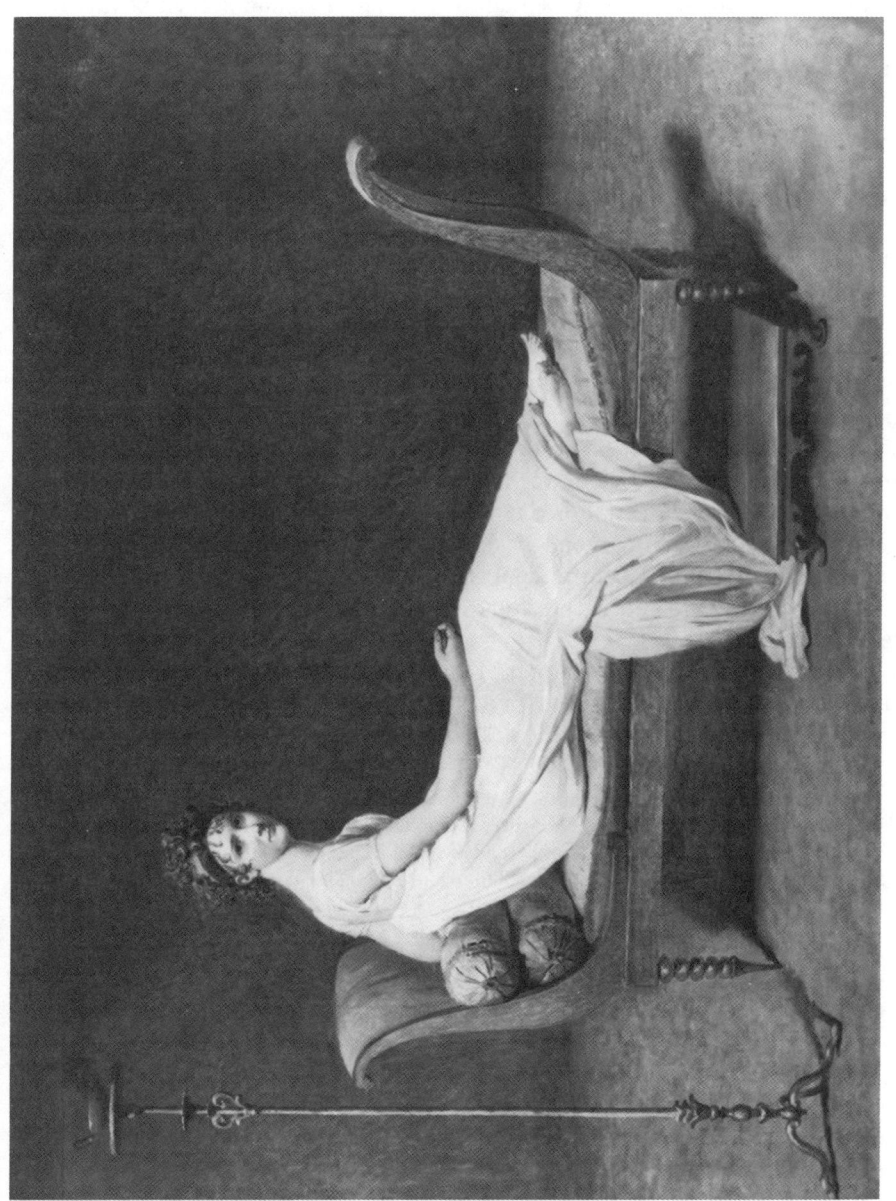

Figure 5. Jacques Louis David, *Portrait de Mme Recamier*. The ideal of feminine frailty and languishing beauty. (© *Giraudon; Photo courtesy Art Resource*)

implications of "natural" and "artful/artistic" beauty in their characterizations and in their characters' beauty. Women of nature and women of art appear as competing heroines in the fiction of this period, and in their beauty is reflected both the long history of interest in art and nature and the nineteenth century's particular conceptions of the problem.

Beginning with the Beginning of *Middlemarch*

Celia Brooke, as *Middlemarch* (1867) opens, surprises her austere sister Dorothea; not only would Celia like to look at their late mother's jewels, but she would go so far as to wear them. Her protest against Dorothea's severity is meek and faltering: "And Christians generally—surely there are women in heaven now who wore jewels."[1] By the novel's conclusion, Dorothea will have matured and her sternness will have been tempered. She will even marry a man of artistic temperament. Although Dorothea is beautiful, Eliot finds fault with her young heroine's character and person; this *Bildungsroman* is the education of Dorothea into the proper expression of both her inner and outer beauty. The dialectic between excess and restraint operative throughout *Middlemarch* finds a metaphor in types of beauty and choices of its expression. The question of art and ornament with which *Middlemarch* opens is thus transformed into a central concern of the novel. Eliot establishes an opposition between art and nature for the reader to use as a touchstone in assessing character.

By the end of the first chapter, Dorothea is already softening. The beautiful gems transmit their spontaneous gleam, and she impulsively selects an emerald ring and bracelet for herself:

> "How very beautiful these gems are!" said Dorothea, under a new current of feeling, as sudden as the gleam. "It is strange how deeply colours seem to penetrate one, like scent. I suppose that is the reason why gems are used as spiritual emblems in the Revelation of St. John. They look like fragments of heaven. I think that emerald is more beautiful than any of them."
>
> "And there is a bracelet to match it," said Celia. "We did not notice this at first."
>
> "They are lovely," said Dorothea, slipping the ring and bracelet on her finely-turned finger and wrist, and holding them on a level with her eyes. All the while her thought was trying to justify her delight in the colours by merging them in her mystic religious joy. (p. 10)

The reader's sympathies are with Celia, who is right to find her sister inconsistent, if not hypocritical. Yet Dorothea's impulses are also right, even if she feels compelled to justify them in religious terms. Eliot has taken pains to point out that Dorothea has a finely-turned finger and wrist, as if to say that they are naturally deserving of ornament, made, as it were, for jewels. Dorothea herself, with her finely-turned parts, is "an art that nature makes."

Figure 6. Jean Auguste Dominique Ingres, *La Belle Zélie*
A larger bodied ideal who wore jewels.
Rouen, Musée des Beaux-Arts.
(©Giraudon; Photo courtesy Art Resource)

In suppressing her natural impulse, Eliot implies that Dorothea goes beyond God's own intentions. Eliot disapproves of Dorothea's asceticism, but she equally disapproves of the religious ardor that turns the "delightful colours" of the ring into fragments of heaven. In this early scene, Eliot establishes that, as far as she is concerned, there are indeed Christian women who wore a few jewels and went to heaven.

Celia's apparently reasonable conviction that jewelled women can go to heaven and Dorothea's recollection of the gems in the Revelation of St. John is Eliot rewriting the Christian textual tradition to suit her own ends. That Dorothea has chosen the emeralds from among all of the jewels reenforces the reader's impression of her piety as well as Eliot's larger purposes because Eliot would have us remember that "round the throne" of God "was a rainbow that looked like an emerald" (Revelation 4:3).[2] But the emerald in Revelation—simply the tail end of a simile—adorns no woman. When the woman who is interpreted as the Ecclesia, the true church, mystically appears, she is

> clothed with the sun, the moon under her feet and on her head a crown of twelve stars; she was with child and she cried out in her pangs of birth, in anguish for delivery. (Revelation 12:1–3)

This woman who wears celestial jewels, suffers the anguish of birth, and takes refuge in the wilderness is entirely a creature of nature. In recalling to us the emerald surrounding God's throne, Eliot suppresses another woman, the one who appears

> arrayed in purple and scarlet, and bedecked with gold and jewels and pearls, holding in her hand a golden cup full of abominations and the impurities of her fornication; and on her forehead was written the name of mystery: "Babylon the great, mother of harlots and of earth's abominations." (Revelation 17:4–6)

The whore of Babylon will be punished: "the beast will hate the harlot; they will make her desolate and naked, and devour her flesh..." (Revelation 17:16). The symbol of Rome's wealth is a jewelled woman; her undoing begins with an undressing.

Dorothea could have remembered the harlot and determined against wearing the jewels; instead, Eliot makes it clear that Dorothea responds first to her impulse and then seeks to justify it in "mystic religious" terms. By highlighting the heavenly connotations of the gems that adorn the throne and omitting their hellish connotations in association with women, Eliot modifies the tradition that associated women in jewels with dangerous artfulness. In contrasting Dorothea and Rosamund Vincy who is, as we shall see, Eliot's artful woman par excellence, Eliot recoils from the values of self-effacing modesty ("modest," in Eliot's time was beginning to have connotations of cheapness and inferiority) represented by such heroines as Amelia Sedley and

Jane Eyre, and speaks for the woman of her own day who could afford an emerald and would go to heaven.

Dorothea's "hypocrisy" typifies her class. All the while that the Victorian middle class continued in its move upward to increased political power and persisted in its belief in universal and limitless progress, it held steadfastly to a religion whose ideals no longer coincided with the practical considerations of changing economic life. In her work on the cottages, to which Dorothea returns immediately after the scene with her sister, Dorothea struggles against this hypocrisy by working to bring Christian ideals to the economic sphere. When she applies this self-sacrificing principle to her own person by marrying Casaubon and denying herself pleasure, she brings, as Eliot sees it, unnecessary misery to herself. Eliot is, above all, judicious, and here, as elsewhere, she distinguishes between essential and superficial reform. Eliot dramatizes Victorian England's social dilemma, a dilemma which G. M. Young describes this way:

> English society was poised on a double paradox which its critics, within and without, called hypocrisy. Its practical ideals were at odds with its religious professions, and its religious belief was at odds with its intelligence.[3]

The incident over the jewels, in which a beautiful woman is self-effacing and self-denying, is Eliot's vehicle for entrance into the subjects of her novel: moderation, exchange of clean capital, and practical reform. To Eliot, these values are threatened by zealous selflessness as much as by blind self-interest. Eliot characterizes her heroines, in part by establishing the nature of their beauty, and in part by making their regard for themselves and their appearances expressive of her most serious concerns about human character and the nature of social and personal responsibility.

To appreciate both Rosamund Vincy's charm and Mary Garth's plainness ("plain" is a distinctively Victorian adjective), the opening conversation between Dorothea and her sister must be understood to lay the ground upon which our expectations of heroism will be built. Eliot arranges for her readers to find Dorothea distasteful for, of all things, her piety; Eliot risks the exaggeration in order eventually to establish a standard of heroism that allows for a new variety of female art. She thereby manipulates her readers into a position of admiration for the liberal views of women such as Lady Dilke, women who were unashamed of their knowledge about art and who recognized the political implications of their interest. If Lady Dilke is the real-life sitter for the portrait of Dorothea, Eliot found a way of presenting Lady Dilke's unorthodox views through the appearance rather than through the beliefs of Dorothea. Not only was Lady Dilke an authority on French painting, but she fought for women's rights in the art world and analyzed art's relationship to politics.[4]

In rescuing Dorothea from her own conservatism, Eliot at once declares the value of art for women (symbolized in the gems) and ensures that someone like Mary Garth cannot be the heroine of *Middlemarch.* As a lively but unspectacular woman of good sense, good humor, and good morals (Eliot may have seen herself in this light),[5] Mary is Eliot's kind bow in the direction of heroines more typical of the earlier half of the century. The bow takes in her readers of old-fashioned piety and modesty, but the gesture of recognition is also one of dismissal. If Eliot wants to prove that heroic acts are small, she would show that heroines are large: statuesque, of generous spirit and manner, and a cut above the common lot of good women who are not distinguished as heroines.

Eliot's effort to create a larger heroine who is willing to ornament herself is symptomatic of changing Victorian values and ideals of beauty. Alison Lurie in *The Language of Clothes* comments on this shift from frail childlike beauty to a new ideal of taller and heavier womanhood in the century's final decades. Lurie writes that "this was the age of the crinoline, and later of the bustle, and the increased importance of women in the domestic and social sphere was signaled by their sheer bulk. The oversize fashions also allowed them to display their father's and husband's wealth to the fullest extent."[6]

This change in fashion towards ornamentation reflects an evolution in values, and to appreciate Dorothea's Christian compunctions and Eliot's victory over them, Dorothea and Rosamund should be understood as late representations in the evolution of a Rebecca/Delilah, Virgin/Magdalen, Ecclesia/Whore, that is nature/art tradition. The mid- to late-Victorian novelists effect an adjustment in the evaluation of beauty, wealth, and art only by wrestling the weight of the Old and New Testaments, Spenser, Milton, and lesser authorities who reenforce the picture and meaning of the Whore of Babylon.

While it may now seem self-evident why evil is symbolized by jewelled woman, the Great Harlot is, of course, a cultural construct. To appreciate the textual resonances of the opening scene of *Middlemarch,* we want to know how evil came to be represented as a jewelled woman in the first place and where else women were united over a maternal casket of jewels. For example, *Middlemarch* begins where Sir Walter Scott's *Ivanhoe: A Romance* (1819) ends, with two women negotiating over a casket of jewels; William Makepeace Thackeray develops the image in a burlesque of *Ivanhoe* and again in *Vanity Fair* (1847). Scott and Thackeray are Eliot's literary godfathers, and in each of these novels a heroine named Rebecca is not only associated with a jewel box, but she is also explicitly confused for Delilah. How had matriarchal power become associated with jewels, and how did the jewel box become an emblem of female sexuality that linked matriarch and whore? To see why Babylon's jewels give her specious charm, we must recognize that she inherits her features from such artful heroines of the Hebrew Bible and Apocrypha as Eve, Rebecca, Jael, Esther, and Judith; their virtue became suspect, however, as the commenting tradition became increasingly wary of the "charms" of female sexuality. The following survey of biblical and rabbinic narratives provides a background against which the Victorian jewel box stands out more clearly.

Mothers and Harlots, Bedrooms and Battlefields: Hebrew Scriptures and Midrash

In Genesis God's principle function is as Creator, and woman, from whose body life stems, must be prevented from usurping that function. In the Garden of Eden story, woman is, therefore, taken from the belly of man, reversing the natural order of things. Then Eve symbolically becomes man's victim as she is seduced by the erect snake.[7] She desires the immortality that it promises, but the only godlike immortality that Adam and Eve come to "know" is sexuality, their own nakedness. God threatens death, the snake promises immortality, and what actually happens is the discovery of sexuality. Sexuality, woman's destruction of man's Edenic peace, is equated with knowledge and with death. The text restrains the victim that it blames; male sexuality (snake) tempts woman, but woman is punished for tempting man (Adam). Her punishment appropriately takes the form of pain in childbirth and subservience to male authority. While Adam's temptation is no more than mentioned in Genesis, the subsequent tradition of representation endows Eve with great seductive beauty and rhetorical skill. Eve's sexual power is imagined in such exaggerated terms that this story justifies male dominance as necessity and phrases it as God's will.

As the first wife and mother and the first temptress, Eve represents woman in all of her contrary aspects. Uncertain that Eve is temptress enough, however, rabbinic commentary, or midrash, invents a rival for Eve, the disobedient Lilith, the wife who refuses to be mastered. Through midrash, collections of stories that much influenced later representations, Lilith enters mythology as *supernature;* unable to bear children herself, she steals sperm and infants to create the world's demons. While Eve is wicked in her own story, compared to Lilith, Eve is both lovely and beloved. The rivalry between Eve and Lilith, who are both temptresses and mothers, repeats itself obsessively in narrative literature.

The barren or virgin mother, a paradoxical irony not unlike Eve's having been born from Adam's body, is an oft-repeated convention of the Bible. The biblical text reasserts the divinity of creation whenever heroes have birth stories, first by insisting that man alone is insufficient to impregnate the mother of a hero, and second by depriving the female of her full creative powers. The beautiful matriarch whose son will carry on the line cannot conceive like other women, and she may be the receptacle of such remarkable seed only if she renounces claim to its issue by allowing her son to leave her and enter God's service.

The Hebrew Bible offers any number of vehicles for female action, but no matter whether her role is as heroine or villainness, mother or whore, her power to create or destroy is ultimately sexual. Each time a woman enacts her role, a man is rendered powerless, and the text's fear of emasculation conveys the message that one must contain she who, if unleashed, wields a threatening weapon.

Female sexual power increasingly becomes associated with jewels in literary and artistic representations. Rebecca and Delilah in the Hebrew Bible are both undescribed beauties, characterized by their actions alone. Later they would become identified through ornamentation. The jewel box was the place where mother and whore were identically beautiful and terrifying.

Rebecca names the middle matriarch, whose barrenness makes her story parallel to that of Sarah before her and Rachel after her.[8] In all of the biblical cases of a loved barren wife, God intervenes to remove the curse of barrenness, and a miraculous birth follows. The special child will be a hero, will hold a special place in the history of the people's redemption. But in each case, the birth is conditional: God removes barrenness and enters into a pact with the mother. She will bear a remarkable son, but she must consecrate that son into divine service.

The significance of barrenness is elucidated elsewhere in Scriptures. If a jealous husband suspects his wife of infidelity, he may put her through the ordeal of bitter waters (Numbers 5:11–31). (Hence, the subsequent association of women and witchcraft resulted in comparable trials.) She swallows a muddy mixture; if she is guilty, she will either die or, perhaps equally devastating, will be barren thereafter. If innocent, she will be fertile and have children. According to one Christian legend, Mary and Joseph admirably survived this ordeal. We discover two contrary interpretations of the barren wife: barrenness proves that she is either the ultimate wicked woman guilty of sexual crimes or the ultimate good woman destined to someday bear heroes.

Whether supremely virtuous or evil, the barren wife carries frightening implications: she emasculates her husband. In the one case she proves him a cuckold, and in the other case, her son is created by and returned to God, the Father. This arrangement erases the human father first as impregnator and second as authority over the child's destiny. In many such stories, like that of Rebecca, the once barren mother prefers the father's youngest son, and the rule of primogeniture is broken. Her favorite child, the weaker, more domestic, prettier, more feminine son carries on the line in preference over the stronger older boys in the family. *The rule of femininity prevails.*

The transfigurations of one biblical heroine illustrate how commentary begins the work of equating female action with gems. Chapters four and five of Judges, the story of Deborah's rule in Israel, includes a brief account of Jael's historic role. Jael is visited in her tent by the enemy general Sisera; she allows him to enter, covers him with a blanket, gives him milk when he asks for water, and then instead of being penetrated by him, she penetrates him. This she does completely, driving a tent peg through his temple; and here a story otherwise spare in detail is painfully explicit: "till it went down into the ground" (Judges 4:21). Jael has successfully deceived Sisera and won for herself glory in Israel; the storyteller has successfully delighted us by deceiving us as well, transforming the sexual drama by reversing the expected sex roles.

Sisera had reason to believe that Jael would protect him, and from her behavior we had reason to believe that he was correct. She has, however, lured both Sisera and the reader into her tent; neither of us is prepared to believe that this woman will do the taking instead of being taken. For Sisera—fearful of the male enemy without, but mindless of the female enemy within—the mistake proves fatal.

The story of Jael and Sisera is embedded in another story about Deborah and Barak, and Jael is produced as a double for the prophetess and judge Deborah. Earlier, Deborah had predicted that because the Israelite general Barak insisted upon a woman's presence in the battlefield, Sisera would be delivered into the hands of "a woman." One heroine is rare enough in the Bible that we do not imagine another readily materializing. The reader assumes, therefore, that the nameless woman unto whom Sisera will be delivered must be Deborah herself. But the text cannot imagine a female conqueror in public space, and Deborah functions in the public sphere. Jael is created, therefore, to accomplish in the bedroom what Deborah is not allowed to accomplish in the battlefield.

Jael is one of the few women in the Bible whose importance is not a function of her role as wife, mother, sister, concubine or prostitute. Jael, like the other heroines, is characterized without any descriptive language whatsoever; her character emerges through action alone. Neither are Jael's motivations explicitly stated, though by the story's conclusion they are clear. Jael has worked a trick; we know that in spite of her family's friendship with Sisera, she is loyal to Israel, faithful to God, brave, and certainly clever. Later rabbinic commentary on this biblical episode insists that Jael is, first and foremost, beautiful, and not simply beautiful, but tantalizingly so: Jael went to meet Sisera "arrayed in rich garments and jewels. She was unusually beautiful and her voice was the most seductive ever a woman possessed."[9] The Bible makes no mention of sexual intercourse, but some writers of midrash, anxious to show that Jael is both virtuous and has not usurped male prerogatives, must choose between sacrificing her chastity on the altar of her femininity or vice versa. One commentary is willing to grant Jael strength and insists upon her chastity, but another argues that Jael had relations with Sisera seven times (once for each verb in the relevant verses) in order to grab hold of him and kill him in a weakened condition.[10] In an attempt to rescue Jael's virtue, this commentator permits sexual transgression committed towards righteous ends. Yet another midrashist increases Sisera's villainy and Jael's virtue. According to this reading, Jael kills Sisera because he is intoxicated and has tried to rape her. Thus, her triumph is made an act of self-defense and only incidentally a military victory accomplished by a woman.

Biblical characters are especially susceptible to revision because the Bible's status as sacred text makes it imperative that its heroes possess only qualities that are valued at the present historical moment.[11] The exegetical tradition continues to restrict female power to sexual power. In making Jael seductive and beautiful, rabbinic commentary makes her conform to the model of other biblical heroines who are bedroom saviors. As a rule, these women work their deceptions by using their beauty—not only natural or God-given beauty—but a beauty artfully supplemented by ornament and adornment. The text specifies that there is a transfiguration as the woman exchanges her rags for finery. The characters who name the book of Esther and the apocryphal book of Judith provide models for midrash.

Esther opens with a royal party, on the seventh day of which the drunken King Ahasuerus orders his wife Queen Vashti to make an appearance "in order to show the peoples and the princes her beauty; for she was fair to behold" (Esther 11:21). In what may or may not be a proto-feminist gesture—but one which proves self-destructive—Vashti refuses to show herself. The king is advised to seek a new queen lest the women of the realm follow Vashti's example of disobedience. Esther is among the beautiful young virgins who undergo the regular twelve months of beautifying ("six months with oil of myrrh and six months with spices and ointments for women," Esther 2:12) before she is brought to the king. "Esther found favor in the eyes of all who saw her" and is made queen "instead of Vashti."

The story opens with a party at which one queen refuses to display her beauty, and the story is brought to its conclusion with two parties at which the replacement queen displays her beauty with a vengeance. Esther's show is calculated to manipulate the king into allowing her influence in the male realm of politics.

Haman, the king's chief adviser, has decreed death for the Jews. To prove her piety to the reader, Esther fasts and puts on sackcloth and ashes. Still mournful on the inside, Esther replaces her rags with her best royal attire. Because the queen's finery masks misery, the reader knows that a deception is planned. The beautiful queen twice risks her life by appearing unsummoned before the king. Twice she touches his royal "scepter" and finds favor in the king's sight; twice she invites Ahasuerus and Haman to dine, and twice she fills them with wine. On the second night, she lets it be known that she is a Jewess. Haman stays behind to plead for his life, but his actions are misinterpreted:

> And the king returned from the palace garden to the place where they were drinking wine, as Haman was falling on the couch where Esther was; and the king said, "Will he even assault the queen in my presence, in my own house?" As the words left the mouth of the king, they covered Haman's face. (Esther 7:8)

Thus, Esther saves her people lying down.

The example of Judith repeats the ancient tradition's insistence upon sad and veiled beauty. Once more a display of finery serves both to signal the reader and to free the heroine for action. Since the death of her husband, the pious and beautiful Judith has worn nothing but black. Now the city is surrounded by the enemy general Holofernes' troops and the Israelites are without an adequate supply of food and water. Just as Esther changes into finery when mourning dress would have better suited her feelings, so Judith, who has been in mourning for three years, prepares the reader for a deception by changing clothes when circumstances are most dire. The description is unusually elaborate:

> she removed the sackcloth which she had been wearing, and took off her widow's garments, and bathed her body with water, and anointed herself with precious ointment, and combed her hair and put on a tiara, and arrayed herself in the gayest apparel, which she used to wear while her husband Manasseh was living. And she put sandals on her feet, and put on her ankelets and bracelets and rings, and her earrings and all her ornaments, and made herself very beautiful, to entice the eyes of all men who might see her. (Judith 10:3-4)

The Latin version, even more emphatic, adds that "God gave her a supernatural beauty because her motive in adorning herself was virtuous and not lustful."[12]

Thus arrayed, Judith goes over to the enemy camp. Several days later, she is invited to Holofernes' party and ends up alone with him in his tent. Like Ahasuerus, Holofernes is drunk, and like Sisera, he is exhausted. Judith's plan resembles that of Jael: Judith decapitates Holofernes and carries his head home. These women all accomplish inside that which is more often accomplished outside; the decisive battle occurs in the bedroom. The texts anxiously assert that the bedroom is the place where man—friend or foe—is most likely to lose his head. Germaine Greer explains how the Judith story functioned in painting; it justified "the portrayal of Jewish beauty (as it did for Rembrandt) or of a mistress's careless cruelty (as it did in the luscious version of Cristofano Allori)."[13]

Figure 7. Artemisia Gentileschi, *Judith Beheading Holofernes* Florence, Uffizi.
(©*Alinari; Photo courtesy Art Resource)*

By overadorning themselves, Judith and Esther only pretend to be whores; at the critical moment, they are not acted upon, but act instead. They turn themselves into works of art to acquire the powers of art, to be artful. When the beautiful widow returns home victorious, she is everywhere sought in marriage. But as if to emphasize that the adornment and masquerade held no secret attraction for Judith, the text overcompensates by adding that although she became very famous, she chose to live as a widow all the days of her life. Not only do virtuous women who masquerade as harlots zealously protect their chastity, but they indicate to the reader that they have no ambition of retaining their power over men. Given the textual company of Esther and Judith, it is not surprising that the subsequent tradition is able to turn Jael into a beauty and seductress as well.[14]

The later tradition invests yet another bedroom deceiver with beauty. Delilah, however, works her deception on an Israelite. The story makes clear that Delilah has been bought by her countrymen, so unlike Jael, Esther, and Judith, Delilah really is a harlot. Because Delilah sells herself, she is closer to the Whore of Babylon than are the other biblical heroines. But the original Samson story disempowers the hero through both figures of female sexuality, the mother and the whore.

Samson's anonymous mother is barren, and as in the case of the matriarchs, the text asserts the divine prerogative over creation. An angel comes to enforce the Nazirite rules upon her during pregnancy and upon her son during the whole of his lifetime: no wine, no haircuts. Samson will have no say in the matter of a vow that he must obey but which is uttered by his mother before his birth. Manoah, Samson's father, tries to insert himself into the story, but the text insists that the matter is between mother and God: the angel comes twice to her. Even as the hopeful mother makes her vow, the Bible reader is soberly aware of how Samson will lose his strength.

In the literary and artistic tradition, Samson is the epitome of masculinity and machismo. When he loses his strength, he loses his hair and his eyesight (as the enemies Sisera and Holofernes lost their heads). In this post-Freudian age, we know what Delilah has done. Blinded like Oedipus, Samson too has been symbolically castrated.

In each of these biblical narratives, the woman, whether adulteress or heroine, enemy harlot or virtuous savior, has extraordinary power. But no matter what role the woman plays in biblical narrative, her power is sexual and supernatural. This message necessitates oppression. In granting women superhuman power, these texts betray a fear of female sexuality, the castration anxiety that Freud would associate with *seeing* that which the Eden story conceals. As the tradition developed, the locus of female sexuality became symbolized in the jewel box, and Rebecca came to look no different from Delilah. In Christian literature, the virtuous heroine therefore distinguished herself from the dark Hebrew, the supernatural, sensual heroine by dressing without ornament.

The New Testament reiterates the message of female sexual power. Mary does the barren mother one better; she is a virgin, and the need for Joseph is thus entirely eliminated. One Mary is a mother, the other a prostitute. Female power is both asserted and restrained, and mother and whore appear again in pairs. Revelations provides us with two symbolic female figures: the Ecclesia is robed with the stars and the moon, and the Whore of Babylon is arrayed in gems. As jewelled women deceive and castrate, it is appropriate that the symbol of Rome's seductive wealth is a jewelled woman. Spenser, in the first book of *The Faerie Queene,* repeats this dichotomous characterization in Una and Duessa, and he emphasizes the association of absence of ornament with female purity, and jewels with power and seduction. In nineteenth-century fiction, Rebecca and Delilah specifically are made paradigmatic of the Eve-Lilith, mother-harlot dichotomy.

Spenser's Una and Duessa; Milton's Dalila

Spenser's Una and Duessa are the Ecclesia and the Whore.[15] As emblems in an allegory, they present reified truths; their bodies express with full clarity the truth of their souls. In the character of Una, Spenser glorifies the virtuous, modest and unornamented woman; with the same stroke, he condemns Duessa, the scheming mistress of art. Spenser's allegory splits the natural beauty who is a mistress of art (Jael, Esther, Judith) and creates one woman of nature and true beauty and another of art and false beauty. In the process he drains the one (Una) of life and the other (Duessa) of value. To the pious of Spenser's day, Una (like Milton's Christ) was fully satisfying. Our modern sensibility prefers Duessa, much as we have been tempted to call Satan the "real hero" of *Paradise Lost,* largely because Victorian writers recover the beauty and heroism of artful women.

Spenser's difficulty is that to divest the woman of art of her powers, he must prove that her attractions are specious. The lure of Babylon finds a psychological explanation in Spenser's personifications which juxtapose the woman whom man does desire with the woman whom man should desire. The women themselves are made into shells that contain worldly ideals on the one hand and religious ideals on the other. Beauty is articulated within a structure of desire; this structure is narrative's principal vehicle for expressing beauty. Spenser operates on the assumption that that which is desired appears beautiful, and because beauty is a container for meaning and value, it is his duty to teach his readers to perceive beauty in the absence of glamour. He revises the type of Esther to show that religion is beautiful in its modesty. Spenser's effort is calculated to reform his readers' vision and make them desire differently.

In the first book of *The Fairie Queene,* Una and Duessa compete for the attention of its hero, the Red Cross Knight. Una's name means "One"; she is humble, good, pure, whole. Her rival has been fashioned from a sprite by Archimago, the arch-magician. As her name suggests, Duessa's skill is deceit. To those of weak faith, she looks like Una. Beauty is ultimately a matter of faith, and Spenser insists that because worldly values are deceptive, faith is necessary to perceive beauty. Duessa, therefore, goes under the alias Fidessa; Duplicity calls herself Truth.

As true beauty is modest, here is how Una is described in the first canto, stanzas four and five of *The Faerie Queene:*

> A lovely Ladie rode him faire beside
> Upon a lowly Asse more white then snow,
> Yet she much whiter, but with the same did hide
> Under a vele, that wimpled was full low,
> And over all a blacke stole she did throw,
> As one that inly mournd: so was she sad,
> And heavie sat upon her palfrey slow;
> Seemed in heart some hidden care she had,
> And by her in a line a milke white lambe she lad.
> So pure an innocent, as that same lambe,
> She was in life and every vertuous lore,
> And by descent from Royall lynage came

Una, "a lovely lady," has whiteness as her only characteristic feature. The significance of white, which later in the poem becomes a dazzling white light, is explicated through extended comparisons with symbolic creatures. Una is whiter than her beast which is whiter than snow, and she leads a white lamb and is as pure and innocent as that lamb. White connotes innocence. Una, white inside and out, is covered entirely by black. She wears a low black veil and a black stole because she is grieving and "inly" mourning. Thus, Una is also black inside and out. Again, as in the instances of both Esther and Judith, the woman of superlative beauty and innocence conceals her beauty and protects herself with dark mourning attire.

Female sadness is linked with piety, just as levity or gaiety characterizes the woman of loose morals. Mourning dress is desexualizing; it points to its wearer's ascetic habits and disinterest in captivating attention (or men). The more valorized, reified, and stylized this association becomes, the sexier it becomes to wear black. Before the nineteenth century, however, mourning was codified as unavailability. Judith wore mourning for three years before circumstances made her (only temporarily) abandon the practice. Because they are natural beauties (a divine sign), Esther and Judith acquire powers when they wear clothes to "entice eyes." In Spenser, such finery and power are made incompatible with purity, and a woman cannot be simultaneously ornamented and untainted. Not until the heroes have completed all of the action on her behalf is Una permitted to change clothes. She then, appropriately enough, wears bridal white and no jewels:

> So faire and fresh, as freshest flowre in May;
> For she had layd her mournefull stole aside,
> And widow-like sad wimple throwne away,
> Wherewith her heavenly beautie she did hide,
> Whiles on her wearie journey she did ride;
> And on her now a garment she did weare,
> All lilly white, withoutten spot, or pride,
> That seemd like silke and silver woven neare,
> But neither silke nor silver therein did appeare.
> (I. xii. 22)

Una had to keep herself covered because God invested her with such natural beauty that it requires no supplement: she seems to be wearing gems ("prides") and silk even when she is not. (Gems and the sin of pride are etymologically related.) Ironically, Una, unveiled and unmarried, might be mistaken for Duessa. The man of faith who learns to read beyond appearance will eventually be permitted to see modest beauty in its unveiled splendor. The poet-speaker claims that his "ragged rhymes are all too rude and base" to do Una justice; not only is beauty an indecipherable cryptogram, but it is left up to the reader's imagination. The poet's most oft-used strategy for asserting beauty is to claim himself unequal to its description. But Spenser effectively conveys Una's beauty by comparing her to the most valorized woman in the textual tradition. As she is transformed into the celestial woman of Revelation, her beauty is given divine authority, and because she becomes an heiress as well, the worldly standard of beauty—birth into the aristocracy—is given divine sanction by implication. Material reward comes to the woman whom God loves, and His love is manifested in her radiance.

Spenser's elaborations upon the descriptions of Ecclesia and Harlot work allegorically to celebrate the beauty of a seemingly unornamented faith. On the literal level, the pious woman hides her beauty, which would otherwise be gemlike in its radiance, while the wicked woman simulates radiance and seduces with gems. Gems are thus retroactively attached to those biblical women who seduce. While the biblical text makes nothing at all of Delilah's appearance, in our cultural imagination she is over-adorned, a woman whose makeup reveals, at the same time that it masks, evil. (Esther's and Judith's paint and ornament, by contrast, supplement their sad and divine loveliness.) Moreover, while the biblical story implies that Samson grows up to be something of a fool, the later tradition does not really blame Samson for succumbing to the *femme fatale*, Delilah. As the woman acquires the power of gems, the man becomes less responsible for his actions.

Milton's *Samson Agonistes* contributes to our image of Delilah as an ornamented beauty. Milton's Samson laments that he has fallen into the snare "Of fair fallacious looks, venereal trains/ Soft'n'd with pleasure and voluptuous life;" (11. 533-34). Merritt Hughes' annotation to these lines explains that "venereal trains" are tricks to arouse physical passion.[16] "Venereal" also refers to another mythology and branch of the textual tradition; the word comes from "Venus," who as she is described in Edith Hamilton's popular *Mythology* is

> Goddess of Love and Beauty, who beguiled all, gods and men alike; the laughter-loving goddess, who laughed sweetly or mockingly at those her wits had conquered; the irresistible goddess who stole away even the wits of the wise.[17]

"Trains" are lures or traps, making Milton's Dalila something like a Venus's flytrap. The phrase "venereal trains," when applied to Delilah, instantly conflates two traditions, collapsing the biblical women of art into those of Greek mythology. Moreover, the poet has the word "fair" modify "fallacious" and uses alliteration to reenforce the association of beauty and treachery.

When Dalila comes to plead for forgiveness, seen from a distance, she seems supernatural. The chorus describes her:

> But who is this, what thing of Sea or Land?
> Female of sex it seems,
> That so bedeckt, ornate and gay,
> Comes this way sailing
> Like a stately Ship
> Of *Tarsus,* bound for th'Isles
> Of *Javan* or *Gadire*
> With all her bravery on, and tackle trim
> Sails fill'd, and streamers waving
> Courted by all the winds that hold them play,
> An Amber scent of odorous perfume
> Her harbinger, a damsel train behind;
> Some rich Philistian matron she may seem,
> And now at nearer view, no other certain
> Than Dalila thy wife.
>
> (ll. 710-24)

In this way, the tradition elaborates upon itself; Milton creates an image of and body for Dalila in spite of the fact that the character on whom she is based has no specified appearance whatever. In so doing, Milton makes Samson a more sympathetic and plausible character, one who is deceived not because he is dense but because his bedecked, ornate wife had the means with which to dupe him. Delilah, as Milton describes her, is preceded by perfumes to lull the senses, dazzles with her ornaments and possesses the power of a ship of state to captivate attention and subdue rebellion.

What enabled Milton to create an ornamented Delilah without seeming to change the text was a tradition that had already assigned jewelled beauty to seductive heroines. In the biblical narrative, Samson stupidly cannot read God's repeated signs; in *Samson Agonistes,* Dalila is so good at what she does that Samson cannot help himself. Thus, the tradition recovers one character at the expense of another. The impulse to rewrite biblical stories, here as in *Paradise Lost,* "to justify the ways of God to man," is the effort to reconcile contemporary ideology with the texts to which it appeals for authority. In making Delilah a beauty, Milton rewrites the Bible, just as the Rabbi rewrites the Bible when he makes Jael beautiful. To the authors of the Bible, Jael's appearance is irrelevant; the rabbis would, however, uphold their own standard of femininity. The Bible is similarly unconcerned with Samson's reputation, but Milton, who identifies with Samson, sees him as a symbol of the English revolution and as a type for Christ, must make Samson's failure psychologically plausible.[18] In both cases these ends are achieved by refashioning the female character into a woman of art. She uses art first on herself and then on others. Her adornment signals deception. Milton, like any midrashist, has no shortage of bedroom deceivers upon whom to model his own creation.

The characters in this tradition share pronounced features of family resemblance. Equally telling, however, are the mutations, those revisions that adapt a later character to new social conditions. The rabbis betray their own anxieties about the nature of female power and male weakness when they make Jael as seductive as Esther and Judith. These stories protest anxiously that a woman must have the special powers of a special beauty (plus charms) to overcome a man. When Milton transforms Delilah in this fashion, he reveals his own worries over Samson's heroic qualities.

With every revision, however, one association is reenforced: adornment is linked to calculated action. "Art" acquires its two senses as beautification and craft; "craft" has a double sense of "a developed skill" and "slyness." "Design" is planned creative invention (the design of the universe) and calculated manipulation (to operate by design). Only the distinction between "artisan" and "artificer," both of whom practice art, seems to keep separate the opposite connotations that struggle within the word "art" and its synonyms.

Although modesty is an implicit value in each of these stories, both Esther and Judith are unquestionably good and heroic in spite of their displays of beauty and craft. Their suffering neutralizes their art and naturalizes their characters. The rabbinic revision of Jael compromises her virtue, and once we reach Milton's comparable elaboration upon Delilah, the change is meant to cement her status as temptress and villainness. Milton's ornamented and wily Dalila is a composite of Old and New Testament heroines, Greek goddesses, and most forcibly, the whore of Babylon. When Eliot works to erase the Great Harlot in the first chapter of *Middlemarch*, she must contend with these other crafty, artful women whom tradition unceremoniously melded together.

The literary tradition thus created a new configuration that combines the heroines of art—Hebrew beauties, Delilah, Venus, and the Great Harlot—and makes the jewelled woman a unique symbol of evil. The fear of female power lurks behind this emblematic woman, who uses her charms, through the practice of a kind of sexual witchcraft, to entrap men. Jael and Judith murder; the Great Harlot deprives the soul of life. Ornament indicates the woman's awareness of her own powers and her ambition to penetrate male domains. By associating such beauty with evil and seduction, the literary tradition marks the active woman as a false beauty, one who is ugly beneath her superficial and purchased attractions. The message of this configuration is that the active woman is unchristian, dangerous to herself and to others. The message urges women to avoid luxury and ambition and to cultivate modesty, and this configuration presents itself to men as the picture of womanhood that promises pleasure but delivers death. Thus, while art is coded as activity and undesirability, nature is coded as passivity and desirability. The lovable beauty is the natural beauty, and womanhood is naturalized as humble and unpretentious obedience. More than Eliot's tolerance for jewels, it is her irritation with the value placed upon women who minimize their beauty and sacrifice their power that prompts her to ignore the Whore of Babylon and reinvest art, and the power that it unleashes, with positive value. One can only challenge old oppositions by imagining new ones, and Eliot is able to modify the woman of art because the literature of the early nineteenth century had begun the process of reassessing art and nature, romanticizing supernatural powers and devaluing conventional symbols of passive religious duty.

The Bequest of the Jewel Box: Scott's *Ivanhoe*

The jewels worn by biblical heroines, virtuous women in their original contexts, are passed on to the true English beauty in a poignant and memorable ceremony: "She entered—a noble and commanding figure, the long white veil, in which she was shrouded, overshading rather than concealing the elegance and majesty of her shape." Rebecca desires an interview alone with Rowena, and the attendants leave. It is a scene of parting. Rebecca says:

"Farewell; yet, ere I go, indulge me one request. The bridal veil hangs over thy face; deign to raise it, and let me see the features of which fame speaks so highly."

"They are scarce worthy of being looked upon," said Rowena, "but, expecting the same from my visitant, I remove the veil."

She took it off accordingly; and partly blushing from the consciousness of beauty, partly from bashfulness, she blushed so intensely that cheek, brow, neck, and bosom were suffused with crimson. Rebecca blushed also; but it was a momentary feeling and, mastered by higher emotions, past slowly from her features like the crimson cloud which changes colour when the sun sinks beneath the horizon.

"Lady," she said, "the countenance you have deigned to show me will long dwell in my remembrance. There reigns in it gentleness and goodness. . . . Long, long will I remember your features, and bless God that I leave my noble deliverer united with—"

She stopped short—her eyes filled with tears. She hastily wiped them. . . . "One, the most trifling, part of my duty remains undischarged. Accept this casket; startle not at its contents."

Rowena opened the small silver-chased casket, and perceived a carcanet, or necklace, with ear-jewels, of diamonds, which were obviously of immense value.

"It is impossible," she said, tendering back the casket. "I dare not accept a gift of such consequence."

"Yet keep it, lady," returned Rebecca. "You have power, rank, command, influence; we have wealth, the source of both our strength and weakness; the value of these toys, ten times multiplied, would not influence half so much as your slightest wish. To you, therefore, the gift is of little value; and to me, what I part with is of much less. Let me not think you deem so wretchedly ill of my nation as your commons believe. Think ye that I prize these sparkling fragments of stone above my liberty? or that my father values them in comparison to the honour of his only child? Accept them, lady—to me they are valueless. I will never wear jewels more."

Rowena urges Rebecca to abandon her erring faith and remain a sister to her. "'No, lady,' answered Rebecca, the same calm melancholy reigning in her soft voice and beautiful features, 'that may not be.'" Rebecca reaffirms her faith and vows to be a healer among the sick and a feeder of the hungry. When she bids Rowena tell as much to Ivanhoe, "there was an involuntary tremour on Rebecca's voice, and tenderness of accent, which perhaps betrayed more than she would willingly have expressed. She hastened to bid Rowena adieu." She says farewell and blesses Rowena:

She glided from the apartment, leaving Rowena surprised as if a vision had passed before her. The fair Saxon related the singular conference to her husband, on whose mind it made a deep impression. He lived long and happily with Rowena. . . . Yet it would be inquiring too curiously to ask whether the recollection of Rebecca's beauty did not recur to his mind more frequently than the fair descendant of Alfred might altogether have approved.[19]

With this scene, followed by a paragraph on the fate of King Richard the lion-hearted, Ivanhoe closes. The transaction between these famed beauties, both of whom love the hero Ivanhoe, is untainted by competition or jealousy. Fair Saxon and dark Jewess, each of whom embodies the values of her

Figure 8. Elizabeth Taylor as Rebecca in *Ivanhoe* (Metro-Goldwyn-Mayer, 1952) The film domesticated the heroine, as Rebecca is without jewels in a distinctively Christian posture.
(Photo courtesy Phototeque)

cultural heritage, enter into a cultural exchange. In the novel's final episode, they confront each other, as alien cultures always confront each other, veil to veil. Once alone, both women agree to remove their masks, the symbols of modesty that protect them and protect others from them. Blushing, their beauty naked and exposed, they take one another in visually, each branding the other on her memory.

The gesture which follows is remarkable. The Jewess, who has wealth, gives her jewels to the Saxon beauty, who has influence. The narrator declares that the jewels are "obviously of immense value," but Rowena is persuaded to accept them because Rebecca convinces her that their value is illusory and that the gems are of less value in Rebecca's hands than they will be in Rowena's. Rebecca's argument is profound: the traditional Christian heroine, passive and beloved, has had no need of jewels, and the exiled Jewess, active and lonely, has been despised because of them. Rowena will take the jewels because she is made to understand that Rebecca does not lose by the exchange. At first Rowena hesitates, declaring that the gift is of too much "consequence"; by accepting the jewels, she agrees to accept that the Jewess has been falsely accused for her arts; she agrees to be uncommon and to reconsider her own judgment upon the alien nation. Rowena hesitates, and if she pities the proud Jewess, she also fears the burden of a pact with a disbeliever. Rowena therefore suggests that Rebecca convert and be a sister to her. In effect, she bids Rebecca keep her jewels and do the business of reintegrating the woman of art into English culture for herself. Rebecca is uncompromising; she refuses sisterhood, refuses England and refuses to abandon her people, but she has accomplished her purpose by imprinting the image of her beauty on the English imagination. Rebecca, a vision out of Hebrew Scriptures, a Hebrew beauty, disappears out of the apartment, out of England, and out of the world of this fiction, having left her diamond ornaments behind in the hands of the Saxon woman, the future of England.

Rebecca is brilliant and powerful. In the art-nature dichotomy, Rebecca is closer to art: she is exotic in her costumes and customs; her eyes are black and brilliant; she has a "profusion of sable tresses" and she wears a wealth of diamond jewelry for which she is envied and derided (p. 94). In the vocabulary of Romanticism, Rebecca possesses "supernatural" beauty. Romantic and Gothic literature express the appeal of the unconscious in their characterizations of dark, alien or wild beauty, and if Heathcliff and Bertha Mason, for example, are dangerous and mad, they are also portrayed as having once been inescapably alluring and attractive. Much Romantic literature suggests that the dark depths within the human psyche are natural, dangerous and unpredictable, but filled with promises of pleasure. Because naturalizing what is darkly beautiful implies rejection of the forces of repression, most importantly, religious and social laws, Romantic texts

Figure 9. Joan Fontaine as Rowena in *Ivanhoe* (Metro-Goldwyn-Mayer, 1952) (*Photo courtesy Phototeque*)

usually stop short of naturalizing the supernatural; this literature unsettles, but does not collapse, the art-nature opposition. Rebecca is a complex figure because her qualities have contradictory connotations: she is foreign, unbelieving, and almost magically powerful, and yet this dark fairy is always benevolent. The dark heroine of this historical romance is appropriately a Jewess removed to the distant past, a woman who is feared because of her brilliance and powers.

Scott sets out to naturalize the supernatural, in Coleridge's sense, by showing us that the foreign beauty of art has a suffering human nature. Women of art who are good are complex because their suffering contradicts their flashy beauty; Jael, Esther, and Judith, like Scott's Rebecca, masquerade and wear finery to conceal unhappiness. By contrast, the evil women of art, Delilah and Babylon, have no redeeming human nature. In his historical fiction, Scott indicts those whose fear of cultural minorities is so great that they call difference of belief "disbelief." Thus would those in power convict the disinherited beauty of sorcery or treason rather than suffer the threat of her charms; thus is Jael taken for a whore. Scott takes history seriously and he recovers the Disinherited (the gallant knight's shield proclaims the novel's theme) by laying bare the conditions that have made them what they are. Even Isaac of York, whose portrait owes much to Shakespeare's Shylock, is as long suffering as he is mean. In his characterization of Rebecca, Scott succeeded in recovering her human nature all too well.

Modern critics find *Ivanhoe* too sentimental, although Scott's original readers didn't find it sentimental enough.[20] Scott himself defended the case against Ivanhoe's marriage to the Jewish beauty in his 1830 preface, and modern criticism has put the case more elaborately.[21] But no one knows better than Rebecca why she may not marry the novel's handsome hero. In *Ivanhoe* the punishment for consorting with those not of one's nation is nothing less than a name of shame and premature disfigurement. The character of Ulrica/Urfried, once a great beauty now become hideous and prematurely aged, is introduced to prove that a female beauty who lies with her oppressor is damnable. Damnation occurs on the surface of the body. Rowena's father Cedric exhorts Ulrica, asking her why she did not kill herself before sharing the enemy's bed. Rebecca is, of course, prepared to die rather than submit to the Templar Brian de Bois-Guilbert. Even her admiration of Ivanhoe distresses her, and she calls herself an "unnatural child" when she "looks upon the comeliness of a Gentile and a stranger." Because Rebecca refuses to be naturalized into the corrupt system of the Templar, she is tried for witchcraft.

It is for her arts and accomplishments that Rebecca is charged with "sortileges and witcheries; whereby she had maddened the blood and besotted the brain" of Bois-Guilbert (p. 376). Rebecca possesses all that is threatening in the woman of art: as active as Rowena is passive, Rebecca is a physician, a

Figure 10. Elizabeth Taylor and Robert Taylor in *Ivanhoe* (Metro-Goldwyn-Mayer, 1952) "...an unnatural child for loving a Gentile and a stranger"—Scott, *Ivanhoe*. *(Photo courtesy Phototeque)*

linguist, a banker, and a lawyer. For these crimes the tribunal would condemn her and vindicate the Knight Templar. The Grand Master argues: "But if, by means of charms and spells, Satan had obtained dominion over the knight, perchance because he cast his eyes too lightly upon a damsel's beauty, we are then rather to lament than chastise his backsliding" (p. 377).

The Grand Master's suspicions are founded upon

> a general belief... that the Jewish rabbins were deeply acquainted with the occult sciences, and particularly with the cabbalistical art, which had its name and origin in the studies of the sages of Israel. Neither did the rabbins disown such acquaintance with supernatural arts, which added nothing—for what could add aught?—to the hatred with which their nation was regarded....
>
> The beautiful Rebecca had been fully brought up in all the knowledge proper to her nation, which her apt and powerful mind had retained, arranged and enlarged, in the course of a progress beyond her years, her sex, and even the age in which she lived. Her knowledge of medicine and of healing art had been acquired under an aged Jewess....
>
> Rebecca, thus endowed with knowledge as with beauty, was universally admired by her own tribe, who almost regarded her as one of the gifted women mentioned in the sacred history. (p. 267)

Rebecca's beauty is linked to her wisdom and knowledge, for which reason her own tribe connects her to the beautiful and gifted women of Scriptures. But Eve's sin is also lust for knowledge. The Grand Master therefore interprets the same signs differently, and associates Rebecca with the other type of the female biblical artist. Invoking the aid of the saints and angels, he says,

> we will counteract the spells and charms with which our brother is entwined as in a net. He shall burst the bands of this Dalilah as Sampson burst the two cords with which the Philistines had bound him.... But concerning this foul witch, who hath flung her enchantments over a brother of the Holy Temple, assuredly she shall die the death. (p. 368)

The Templar is said to lust after a "painted piece of Jewish flesh and blood," but when the Grand Master insists that she face her trial unveiled, he loses the sympathy of the crowd:

> Her exceeding beauty excited a murmur of surprise, and the younger knights told each other with their eyes... that Brian's best apology was in the power of her real charms, rather than in her imaginary witchcraft. (p. 382)

The crime against Rebecca is that she is taken for Delilah; the matriarch is confused with the whore. Though the enlightened hero Ivanhoe would be Rebecca's champion, Scott calls upon a higher authority to save Rebecca. Bois-Guilbert falls dead miraculously, because of the conflicts within his own conscience.

Rebecca is so well vindicated of the charge of witchcraft that nineteenth-century readers were disappointed that she is not rewarded for her suffering by marriage to the hero. But Rowena is meant to be the real heroine of Ivanhoe. Scott's marriages are endogamic and Ivanhoe's love for Rowena, a woman of his own tribe, has been nurtured since childhood. Rowena's only characteristic feature is her fair beauty—her body is a repository for Saxon values—and if she is less accomplished than Rebecca, there is less need for her to be skilled and crafty. Like Heathcliff and Cathy, Ivanhoe and Rowena were raised as brother and sister. While such a bond should be enough to satisfy us in nineteenth-century fiction, the Romantic novelist has so successfully naturalized the supernatural, has made Rebecca so complex and interesting, that she threatens the status of the conventionally virtuous, placid, and beautiful Christian heroine. Though Rebecca and Rowena are not rivals for Ivanhoe's affection, they become rivals in the mind of the reader. The marriage of Rowena and Ivanhoe is meant to symbolize the rebirth of England after the Norman conquest, but this new Adam and Eve have also been threatened by a seductive artist; though Rebecca proves benign in Scott's fiction, she is a snake in Thackeray's.

Thackeray's Rebeccas

Thackeray's *Rebecca and Rowena: A Romance upon Romance,* a broadly comic burlesque conceived in 1846 and published in *Punch* in 1850, mediates between *Ivanhoe* and *Vanity Fair*. The setting is after the marriage of Rowena and Ivanhoe in the late twelfth century, but their castle could easily house a nineteenth-century middle-class couple. Rowena is a religious prude, and poor Wamba the jester is not suffered to crack a joke. Rowena wears Rebecca's jewels everywhere, but torments Ivanhoe with her jealous memory of the Jewess. Ivanhoe is henpecked by a domestic tyrant, and Thackeray at once burlesques the conventions of the romantic plot at the same time that he satisfies his readers by marrying Ivanhoe to the more accomplished beauty. Compton McKenzie summarizes the plot:

> Ivanhoe soon gets bored by Rowena and goes off to the wars again. He is reported dead and Rowena marries Athelstane. Ivanhoe comes home to find another siege of a castle going on, in which Athelstane is killed. Then Rowena dies, after making Ivanhoe promise that he will never marry a Jewess. After various adventures Ivanhoe rescues Rebecca who has been imprisoned by her father for turning Christian, and marries her.[22]

Rebecca's people weep bitterly for their loss, in high comic style, but Thackeray knows that his readers will only tolerate the marriage if Rebecca is transformed into a Christian beauty. If Victorian readers loved Rebecca for

Figure 11. "A Court Ball"
Print from Thackeray's *Rebecca and Rowena*.

her vital and exotic beauty, they also wanted her domesticated. Scott's romance is at odds with itself because the appeal of the passive romantic heroine is threatened by a foreign attraction who is not only a Jew but who is also a busy professional. The constraints of Scott's fiction keep Rebecca on the margin by precluding the possibility of her domestication. But these constraints are too weak. Rowena doesn't seem to have earned the hero and if foreignness is an obstacle, certainly Scott might have done what Thackeray did: simply convert her.

The tensions of an era in which creeds of progress coexisted uneasily with time-honored religious creeds forced novelists to create a new beauty, one who is as "commanding" as Rebecca (Scott's favorite adjective for her) and as Christian as Rowena. Yet there were few models for such a heroine; since the great harlot, artistry and jewels had been incompatible with virtue. A compromise needed to be struck and two words in the art-nature vocabulary were reassessed: "piety" and "vitality." Eliot is able to moderate Dorothea's piety because Scott demonstrates that piety results in an injustice against the modern bejewelled beauty who has been accused of sorcery in the name of religion. Without the reappraisal of values that made the chain of Rebecca characters possible, Dorothea would have been unimaginable.

Fast changing economic life in Europe, revolutions, and industrialism made Victorians sensitive to the issue of hypocrisy. Out of the two kinds of beauty—that of Rebecca and that of Rowena—Victorian novelists sought to produce a compromise that would satisfy middle-class readerships. *Vanity Fair* is "a novel without a hero" (or heroine) because Thackeray takes hypocrisy for his subject and uses his heroines' bodies to expose the advantages and disadvantages of Christian nature on the one hand and modern invention on the other. Thackeray reinvents the Rebecca figure that had been naturalized in *Ivanhoe* to show both sides of such vitality. Energy made one self-sufficient and was necessary for upward mobility, but sexual energy was not without its dangers. Thackeray's Amelia and Becky undermine the very ideals that they represent.

Unlike the Romantic *Ivanhoe*, a fiction that is unthreatened by the jewelled beauty, *Vanity Fair* is judiciously Victorian in its memory of the message of the Bible. Thackeray jests about potential female power when he describes his own Rebecca's "artful" ways: "And this I set down as an absolute truth. A woman with fair opportunities, and without an absolute hump, may marry WHOM SHE LIKES. Only let us be thankful that the darlings are like beasts of the field and don't know their own power. They would overcome us entirely if they did."[23] At the same time, Thackeray can no longer return to a passive Christian ideal. Because Thackeray refuses to choose between Amelia and Becky, he has been accused of not knowing his own mind.[24] The effect of Thackeray's refusal is that he produces a drama that depicts Christianity in a

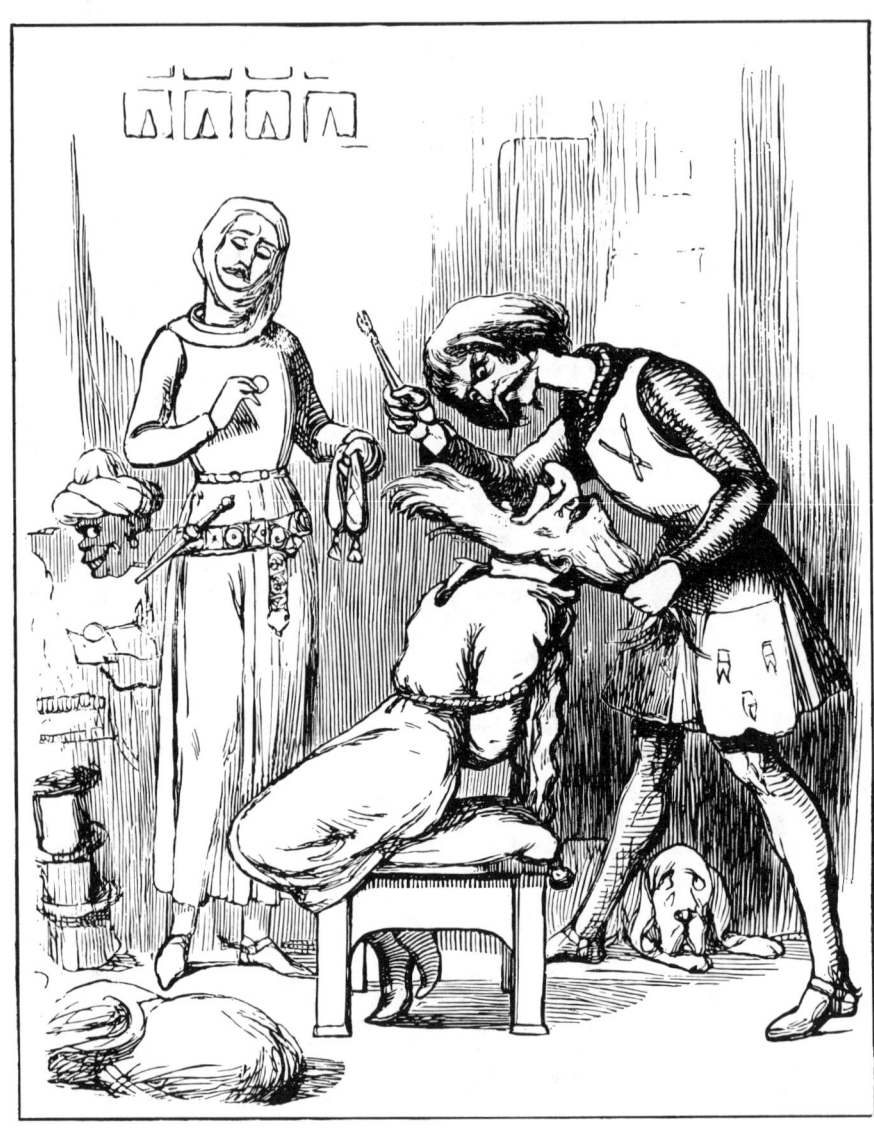

Figure 12. "Ivanhoe Ransoms a Jew's Grinder"
Thackeray burlesques Scott's sentimental portrayal of the Jews.
Print from Thackeray's *Rebecca and Rowena*.

power struggle with modernity. Thackeray repeats the contrast between Una and Duessa in Amelia and Becky, destabilizing the values that Spenser, and the tradition that he represents, had worked to create. By animating these types, Thackeray allows their values to fluctuate, making his characters ambiguous and open to interpretation.

The new Rebecca, both that of Scott and that of Thackeray, is vital in her beauty, like Spenser's evil Duessa. Thackeray highlights the association of art and energy on the one hand, nature and passivity on the other. That Una is as lacking in vitality as she is sparing of ornament would not have troubled Spenser, who wrote at a time when the rich could afford to value Christian passivity over competitive energy. By the nineteenth century, however, middle-class readers needed to reconcile piety and vitality.

Vitality became a valued quality in women and therefore a criterion for beauty during the middle of the nineteenth century. The word "vitality" was not used in its modern sense much before Thackeray's day. Reformation Protestantism, scornful of worldly pride—both as quality and as ornament—found virtuous beauty in life-denying women and put the opulently attired in the devil's company. The Hebrew beauty who supplemented her natural attractions with ornament in order to act heroically had been thoroughly revised by the tradition. She was rived in two: her veiled aspect was valorized and her adorned figure was debased. With *Ivanhoe,* the commanding, vital, and jewelled heroine is reintroduced into the English tradition and offers her charms to the English woman, but she is a problematic figure, even for Scott. Romanticism suggested a new standard of beauty and value that Scott's Rebecca typifies, but Victorianism was often wary of Romantic innovations. When Thackeray sets out to review and revise Rebecca, he returns to the woman-of-art configuration and weighs Rebecca's charms against the whore's dangers. In his characterizations, Thackeray sets up a competition between vital and pious beauty.

Amelia's innocence is contrasted with Rebecca's resourcefulness. Is Amelia's frailty, lovely and unthreatening, so valuable that society wants to shoulder the burden of helpless individuals? While Amelia's old-fashioned modesty carries none of the risks of radical moral codes, she cannot fend for herself, and she is a drain on the resources of her friends. Moreover, Amelia's goodness is accompanied by shortsightedness, and she reads character poorly. Becky, on the other hand, possesses clarity of vision (she is society's best reader) and she is the life of the party. But she is also an artful magician, and Thackeray wonders if her energetic cleverness is worth the risk of looser morals and upstarts rising from the lower classes. Thackeray may recall that Romantics and revolutionaries had invoked nature to sanction such radical ideas as sexual license and political revolt. At the same time, Rebecca's appeal—for equal rights and to man's appetite for pleasure—could not be dismissed with the same conviction that would have been possible in pre-romantic and pre-revolutionary days. For Spenser, Duessa poses a superhuman threat, and as the Grand Master later points out, one forfeits one's rights simply by disbelieving. Although Amelia physically and spiritually resembles Una as Becky resembles Duessa, Thackeray—who has heard the spirited self-defense of Scott's Rebecca and who has grown suspicious of Una's promises—lacks Spenser's certainty about which female type is more deserving and more desirable.

Thackeray's Amelia and Rebecca are variations of Una and Duessa. Amelia's purity is appreciated only by Dobbin, and because he is beauty's most capable beholder, his self-sacrificing love for Amelia suffices to ensure his status as the hero of the novel "without a hero." The others in Vanity's Fair find Becky more beautiful. Like Duessa, Becky has been fashioned by art; her mother was an actress and her father was a painter. From them, she inherited wit and learned that the art of mimicry works wonders: "Many a dun had she talked to, and turned away from her father's door; many a tradesman had she coaxed and wheedled into good humour, and the granting of one meal more." In *Vanity Fair,* however, the art of mimicry is the art of survival, and as it had been for Scott's Jewess, it is imperative that the disinherited girl be a linguist. Thackeray's Rebecca uses her knowledge of French to intimidate Miss Pinkerton. Becky's early education in art, learned in the school of the poor, gains her entry into the school of the rich.

Miss Pinkerton is deceived into letting Miss Sharp (whose surname imports her wit and its dangers) become a student. Even Rebecca's appearance conspires in her favor: "By the side of many tall and bouncing young ladies in the establishment, Rebecca Sharp looked like a child.... But she had never been a girl... she had been a woman since she was eight years old." Thus, the artist's daughter, small and poor, acquires charity only because she appears weak and behaves unthreateningly; in Thackeray's words, she admirably performed "the part of the ingénue." The narrator takes some delight in conjecturing "how Miss Pinkerton would have raged had she seen the caricature of herself which the little mimic, Rebecca, managed to make out of her doll" (p. 21).

Rebecca enters the Sedley home in the guise of an angel, all the while playing enchantress and using her covetous green eyes to feign modesty and dart arrows, in the form of glances, through the pompous comic figure Jos. Becky has turned herself into a foreign exotic beauty. In her fancy, to which the narrator admits us, "she had arrayed herself in an infinity of shawls, turbans and diamond necklaces" (p. 28). Like Duessa, Rebecca masquerades as Una. Down the stairs she goes on Joseph's arm, "Rebecca very modest, and holding her green eyes downwards. She was dressed in white, with bare shoulders as white as snow—the picture of youth, unprotected innocence and

Figure 13. "Mr. Joseph Entangled"
Print from Thackeray's *Vanity Fair*.

humble virgin simplicity" (p. 30). Rebecca's shoulders do double duty: the word "bare" generates the word "unprotected," which, Thackeray repeatedly reminds us, is the truth of the poor orphan's situation; at the same time the bare shoulders that are read as "humble virgin simplicity" are meant to be understood by the reader as another immodest gesture among Becky's other acts of calculated immodesty. The description is typical of Thackeray's strategies for assigning double meanings without calling too much attention to his ploy. Bare and unprotected, there is little irony in the fact that Becky is an orphan among society's disinherited who behaves, therefore, justifiably. Yet we know that the narrator is sarcastic because he explicitly assigns one meaning to Becky's bare whiteness, while we have been given the keys to interpret it more skillfully than the company for whom Becky attires herself (and whom the narrator counts himself among). Moreover, Thackeray depends upon our knowing that true virgin simplicity—something that we remember from our whole series of veiled beauties—keeps its shoulders covered.

Amelia Sedley is modeled on the natural beauty of Christian goodness as she had been incorporated into the eighteenth-century benevolent tradition as a woman of good nature. In fact, "good nature" is Thackeray's tag phrase for Amelia. We first meet Amelia on her return from school, prepared, presumably, to begin adult life. Within a short space she becomes Mrs. George Osborne and six weeks later, she is a widow. For the remaining decade and a half that the novel covers, pale Emmy wears black. Amelia's mourning casts her in the mold of the natural beauty, Una, and it also serves to explain why Becky outshines her. At long last, Amelia removes her mourning to marry Dobbin. Thackeray's twist is that Amelia mourns for a husband who was vain, disinterested, and unworthy. Her years of widowhood, while still signifying her unfailing virtue, are a mockery because they are marked only by her blindness to that which stands plainly before her and by the doting, wearisome attention that she pays her son. While Thackeray is not unmindful of the time-honored ability of pallor and mourning clothes to convince the reader of a heroine's goodness and underlying beauty, he seems to have little patience for such unflagging virtue. The sadder Amelia is, the more vapid she seems. Ironically, it takes wicked, but astute, Becky to bring Amelia to her senses. Immediately, through the storms comes Dobbin, loyal, natural creature that he is.

As Geoffrey and Kathleen Tillotson hold, Dobbin is "in, yet not of, the world of *'Vanity Fair.'*"[25] Like the lion in Book One of *The Faerie Queene* who becomes Una's protector rather than her ravisher, Dobbin is a creature uncorrupted by culture, who sees through veils and licks the feet of the woman of nature. Had Una been a woman of art, nature's beast would have devoured her.[26] E. M. Forster writes that "we know too little of animal psychology" to introduce them into fiction,[27] but Dobbin is consistently described by appeal to a code of animals and is valorized in terms of his canine qualities. He has big feet, and Amelia is guilty of treating him like a "Newfoundland dog" (p. 641). The Tillotsons have shown that Dobbin was added by Thackeray at the stage of revision and that he lacks the necessary dash to be a real hero.[28] The narrator's ironic view of his characters is well balanced: by making Dobbin a "Spooney" and by making Becky a fascinating snake, Thackeray devalues both the potential beauty of nature and the beauty of art, showing that the former is insipid and the latter is dangerous.[29]

Amelia, like the Ecclesia and Una, is represented in exile. Her wilderness is her isolation, particularly at parties. When Becky arrives, she behaves like the whore and Duessa by usurping Amelia's rightful position. As the Red Cross Knight had been misled, so is Amelia's husband George, who slips Becky a note which is "coiled like a snake among the flowers." Their eyes meet (p. 278). The snake imagery of Genesis and Revelation surrounds Thackeray's Rebecca, but few besides the reader see her as a snake. Because beauty is a matter of faith, the Red Cross Knight receives a prophesy in which Duessa is described as a snakelike monster (I. viii. 46–49), and at the end of *Vanity Fair* Rebecca is also fully described as a serpent-siren whose "monster's hideous tail" "peeps diabolically above water"; she is "writhing, diabolically hideous and slimy" (pp. 617–18). Roger B. Henkle points out that Thackeray is clumsy in finishing Rebecca off in this way,[30] but by completing the connection between the dark jewelled beauty and the serpent-siren, Thackeray does not simply make Becky repulsive; he also makes the snake attractive. The snake's wisdom affords pleasure and profit and the basilisk's eyes are fascinating for good reason.[31]

Just as Amelia's characteristic features are the pallor and dark dress which associate her with Una, so Becky is a basilisk whose characteristic feature is her eyes, eyes which are green gems that charm and work spells. Green, they are jealous (p. 296); bright, her intelligence shines through them; and deadly—"Reverend Crisp... fell in love with Miss Sharp... being shot dead by a glance of her eyes, which was fired" from a great distance (p. 21); and Joseph, "encountering the eye of Miss Sharp stopped all of a sudden, as if he had been shot" (p. 27)—Becky's looks are killing. Green, bright, and killing summarize Becky's character and appearance. These adjectives penetrate her body and reach to her soul. Perhaps Becky is a murderess. Green, bright and killing (who would scorn to have looks that kill?) are all ambiguous qualities.

The interview between Rebecca and Amelia, while Amelia fears for a husband who unbeknownst to her already lies dead, is a play of Rebecca's eyes against Amelia's cheeks. Amelia's hair is loose in the style of one without sense (Thackeray touches Emmy with signs of madness now and then) and her eyes are "fixed and without light." We join Rebecca as she enters the chamber:

Figure 14. "Mrs. Osborne's Carriage Stopping the Way"
Print from Thackeray's *Vanity Fair*.

> Rebecca's appearance struck Amelia with terror, and made her shrink back. It recalled her to the world and the remembrance of yesterday....
>
> After the first movement of terror in Amelia's mind—when Rebecca's green eyes lighted upon her, and rustling in her fresh silks and brilliant ornaments, the latter tripped up with extended arms to embrace her—a feeling of anger succeeded, and from being deadly pale before, her face flushed up red, and she returned Rebecca's look after a moment with a steadiness which surprised and somewhat abashed her rival. (p. 297)

The context doesn't clarify for us if the terror caused by Becky's appearance refers to her entry into the room or to the way she looks. As Thackeray makes a good deal of Rebecca's inappropriate finery, the text favors the latter reading, though the former is more logical. Amelia is terrified, significantly, not when her eyes light upon Rebecca, but on the contrary, when Rebecca's eyes light upon Amelia. What power is in those eyes that they terrify those upon whom they are cast? Thackeray is subtle; the passage would make ordinary sense only if Amelia's fright had been a consequence of seeing rather than of being seen. Thackeray drives this point home because Rebecca is momentarily bested when Amelia is uncharacteristically able to return Rebecca's gaze.

Amelia is able to look Becky in the eye, to see Becky for whom she is, because she has been permitted to get angry for the first time in the novel. Anger animates her and her face turns from white to red. The shift in color is a shift from passivity to activity, and very briefly the power relation between the rival women is reversed. At the novel's outset, its heroine Amelia was rich, healthy, and rosy, while Rebecca was poor, pale, and dressed in virgin white. Once Becky comes into money and attires herself in jewels, she becomes the picture of health, while Amelia has been transfigured into an emblem of sad, impoverished, even sickly, piety and passivity. As such, Amelia is unable to sustain her anger; she lapses back into delirium, and Rebecca slips away to tell the household that Amelia is ill.

Amelia's virtue is linked with lifelessness, because Thackeray modifies pale with "deathly" and pictures Amelia in delirium and in sleep (p. 280). With the progress of the novel, Thackeray transforms Amelia from a rosy youth into a dull adult. The opening description of Amelia endows her with the physical attributes that will later attach themselves to Becky:

> As she is not heroine, there is no need to describe her person; indeed I am afraid that her nose was rather short than otherwise, and her cheeks a great deal too round and red for a heroine; but her face blushed with a rosy health, and her lips with the freshest of smiles, and she had a pair of eyes, which sparkled with the brightest and honestest good-humour, except indeed when they filled with tears, and that was a great deal too often for the silly thing would cry over a dead canary bird.... (pp. 14–15)

As Amelia's eyes and cheeks get duller, so does her personality. She is rosy, bright and alive in the days when she can afford, and wears with pleasure, fine clothes and expensive gems. Rebecca is as conspicuously poor of friends and possessions as Amelia is rich. As Thackeray strips Amelia of wealth and her husband, giving her real reason to cry, he strips her of color both literally and figuratively.

Rebecca acquires all that Amelia loses: money, ornament, and society. Rebecca succeeds because she is artful, and to the novel's end, she is a pleasure-giving enchanting demon: "Jos went away convinced that she was the most virtuous, as she was the most fascinating of women" (p. 633); In Rebecca, Dobbin sees the devil: "That little devil brings mischief wherever she goes," and the narrator exploits the ambiguous value of a woman practiced at giving pleasure: "we know that she was eminent and successful as a practitioner in the art of giving pleasure" (p. 650). This statement, far from innocent, is made when Rebecca is innocently making Amelia happy. In this way, Thackeray manipulates his contexts to achieve irony. Once Amelia is widowed and impoverished, she affords little pleasure to her friends and family. Thus unpracticed at female art, however, Amelia's virtue and maternal nature remain intact. Amelia is drained and Rebecca is filled; Rebecca is drained and Amelia is filled; material goods oppose spiritual value. The reader remains on Thackeray's seesaw, a balance that has art, wealth, and pleasure on one side and nature, poverty, and boredom, on the other.

To be thoroughly an artist is to renounce nature. Becky's most damning trait is that she is an unnatural mother. Rebecca's son looks on her with wonder:

> Sometimes—once or twice a week—that lady visited the upper regions in which the child lived. She came in like a vivified figure out of the *Magasins des Modes*, blandly smiling in the most beautiful new clothes and little gloves and boots. Wonderful scarfs, laces, and jewels glittered about her.... She was an unearthly being in his eyes... to be worshipped and admired at a distance.

This "unearthly being" seems supernatural to her child, like Milton's Dalila or Scott's Rebecca. On a carriage ride the child learns that power lurks in his mother's eyes: "he gazed with all eyes at the beautifully-dressed princess opposite to him. Gentlemen on splendid prancing horses came up, and smiled and talked with her. How her eyes beamed upon all of them!"

Sometimes the maid allows the child into his mother's room in her absence:

> It was as the abode of a fairy to him—a mystic chamber of splendour and delights. There in the wardrobe hung those wonderful robes—pink and blue, and many-tinted. There was the jewel case, silver-clasped; and the wondrous bronze hand on the dressing table, glistening

Figure 15. "The Letter before Waterloo"
Print from Thackeray's *Vanity Fair*.

all over with a hundred rings. There was the cheval-glass, that miracle of art.... O; thou poor lonely little benighted boy! Mother is the name for God in the lips and hearts of little children; and here was one who was worshipping a stone. (pp. 368-69)

The child secretly goes to see his mother's jewel case in her absence, and Thackeray thus portrays what would become a classic Freudian scenario. As we are made to see Rebecca's room through her child's eyes, we find ourselves in a magician's den, filled with gems, wonders, and miracles of art. Thackeray's metonymic use of "stone" for Rebecca goes far: She is "as cold as a stone," "with a heart of stone," but most importantly, she is mistaken for (and not by the child alone) the valuable stones that she wears. Our own admiration for Rebecca numbers us among the inhabitants of *Vanity Fair*. As beauty's beholders, we do not escape Thackeray's characterization. We are charmed by Rebecca because she succeeds at what nearly every one else tries. She is not to be blamed for her success; in the vain and unjust world of society, Thackeray often reminds us, it is to the orphan girl's credit that she beats them at their own games. Thackeray has good fun with us, alternately making us admire and condemn Rebecca.

Vanity Fair exaggerates the attributes of the woman of nature and the woman of art, and Thackeray uses models of their representative characters to effect his own characterizations. Amelia, like Rowena and Una, is fair and uninteresting, but as a type of veiled beauty, she is also a natural mother and a virtuous Christian. At the same time, Amelia spoils her child badly; if Rebecca is an unnatural mother, Amelia is too natural a mother. Becky is disinherited, like Scott's Rebecca, but when Thackeray's bejewelled heroine is accused of being a Delilah, the charge is not unfounded. Of Becky's husband, Rawdon Crawley, Thackeray writes that,

> He was beat and cowed into laziness and submission. Dalilah had imprisoned him and cut off his hair too. The bold and reckless young blood of ten years back was subjugated, and turned into a torpid, submissive, middle-aged, stout gentleman. (p. 433)

Here Rebecca Sharp, guilty of disempowering her husband, is named Delilah with some justice.

Thackeray exposes Victorian hypocrisy as a contradictory desire for innocence and experience, old-fashioned religion and ruthless competition. By developing his heroines in the tradition of the biblical women of art and nature, Thackeray articulates on the surface of his heroines' bodies the incompatible values that his society admires. For Thackeray, Evangelicalism and Romanticism produced a tension between current beliefs that left no coherent ideal of beauty or value.

Changing ideals in beauty respond to these tensions, but as a satirist, Thackeray is unwilling to produce a heroine who effectively reconciles competing values. He asks us to choose between Rebecca and Amelia. By the novel's end, however, he has undercut them both. To enjoy Rebecca's vitality and benefit from her energy and wisdom, we must accept her loose morality and sacrifice innocence as a female virtue. On the other hand, to protect Amelia's piety, we must suffer her to be a burden upon us, and we must forgive her dullness of vision and personality. Even Dobbin comes to find Amelia shallow, and Thackeray thus contradicts himself on her one saving virtue, the capacity to love. Becky offers a model of beauty that valorizes art at the expense of heretofore "natural" morality, but to preserve the morality of frail and sheltered women means reassessing the premium that had recently been placed on the free expression of sexual energy. To decide which system of morality is better, each with its manifest drawbacks, depends upon whether one finds Amelia or Becky more attractive. Most Victorians championed Amelia, and as recent criticism shows, we suppose Thackeray to have preferred Rebecca. It is only natural that we should think so, but history, and not Thackeray, made her victorious.

Concluding *Middlemarch*

George Eliot, who is well familiar with this tradition, takes up the challenge to produce an ideal beauty in *Middlemarch*. Eliot spares no details in the portraits of her characters. Neither are these details superfluous; each figure in the novel is defined with respect to both traditions of beautiful heroes and heroines and to contemporary models of loveliness. Beauty is of no small concern to Eliot's characters, who talk of beauty tirelessly among themselves, weighing the advantages and disadvantages of its various manifestations. And well might they do so, as Eliot attaches dire consequence to reading the character of beauty, in a world in which life's most serious decisions concern the selection of one's partners.

Exploiting the distance between Dorothea's self-perception and her "nature," Eliot writes within and rewrites the art-nature tradition. "If Miss Brooke ever attained perfect meekness, it would not be for lack of inward fire" (p. 10): the narrator is bemused by the paradox of Dorothea's ardent efforts at self-erasure. Dorothea, whose limited education afforded her few models of behavior, is a self-fashioned Una or Amelia; she associates piety with absence of ornament, severity of dress, and quiet self-sacrificing servitude. Eliot has, however, lost patience with the Quakerish Jane Eyre-type heroine who wishes only to be granted "a new servitude," and Dorothea's beauty, resembling neither that of Amelia nor that of Jane, bespeaks inner traits that thwart Dorothea's own effort to transform herself into an Ecclesia in the wilderness. Dorothea, dark, statuesque and sensuous, is pictured on the model of Rebecca. But Rebecca, whether good or evil, has enjoyed few rewards; Scott's Rebecca renounces her jewels and opts for celibacy; Thackeray's Rebecca wears a treasury of jewels and is stripped of them because she is wanton. Eliot is determined to recover and refine the values embodied in the woman of art without destroying her in the process. She shows that by opting for the wrong model of beauty and heroism, women like Dorothea have restricted themselves; Dorothea's decision to harness her independent spirit by marrying Casaubon proves a crime against her sex and her sexuality.

Dorothea and Casaubon are incompatible for more reasons than one. Derek Oldfield makes much of their different styles of speech, demonstrating that Dorothea becomes more controlled and eloquent as she matures.[32] She also grows more beautiful as Eliot cures her of the misperceptions that allow her to marry Casaubon in the first place. Their incompatibility is evidenced most obviously in their respective appearances: Casaubon, who is old, ugly and shrouded in darkness, is described as "faded," and Dorothea, young, beautiful and beaming, is described in terms of her "bloom." Yet Casaubon has been too long shut up with his books and Dorothea has too little worldly experience to properly appreciate the appearance and character of the other. The novel educates Dorothea in art appreciation, and the twice disinherited young artist Ladislaw is her teacher.

Against the background of the art-nature tradition—the implications of which Dorothea imperfectly understands—it is clear why Dorothea is surprised by Celia's eagerness to wear jewels. In light of Dorothea's proud dark beauty and its literary and graphic models—which Ladislaw, as a museum visitor knows well—it is clear why Ladislaw is surprised by Dorothea's eagerness to renounce jewels.

A cameo bracelet in her hand, Dorothea no sooner greets Ladislaw at her apartment in Rome than she appeals to his expertise and asks his opinion of the jewelry. Ladislaw approves, adding that they will suit her well; Dorothea quickly replies that these fragments are being purchased for Celia at Celia's own request. Dorothea's seemingly simple tastes are subjected to Ladislaw's analysis in a step-by-step argument that leads to surprising ethical questions. First Ladislaw observes that Dorothea doesn't seem to care for cameos; she confirms this to be the case. Ladislaw takes the leap from jewels to art and beauty: "I fear that you are a heretic about art generally. How is that? I should have expected you to be very sensitive to the beautiful everywhere." Dorothea confesses that she is not only ignorant of art but that she is unwilling to indulge in appreciating "the immense expense of art" while there are others who cannot afford the same pleasures. (Rowena's words echo unmistakeably here.) Ladislaw has a ready response to Dorothea's Victorian anxiety; Will equates Dorothea's definition of piety with fanatacism:

> "If you carried it out you ought to be miserable in your own goodness and turn evil that you might have no advantage over others. The best piety is to enjoy—when you can.... I suspect that you have some belief in the virtues of misery, and want to make life a martyrdom." (p. 163)

In so saying, Ladislaw questions the equation of "natural women" and suffering women. Ladislaw, who worships Dorothea as a "beguiled angel," answers her in her own terms by redefining piety as pleasure, for how can one appreciate beauty if one does not permit oneself joy? Ladislaw goes on to give Dorothea her second lesson in the appreciation of Rome's works of art, which has, to this point in the novel, been their favorite topic of conversation.[33]

The private opinion of the artists, however, is that the finest work of art in Rome at present is the one that nature made: Dorothea herself. The studio painter Naumann and his friend Ladislaw are in the Vatican when they first spot a figure who shames neither the Ariadne nor the Cleopatra, a figure in "Quakerish grey drapery" whom Naumann would cast as a nun were she not wearing a wedding band. The artist tries another image on Dorothea (who does not know that she is being watched) and tells Ladislaw that she is "the most perfect Madonna I ever saw." Finally he discovers the truth of Dorothea's beauty: "an antique form animated by Christian sentiment—a sort of Christian Antigone—sensuous force controlled by spiritual passion" (pp. 140–41). Naumann will paint Dorothea as Santa Clara. Eliot will compare her as well to Santa Barbara and Saint Theresa (who is sculpted "in ecstasy"), and finally to Antigone again (p. 612), though Dorothea, whose antique form is animated by Christian spirit and who is both sensuous and spiritual, must be heroic in nineteenth-century style. Dorothea soon wears mourning because her husband is dead, and she exchanges her chosen drab clothes for a widow's attire. Dorothea removes her mourning to marry the man of artistic temperament who best appreciates her worth as a thing of beauty and a work of art.

Middlemarch's underlying subject is the education of women. The ending of the first edition included a direct statement of this concern: "it was never said in the neighborhood of Middlemarch that such mistakes could not have happened if society... had not smiled... on modes of education that made a woman's knowledge another name for motley ignorance." Dorothea laments that she has received an inadequate training in aesthetics, history and languages; if Eliot is to recover the Rebecca figure, she wants to be certain that she is educated in the manner of Scott's Rebecca and not Thackeray's. And indeed, according to Eliot's view, Dorothea's ignorance led her to mistake pedantry for genius and beauty for sin.

Dorothea must "learn what everything costs," as she promises Ladislaw, because in *Middlemarch* the ability to discriminate values is the essential ingredient of heroism. Ladislaw recommends himself as a hero because he is the rare character who knows the difference between a woman who is a thing of beauty and a woman who practices artistry. He alone rejects Rosamund for Dorothea. Rosamund's education at Mrs. Lemon's tempts Eliot to caricature; the narrator remarks that Rosamund's apparently natural movements are as pretty as those of a kitten: "Not that Rosamund was in the least like a kitten; she was a sylph caught young and educated at Mrs. Lemon's" (p. 118). Rosamund's fair beauty and her schooled manipulations ensnare Lydgate, who falls for an actress for the second time in his life. Thus, Eliot contrasts Dorothea's excessive spirituality with Rosamund's false appearance of spirituality and makes Rosamund's beauty her vice. Because she has been too much admired and too little trained in proper values, Rosamund cannot see beyond herself; she is characterized as vain and spoiled. Like Amelia, Rosamund is a burden upon all with whom she is associated and like Becky Sharp, she is overly fond of finery and overly ready to entice the eyes of men. Rosamund's snakelike neck offers an image that fully connects her with the woman-of-art configuration, because like Duessa and Becky Sharp, Rosamund masquerades as Una. Although there are those in Middlemarch prepared to confuse the emancipated Dorothea with a harlot, Eliot convinces us that it is not the liberated or educated woman who is a danger, but the conventional ideal of womanhood who has been trained only well enough to ensure her security by exploiting the vulnerability of others.

Rosamund, the conventional fair beauty, is set against plain Mary Garth:

> Rosamund took off her hat, adjusted her veil, and applied little touches of her finger-tips to her hair—hair of an infantine fairness, neither flaxen nor yellow. Mary Garth seemed all the plainer standing at an angle between the two nymphs—the one in the glass and the one out of it, who looked at each other with eyes of heavenly blue, deep enough to hold the most exquisite meanings an ingenious beholder could put into them, and deep enough to hide the meanings of the owner if these should happen to be less exquisite. Only a few children in Middlemarch looked blond by the side of Rosamund, and the slim figure displayed by her riding-habit had delicate undulations. In fact, most men in Middlemarch... held that Miss Vincy was the best girl in the world, and some called her an angel. Mary Garth, on the contrary, had the aspect of an ordinary sinner: she was brown; her curly dark hair was rough and stubborn; her stature was low; and it would not be true to declare, in satisfactory antithesis, that she had all the virtues. Plainness has its peculiar temptations and vices quite as much as beauty; it is apt to feign amiability, or not feigning it, to show all the repulsiveness of discontent: at any rate, to be called an ugly thing in contrast with that lovely creature, your companion is apt to produce some effect.... Advancing womanhood had tempered her plainness which was of a good human sort.... Rembrandt would have painted her with pleasure, and would have made her broad features look out of the canvas with intelligent honesty. For honesty, truth-telling fairness, was Mary's reigning virtue: she neither tried to create illusions nor indulged in them for her own behoof.... (p. 84)

In this juxtaposition, both Rosamund and Mary suffer by the comparison. Eliot insists that plainness has its disadvantages, disadvantages that are explicitly connected with self-denial. At the same time, Eliot legitimates plainness as a kind of beauty more artistically noble than the apparently angelic beauty of Rosamund. Rembrandt would have enjoyed painting Mary; her beauty points to qualities of education and mind of which Eliot essentially approves. With the same stroke, Eliot exposes the tradition of beautiful women pictured before their mirrors and warns her readers that the beholder of such art is likely to fall victim to false readings. The heavenly blue of Rosamund's eyes, in actuality empty, is invested with meaning by the ingenious beholder.

The contrast between Rosamund and Dorothea is meant to distinguish "art" in its negative sense from "art" in its positive sense. Rosamund works illusions; Dorothea is real in her beauty and charms. Mary Garth, who is low in stature and may be falsely amiable, stands between these two ideals as an average-looking woman whose virtues are sense and strength of character. From Mary we learn that the average woman profits by admiring an ideal of courage and stature.

Dorothea is a Christian Antigone because she returns to right an injustice even though she is threatened with punishment. She lifts the veil from her own face, in spite of the fact that the world calls it shame, and displays herself, with confidence and defiance, to the world. All of Middlemarch may protest Dorothea's marriage to Ladislaw, as critics of the novel have as well, but Dorothea can withstand the attack. Strong men such as Lydgate, brown and broad-shouldered, are easily enchanted. But feminine, Romantic Ladislaw, with his halo of curly hair, is the sensitive connoisseur who willingly educates and admires a strong and vital beauty. The marriage of Dorothea and Ladislaw may be less than satisfying because while Eliot has worked hard to establish Dorothea as a modern heroine, she has devoted less effort to establishing Ladislaw as a modern hero. As we shall see in the following chapters, Ladislaw's beauty was of a type that was becoming increasingly suspect as literature came to prefer dark, masculine, brute strength.

In *The Madwoman in the Attic,* Gilbert and Gubar show how Eliot's "The Lifted Veil" informs her major fiction. They demonstrate Eliot's preoccupation with lifting veils, and they lift some themselves:

> According to Saint Paul, only the veiled woman can prophesy in the temple because the head of every man is identified with Christ and the spirit, while the head of every woman is associated with the body and therefore must be covered (1 Corinthians 11). As in purdah, acceptance of the veil becomes a symbol of the woman's submission to her shame: the unveiled Salome will damn and destroy men, but the Virgin Mother remains a veiled goddess whose purity is shared by religious Jewish women who shave their heads, and by nuns who, as the brides of Christ, perpetually wear the veil.... Wearing the mantle of invisibility conferred by her omniscience and the veil of the Madonna conferred by her message of feminine renunciation, Eliot survives in a male-dominated society by defining herself as Other.[34]

I am less convinced that Eliot defines herself as Other than that Eliot redefines the "other woman." Scott's Rebecca had been "the other woman," the veiled other. Dorothea naturalizes this figure of "other woman." Above and between Rosamund, the charming artist, and Mary Garth, good nature, Eliot inserts Dorothea, a woman whose beautiful appearance is consistent with her vitality and strength, a woman for whom being a Christian Antigone is neither contradiction nor shame. Dorothea is "an art that Nature makes," a fully naturalized woman of art because she was once a model of ascetic piety. But Middlemarch cannot domesticate Dorothea, and the novel ends with the hero and heroine leaving the world of the novel. Eliot makes Dorothea virtuous to the reader, but she is unwilling to suggest that Middlemarch society has a place for Dorothea and Ladislaw. We may be disappointed that Dorothea's large resources must be used to tend to small things.

Jewel Caskets after *Middlemarch*

The dramatic action of Anthony Trollope's *The Eustace Diamonds* (1873) consists largely of the beautiful Lizzie, whom the novelist meaningfully calls "a second Becky Sharp,"[35] ponderously transporting a heavy box containing the family diamonds wherever she travels. Like Becky Sharp, Trollope's Lizzie is wicked, so much so that she and her diamonds nearly seduce Lucy's lover; but if the man goes to Lucy, the reader stays with Lizzie. We see that as Scott's originality consists in his having revised the familiar portraits of dark and light heroines by making *both* appealing, Thackeray and Trollope ingeniously make *neither* type of heroine entirely desirable. Because the blond is dull in the minds of readers—perhaps against the wishes of the creators of these fictions—the wicked jewelled woman holds the greater attraction. Piety continued to lose ground to vitality.

In *Middlemarch,* Eliot succeeds in creating a heroine who learns to wear jewels, to be sensual, and to love art without sacrificing her virtue. The novel begins where Scott's romance ends: two women negotiating over a maternal casket of jewels, and the reluctant heroine is finally persuaded to take jewels of "consequence." Beyond Dorothea's learning to be comfortable with her own pleasures, Gilbert and Gubar find further evidence that this novel does not tolerate female renunciation, not even from Rosamund whom they explain is *Middlemarch*'s "Becky Sharp." They add that "the Lilith to Dorothea's Mary, Rosamund is associated... with sirens, serpents, and devilishly alluring charms." But they go on to demonstrate that Dorothea and Rosamund share more characteristics than not, both being "angels," and both being beauties: "The meeting between Rosamund and Dorothea is... the climax of *Middlemarch.* Both women seem childish because both have been denied full maturity by their femininity.... Each is jealous of the other, yet self-forgetful" (pp. 514–18). They hold hands, and they save each other. As Rebecca and Rowena approach one another in friendship, Becky Sharp is uncharacteristically generous to Amelia late in *Vanity Fair.* On the model established by Scott, the rival women in *Middlemarch* are also able to forget their suspicion.

In *Daniel Deronda* (1876) Eliot tries to recover the Jewess (literally) for English literature. To do so, she attacks the stereotype of the sensuous Hebrew by depicting Mirah as a passive unadorned virtuous and suffering beauty. This portrait proves a strategic error. The beauty of Mirah and Gwendolen reverses that of Rebecca and Rowena. Mirah fails to engage the reader because Gwendolen—the woman in the novel who acquires the jewel-case— keeps our attention. As Nancy Nystul has shown, motherhood, Judaism, and jewelry go hand in hand in the symbol system of *Daniel Deronda*.[36] And just as Rebecca gave a casket of jewels to Ivanhoe's legitimate bride, so too does Lydia Glasher, Grandcourt's mistress, send Gwendolen, Grandcourt's bride, the "family jewels"; the note accompanying the casket ominously predicts that Gwendolen's happiness will be buried with that of Lydia and her children. Although Gwendolen, like Rebecca Sharp (and Jael and Judith), may be guilty of murder, the late Victorians had come to value complexity of character and the vitality that height and gems signified over "plain" goodness. Here the Jewess is rewarded with marriage to the hero—something of a knight himself—but the reader may wish that Mirah had something of Gwendolen's charm.

Freud, who taught us to regard repetition with suspicion because it is symptomatic of deeper anxieties, himself repeats a story about transference and a maternal jewel box. He reports in *Dora: An Analysis of a Case of Hysteria* (1905) that his patient recurrently dreamed of her mother's jewel-case and that the jewel-case is the site of female sexuality.[37] According to Freud the sight of the "jewel casket" traumatizes. As in the myth of *Pandora*, the source of the world's troubles is located in the first woman's box.

The jewel-case, shared by mother and harlot, divided mother and daughter. This literary scenario provides Dora with a metaphor for her illness. Freud speaks for her: "My jewel-case is in danger, and if anything happens it will be Father's fault." Freud explains that therefore

> in this part of the dream everything is turned into its opposite.... As you say the mystery turns upon your mother.... You would have been glad to accept what your mother rejected. Now let us put "give" instead of "accept".... [Herr K.] gave you a jewel-case; so you are to give him your jewel-case. (p. 87)

In an entirely different context, Marie Balmary writes of Freud:

> Let us return first of all to Rebecca and to the famous letter in which Freud begins by renouncing a theory that made the father guilty of provoking symptoms in his daughter.... Because of Rebecca, the hidden wife whose disappearance must constitute a fault for the father [Jakob], Freud cannot persevere in the... discovery. To speak of Rebecca, however, is to do the opposite of what he says. (p. 65)

Thus, Balmary finds that Freud's repression of his father's second wife, Rebecca (to save Jakob, the father) results in the repression of a theory that can see clear to blame fathers for the sexual neuroses of daughters. For his own psychological comfort, Freud needed to repress Rebecca. Balmary shows that he did not completely succeed.

Because the Jewess and her jewel box provided effective metaphors for such Romantic concerns as supernaturalism, the rights of minorities, sexuality, and secularism, the time was ripe for their assimilation.[38] Several Victorian writers recreate the relationship between Rebecca and Rowena type characters—they even return to scenes of two women over a jewel box—but try as they did, such overshadowed heroines as Thackeray's Amelia, Trollope's Lucy, and Eliot's Mirah suggest that after *Ivanhoe* the nineteenth century had difficulty inventing a vital dark Rebecca who did not capture the reader's interest more fully than her pious blond rival. Rowena is, after all, persuaded to accept the casket of jewels, and finally Dorothea Brooke does the same.

The Future of an Allusion

The mere difference of a vowel in the words "allusion" and "illusion" points to an identical origin: according to the *OED,* both words derive from verbs that meant "to play with," "to jest," or "to mock." The refinements of literary theorizing have long since led to definitional distinctions between allusion and illusion, though ever more complex theories about textual dependencies begin to threaten the future of the term "allusion" as a meaningful theoretical concept. The example of Dorothea's allusion to the jewels in The Revelation of St. John suggests that allusion lends the reader access to deeper, more complex textual relationships. The example demonstrates that an allusion can function as a distraction to create the illusion of cultural consensus where none actually exists. Inasmuch as tracing allusions engages the reader in the analyst's game of recovering, or inventing, origins, the lessons of psychoanalysis invite us to recover as well the original connection between allusion and illusion.

Illusion, Freud explains, is an effect of repression; related to sublimation and wish fulfillment, illusion is a psychological device that has consolatory power.[39] While acknowledging the possibility that his own prediction may be wish-fulfilling, Freud reasons that the illusion, which served the primitive psyche, has no future. The illusion to which he refers is religion.

As a literary device (usually associated with poetry), allusion distinguishes itself from illusion as a product of the hyperconscious, rather than of the unconscious mind. However much it enjoys hiding, allusion means to be detected because it ultimately exists to clarify rather than to conceal. In the words of Earl Miner's standard definition, allusion refers clearly to "another art, to history, or to contemporary figures or the like."[40] As such, we understand that allusion works to include that to which it refers, while illusion means to exclude that which it works to repress. Finally, because an allusion is only realized in the discovery of its referent, an allusion is all future.

When we find ourselves in the presence of an allusion, we assume the role of a puzzle-solving detective. We reserve our psychoanalytic skills for deeper literary questions. While Miner does distinguish allusion from less sophisticated devices such as source borrowing—allusion "requires the reader's familiarity with the original for full understanding and appreciation"—and from "mere reference"—allusion "is tacit and fused with the context in which it appears"—allusion shares with these devices authorial intention and a directive function. If the clues are properly pursued, questions of meaning are resolved.

While plain "source-borrowing" and "mere reference" still seem to have some explanatory function, the once lofty term "allusion" yields to more comprehensive identifications. Michael Riffaterre, for example, uses "intertextuality" to name codes of textual reference to as much as whole traditions; Hegel's phrase "the historical unconscious" has come to be used to identify textual evidence of a shared living history; Umberto Eco's encyclopedia contains the cultural information that we need to understand all textual references, no matter how small; and Harold Bloom finds "the anxiety of influence" responsible for other kinds of textual echoes. And the list continues. To do the work required by users of these terms, the literary critic must be a psychoanalyst of texts. This job of detection involves moving from superficial symptoms to the cultural unconscious in order that we may discover what the text (or its author) has tried to repress.

The accepted definition of allusion has limited the term's critical usefulness. Rather, in its very hyperconsciousness, allusion is a product of the unconscious; it conceals as it clarifies, excludes text as it includes text, and is a symptom of the repressed. Writers of realism in particular depend upon their ability to distract us with references and details in order to repress those traditional values that the writer wishes to avoid. It then becomes the analyst's task to regard allusion as a kind of blocking device, displacement, or symptom, a clue to something more deeply troubling. Like illusion, allusion serves a culture and has the power to console.

As a recognizable tacit reference that fuses with its new context, Dorothea's reference to the Revelation of St. John meets Miner's criteria for allusion. Does the reference point to apocalypse in *Middlemarch?* Frank Kermode does find a "muted apocalypse" in *Middlemarch,* and he praises the subtlety of Eliot's early allusion: "the jewels of St. John's Revelation are mentioned early but the context seems to make them serve only as a way of noting Dorothea's priggish attitude toward Celia."[41] We have seen that the reference does more. The Great Harlot is one of many jewelled figures who are repressed here because they serve as emblems of wickedness. The Whore of Babylon, Spenser's Duessa in *The Faerie Queene,* and Milton's Dalila as she is represented in *Samson Agonistes,* demonstrate, by their example, that women who wear jewels do not go to heaven.

A series of allusions surrounding Dorothea Brooke's beauty serves to repress and redefine those Christian values that deprive femininity of the powers of seduction. In Revelation, the symbol of Rome's evil and wealth is a jewelled woman. Rome surfaces in this novel about provincial England as the site of great Christian art. But when Dorothea finds herself there, it is not the Christian tradition that we are asked to admire. To the artists' eyes, Dorothea shames neither the Ariadne nor the Cleopatra, powerful figures of pagan sensual beauty. We are again distracted from the Christian value that distrusts ornamented women. The reader is referred as well to Antigone and St. Teresa.

That beauty is an illusion is a cultural cliché. As such, perhaps more than anything else, beauty can only be defined through allusions, for, as Roland Barthes writes in *S/Z,* "beauty cannot assert itself save in the form of a citation" (p. 33). Woman's beauty always refers to the code of art, but in defining beauty in one way, writers necessarily exclude other historical or cultural ideals. Dorothea, whose education is limited, dresses in Quaker drab because the small self-effacing woman is her imagined ideal of a Christian.

Nancy Nystul argues that jewels in Eliot's *Daniel Deronda* are associated with motherhood, with the mother's awesome power, and the mother religion, Judaism. Nystul puns on Jew and jewel. In *Middlemarch,* even as we disapprove of Dorothea's refusal to wear jewels we disapprove too of her misguided desire for a husband who can teach her Hebrew if she wishes. Later the narrator comments that a stupider or more conceited version of Dorothea would have found "her ideal life...in the perusal of 'Female Scripture Characters'" (chapter 3). Eliot's allusions to Hebrew and to Female Scripture Characters as negative models again work not to reveal but to conceal an affinity.

In the tradition of literary and artistic representation, the tall, dark statuesque Hebrew beauty and the characters in Hebrew Scriptures wear jewels. Dorothea resembles Esther and Judith in appearance and character. Artemisia Gentileschi and Rembrandt are but two of the artists who had codified the image of such power and beauty. This figure of the powerful *femme fatale* had become a cultural cliché. As an emblem of female sexuality, wickedness, and foreignness, however, the type of the threatening Jewish beauty became opposed to the untainted Christian heroine whose virtue resided in her "naturalness" and passivity. Through a system of oblique allusions that drown out the prevailing voices of her contemporary tradition,

Figure 16. Giovanni Lorenzo Bernini, *St. Teresa in Ecstasy*
Dorothea Brooke is modeled on St. Teresa.
Rome, Chiesa da Santa Maria della Vittoria.
(©Alinari; Photo courtesy Art Resource)

Eliot recovers female power and Hebrew beauty for Christianity. She does so for a bourgeois reading public that is acquiring wealth and is ready to display it on their own (or their wives') righteous bosoms. The growing vogue of feminine ornamentation in the late nineteenth century motivates Eliot to repress earlier religious codes that assign negative connotations to jewelled women. Eliot is helped by a growing secularism and a growing interest in the exotic.

I quote a remark by Arnold Kettle with two embedded phrases to illustrate how effectively Eliot has used references to varied traditions of beauty in order to conceal the transformation of Dorothea from a nun into the mythical type of the powerful Hebrew heroine of art. Kettle writes that Eliot's "standards of right and wrong (perhaps her emphasis on Law and her sympathy for Judaism—not revealed in this particular book—are significant) are not quite adequate to the complexity of her social vision."[42] Kettle's doubly parenthetical aside and his double negative arguing that the Judaic tradition is missing in *Middlemarch* suggests to me that he has heard it in this novel, though he does not know precisely where.

Finally, I would add that *Middlemarch*'s standard of moral rectitude, Mary Garth, reads Sir Walter Scott. The reader is—for no apparent reason—so informed. We know that Eliot read Scott as well. Scott may be named here simply because he is among those Romantic writers who "naturalize the supernatural" by allowing jewelled women to be virtuous heroines in his fictions. Particularly in *Ivanhoe,* Scott more than tolerates the power of the Hebrew beauty. He vindicates the jewelled woman of the charge of harlotry as Eliot will so vindicate Dorothea.

By referring the reader to the emeralds that surround God's throne in Revelation, Eliot represses the Whore of Babylon, jewelled women as harlots in Western literature, and a whole tradition of tall dark Hebrew beauties who long functioned in art as emblems of female seductive power. At the same time, she infuses her work with other, *unalluded to,* cultural references. When an author calls us into conspiracy through an allusion that reminds us that we share a cultural tradition, we are flattered by the assumption that we can find the reference. We do well to ask why the writer will, in one place, insist upon a particular consensus by appeal to outside textual authority, while he or she will comfortably assume consensus elsewhere. Allusion can be a kind of overcoding, an attempt to protect the writing self and the reading public from an established traditional value that the writer needs to ignore.

I think that Eliot was unaware of the presence of Hebrew beauty in her own text because she shared some of Dorothea's Puritanism. But Eliot had to describe Dorothea somehow. In the effort to create a powerful heroine, Eliot hid an aspect of her own tradition's misogyny from herself. Allusion can suppress as well as reveal meaning, and because the path's an allusion strikes may elude the writer too, realistic novels—full with apparent excess, static, and extraneous details—are dense and endlessly rich. Therein too lies their powers of manipulation.

In *The Winter's Tale,* a shepherdess, as beautiful as a princess, masquerades as a queen, parries with a king, himself disguised as a common subject, in the course of a play that will discover the artifice to have been more real than the apparent reality: the shepherdess is, by right of birth, a princess. Nature is design, and in Her boundless justice, She stamped such beauty upon the face and figure of the shepherdess/princess as could only attract a prince. Himself in the act of dissembling, King Polixenes means to ensnare the artless peasant, whom he believes has designs upon his son. Both kings in this drama are guilty of nearly fatal acts of misreading; both kings misread beauty's character.

In the lines that are my chapter's epigraph, Polixenes defends the beauty of art by affirming the precedence of nature; all is reducible to nature's creation. He avows a preference for hybrid flowers—the work of human invention—over nature's purer and poorer supply. But that which recommends itself to one as invention, seems artifice to another, and Perdita, fearing that these artificial breeds are sinful, finds neither beauty nor merit in them. The fact of Shakespeare's play, itself art, argues against Polixenes' position, silently affirming that "over that Nature which you say makes for art is a Nature that art makes."

Whether the hybrid flowers are beautiful and therefore worthy of appreciation is of no small consequence. The relative value of art and nature has political, social, and economic implications of which King Polixenes is blissfully ignorant when he undermines his own position against the "unnatural couple" by arguing for the beauty of mixed breeds over that of pure breeds.[43] Polixenes articulates a revolutionary criterion for beauty, staking out the position of democracy that will ultimately devalue the aristocracy by depriving it of inherited beauty. If Perdita looks and acts the part of a princess though she was raised a shepherdess, the time will come when nurture takes precedence over nature, when the likes of Perdita will be written out of the tradition of realism. In the following chapter, we will look at what became of the foundling's beauty in the Victorian novel. When nurture began to compete with nature as an authority of beauty, literature was able to see beasts in the bodies of beauties and beauty in the bodies of beasts.

6

Grace: The Birth of Breeding

The last and noblest part of beauty is grace.
                                    Reid

When in *The Winter's Tale* Perdita scorns art as sacrilege and expresses her conviction that beauty has Nature (God) as its only source, she pays homage to the generous benefactress who graced her with all of her characteristic qualities.[1] The supremacy of Nature's reign goes unchallenged by heroes and heroines who are unambiguously virtuous and beautiful from birth through adulthood. When Polixenes argues that nature can be improved upon through breeding, the audience appreciates the irony of royalty favoring breeding over birth. When privilege is earned rather than inherited, when grace depends upon, rather than predicts, behavior, then nurture acquires limited powers over nature. Breeding subjects nature's raw materials to change, but however much a character is changed by experience, nature recovers herself always as beauty's creator and ultimate judge, as origin and end.

Perdita's grace comes naturally and distinguishes her from those who were born into the class in which she was raised. But grace, an attribute of royalty and a gift of divinity, is one of the many qualities to which the princess has lost her exclusive rights. While we speak of "natural grace," we also regard grace as the sign of an expensive education, more truly a function of nurture than of nature. In the one sense "grace" refers to a state over which the individual has no control: Grace names the sister goddesses who endow beauty and charm, and grace refers to the exceptional favor bestowed by kings and gods. In its other sense, grace means personal control, and even a person not graced with natural beauty can acquire the beauty of natural grace.

"Class" is another of the words that straddles the boundary between nature and nurture. In its sense of social rank "caste" is its nearest synonym, but class also refers to well-bred elegance. While everyone is born into a class, classiness—the class that makes a person alluring—is a skill that may be acquired in the classroom.

In the determination of beauty and character the roles assigned nature and nurture (birth and breeding, heredity and environment) have developed historically. The paradox of such words as "grace" and "class" reflects historical reversals. What was once thought to be natural came to be regarded as cultural. Cultivation (as associated with the land) was itself once a matter of nature, and cultivated people tend to be nostalgic about times gone by when nature was uncorrupted by culture. Indeed, in every generation pastoral literature posits ideal beauty (uncorrupted nature) in the past. Raymond Williams accordingly finds himself on an "escalator" as he tries to locate the moment when we imagine ourselves to have been severed from the golden age of rural purity.[2] That moment of rural purity is infinitely removed.

Male Beauty Contests: *Daphnis and Chloe* and *Wuthering Heights*

Through the depictions of its heroes, Emily Brontë's Gothic romance, *Wuthering Heights* (1847) positions the reader on this escalator. The competition between Heathcliff and Edgar Linton, which is phrased in terms of nature and nurture, relies upon our familiarity with the pastoral tradition. Nelly Dean is grooming her young charge Heathcliff, apparently trying to refashion his soul as well as his body, when Heathcliff challenges her assumptions about beauty's meanings, manifestations and origins:

> "... I'll steal time to arrange you so that Edgar Linton shall look quite a doll beside you: and that he does. You are younger, and yet, I'll be bound, you are taller and twice as broad across the shoulders—you could knock him down in a twinkling..."
>
> "But Nelly, if I knocked him down twenty times, that wouldn't make him less handsome, or me more so. I wish I had a light hair and a fair skin, and dressed and behaved as well, and had a chance of being as rich as he will be!"
>
> "And cried for mamma at every turn... O, Heathcliff, you are showing a poor spirit! Come to the glass, and I'll let you see what you should wish. Do you mark those two lines between your eyes; and those thick brows, that instead of rising arched, sink in the middle; and that couple of black fiends, so deeply buried, who never open their windows boldly, but lurk glinting under them, like devil's spies? Wish and learn to smooth away the surly wrinkles, to raise your lids frankly, and change the fiends to confident innocent angels..."
>
> "In other words, I must wish for Edgar Linton's great blue eyes and even forehead," he replied. "I do—and that won't help me to get them."
>
> "A good heart will help you to a bonny face, my lad," I continued, "if you were a regular black; and a bad one will turn the bonniest into something worse than ugly. And now that we've done washing and combing and sulking—tell me whether you don't think yourself rather handsome? I'll tell you I do. You're fit for a prince in disguise. Who knows but your father was the Emperor of China, and your mother an Indian queen, each of them able to buy up, with one week's income, Wuthering Heights and Thrushcross Grange together? And you were kidnapped by wicked sailors and brought to England. Were I in your place, I would frame high notions of my birth; and the thought of what I was should give me courage and dignity to support the oppressions of a little farmer!"[3]

By arguing that a handsome face is the manifestation of a good heart, Nelly claims that the features of Heathcliff's appearance matter less than how he interprets them. It is descriptive language in which he will be figured, and if he behaves well and schools his heart, it is in his power to be compared to, and taken for, a prince rather than a demon. When Nelly urges him to frame high notions of his birth, Heathcliff answers with a wisdom beyond his years and expresses a typically Victorian sentiment. He says, in effect, that wishing will not make it so. Heathcliff's sense of disadvantage, first expressed as a conviction of ugliness and unworthiness, is the force that propels the story.

Heathcliff challenges more than the advice of an encouraging servant; he rejects the romantic assumption that goodness is rewarded by beauty and wealth. Aware that if he is to own Wuthering Heights and Thrushcross Grange together, no royal parents will materialize to buy them up with one week's income, Heathcliff finds Nelly's advice outmoded. As dark and poor as Linton is fair and rich, Heathcliff's consolation will not come from fantasy. Indeed, Nelly's scenario is borrowed from pastoral romance, and witnessing the rivalry between the two boys for Catherine's affections, she may have been reminded of an earlier beauty contest:

> One day—for it was now Daphnis' turn to realize what love meant—he and Dorcon engaged in a beauty contest. Chloe was the judge, and the prize for victory was the privilege of kissing Chloe.
> Dorcon spoke first to this effect:
> "Well, my girl, I'm bigger than Daphnis. And I'm a cowherd and he's a goatherd, so I'm as much superior to him as cows are to goats. And my skin's as white as milk, and my hair's as red as corn that's just going to be reaped. And I was nursed by my mother, not by an animal. But this fellow's quite short, and he's as beardless as a woman and as dark as a wolf. And he grazes he-goats and smells awful as a result. And he's too poor even to keep a dog. And if it's true that he was suckled by a goat, as people say, he's really no better than a kid."
> When Dorcon had said something like this, Daphnis replied:
> "Certainly I was suckled by a goat—so was Zeus. And the he-goats that I graze are bigger than his cows. And they don't make me smell, because even Pan doesn't smell and he's three-quarters goat. And I've got plenty of cheese, and bread baked on a spit, and white wine, and all that a peasant needs to make him rich. I haven't got a beard, but neither has Dionysus. I'm dark, but so are hyacinths—and Dionysus is superior to the Satyrs, and so are hyacinths to lilies. But this fellow's as red as a fox, and he's got a beard like a he-goat, and his skin's as white as a town lady's. And if you have to kiss someone, you can kiss my mouth, but all you can kiss of him is the hair on his chin. And remember, dear girl, that you yourself were nursed by a sheep—and even so you're beautiful."
> Chloe waited no longer, but partly because she was pleased by the compliment and partly because she had been wanting to kiss Daphnis for a long time, she jumped up and kissed him.[4]

In the cases of both Daphnis and Heathcliff, the foundlings' beauty is expressed as a mystery and a possibility.

The match between Daphnis and Dorcon is verbal rather than visual. Each contestant presents an argument for his beauty by assigning a deeper meaning to the qualities of his own appearance. Dorcon appeals—as Linton might—to his known origins and relative wealth. Rather than stake a claim to extraordinary beauty, Dorcon feels safe on the firm ground of that which is familiar and valued. The metaphors that he chooses associate him with nature's products: his skin is milk-white and his hair is as red as ripe corn. Finally, he argues that because he was nursed at his mother's breast, he is assuredly more beautiful than Daphnis, who is reputed to have been suckled by a goat. A simple exercise in logic proves that Daphnis is no more beautiful than a kid.

More sophisticated than his opponent, Daphnis is able to turn a presumed disadvantage to his favor. If you don't know who I am and what my beauty means, he replies, let us assume instead that I am like the gods. Daphnis systematically replaces base references to the animal kingdom with lofty ones to Olympian heights. He denies that he is like a goat or a wolf by affirming that he is like Zeus, who was raised by goats, and like Pan, who is part goat, and like Dionysus, who is beardless. Nelly Dean is not the first to operate on the assumption that beauty is manufactured by rhetoric.

One metaphor is skillfully exchanged for another. If Dorcon claims that darkness is wolfish, Daphnis can claim that darkness belongs to the hyacinths. By scorning Daphnis for his beardlessness, Dorcon gives offense to Dionysus. And Daphnis can play the same game: he tells Dorcon that his hair is red, not as the corn, but as that of the sly fox, and that his skin is white, not as milk, but as the skin of a town lady. In the code of flowers to which Daphnis has appealed, dark hyacinths are preferred to white lilies. Finally, Daphnis earns Chloe's kiss by reminding her that her origin, and therefore her beauty, is as fantastic as his own. Dorcon, by insulting Daphnis on this ground, has unwittingly insulted the beauty of the woman he wishes to impress. Because Daphnis and Chloe are extraordinary for the same reason, they have a type of beauty in common. This, the narrator tells us, is the winning argument, though Chloe requires no such persuasion; she has loved Daphnis, who has been her constant companion since infancy, best all along.

The plot of Longus' third-century pastoral romance—the basis for Greene's *Pandosto* and, at least indirectly, for Shakespeare's *The Winter's Tale*—justifies Daphnis' argument. Dorcon proves himself a "sly fox" (a brutal animal) when, as the frustrated loser of the beauty contest, he attempts to rape Chloe by disguising himself in animal skins. Moreover, by boasting of riches, Dorcon proves himself ugly for his ambitions while Daphnis, content with the wealth that suffices to make a peasant rich, is an innocent child of nature. Daphnis naively walks away arm in arm with his dangerous rival, and the conventions of pastoral romance ensure that appropriate justice is meted out: Dorcon is killed, and Daphnis and Chloe are preserved through many life-threatening adventures, until they are discovered to be a lost prince and princess, marry each other, and recover the rights that are theirs by birth.

It is on this model that Nelly finds encouragement in the mystery of Heathcliff's birth. Though Nelly urges Heathcliff to count his strength, exoticism and darkness as potential advantages, Heathcliff is convinced that his society places a premium on the fairness, grace, and class sported by Linton. Indeed, the same features that suggest to the servant that Heathcliff may be the son of a Chinese Emperor and an Indian queen persuade the more powerful Lintons and Hindley that Heathcliff is likely to be a gypsy's child. And the steps from gypsy to demon, from demon to fiend, and from fiend to beast turn out to be small. In spite of Nelly's efforts to fashion a beauty, the others persist in seeing only a beast.

Although Nelly's hopes seem unrealistic, her attitude is, in one sense, more advanced than that of the narrow-minded families she serves. The possibility of the beast having beauty had reemerged in the eighteenth century in less fantastic genres than the fairy tale. Early in the seventeenth century, man in a state of nature was imagined to have been a vicious and brutal beast. Hobbes, the most eloquent spokesman for this theory, advocated strict government: if nature is evil, nurture is all important. Caliban in *The Tempest* embodies the characteristics of uncultivated man. Not only is he ugly, but he is dangerous. He is prepared to take Miranda by force, and raping the innocent daughter is the ultimate brutality. Rape is a continuous metaphor for beastliness, and fear of rape often justifies the oppression of those who are called "primitive men."

Writing a century after Hobbes, Rousseau pictured a primal man who bears a closer resemblance to Daphnis than to a beast. To describe his hypothetical primitive, Rousseau coined the phrase "noble savage." The allure of beauty in the beast made Victorian high society ultimately befriend the one whom they called "the elephant man." Edgar Rice Burrough's Tarzan, a beautiful beast, exemplifies this reversal, though *Tarzan of the Apes* (1912) betrays a reactionary attitude in its identification of the source of Tarzan's merit. Like Dorcon and Caliban, Tarzan is also prepared to rape Jane, but in a chapter entitled "Heredity" the narrator reports that "a lifetime of uncouth and savage training and environment could not eradicate" Tarzan's "instinct of graciousness." At the moment when Tarzan wishes to take Jane, "in every fiber of his being, heredity spoke louder than training," and he shelters her instead.[5]

With Rousseau's "noble savage," the connotations of nature and nurture appeared to have undergone a reversal, and the political uses towards which Rousseau's theories were put are familiar and dramatic history. Less momentous than the French Revolution, but perhaps an equally significant symptom of the reorganization of political, economic, and philosophical categories, is a changing ideal of beauty. To appreciate the stakes for the reader in the beauty contest between Heathcliff and Edgar Linton and to measure the ideological distance from Daphnis and Dorcon to Heathcliff and Edgar, we want to know how nobility and savagery, beauty and beastliness, lost their identity some time after Daphnis and how Rousseau imagined that he could yoke them together again for his own age.

While the criteria for beauty depend upon the assessment of human nature, that assessment is unstable: does man inherit nobility or savagery? If man is naturally angelic (spiritual) and naturally animal (sexual), how can these contradictory natures be reconciled? Religious and naturalistic metaphors were confused: if man is savage, does it not follow that he is demonic? Rousseau's construction represents an attempt to reclaim that which centuries of representation had denied: according to Rousseau, beauty and virtue were most likely to be found in the absence of law and God. The redistribution of wealth and evolving political systems made Rousseau's ideas singularly appealing. A consequence for literary idealizations was that Daphnis and Chloe had come to look unrealistic because the beautiful prince raised among peasants implied a definition of nature—inherited beauty and privilege—that was increasingly unacceptable in developing democracies.

At the turn of the nineteenth century, questions of nature and nurture so charged the atmosphere that an increasingly educated European population seemed to be waiting for a character—real or imagined—who could settle once and for all the question of whether Hobbes or Rousseau painted a more accurate picture of natural man. Popular speculation led to the depiction of beautiful beasts as heroes in some texts and beastly natural men in others. Much discussed was the obviously untenable experiment of isolating a child in nature; but even imagining such a situation provided material for enlightening fictions. When, in 1800, a real wild boy stepped out of the woods, Europe's eyes turned towards him. This child could, people seemed eager to believe, settle the questions of nature and nurture. As a result, he grew larger than life and today proves emblematic of the ambiguous character of beauty in the nineteenth century.

The Wild Boy of Aveyron: Itard's Diary and Shattuck's *The Forbidden Experiment*

Jean-Marc-Gaspard Itard, who undertook the project of civilizing the Wild Boy, wrote in his report that "the most brilliant but unreasonable expectations were formed by the people of Paris respecting the Savage of Aveyron before he arrived."[6] Itard noted that even persons of "eminent understanding"

> thought that the education of this individual would be the business of only a few months, and that they should very soon hear him make the most striking observations concerning his past manner of life. Instead of this, what did they see?—a disgusting, slovenly boy... continually balancing himself like some of the animals in the menagerie, biting and scratching those who contradicted him, expressing no affection for those who attended upon him; and in short, indifferent to everybody, and paying no regard to anything. (p. 41)

The Wild Boy is described as capable of "uttering only a guttural and uniform sound" (p. 97). Itard writes that his charge's senses were "very inferior to those of some domestic animals," that the child's feeling was "limited to those mechanical functions which arose from the dread of objects that might be in his way."

Whether or not Brontë was very familiar with reports on the Wild Boy, her character much resembles him. When Heathcliff first arrives at Wuthering Heights he is "a dirty, ragged, black-haired child" who speaks "gibberish that nobody can understand" (p. 41). Most remarkably, Heathcliff frustrates his tormentors by his apparent indifference, and like the wild child, he even displays indifference to physical pain.

In his second report of 1806, Itard writes that the outcome of his work "offers less a story of the pupil's progress than an account of the teacher's failure" (p. 141). Itard remembers "the dreadful picture of the man-animal as he was when he left his wild forests," when, like the molten idols of Psalm 115, "his eyes looked but did not see, his ears heard but did not listen," and he marvels at the "prodigious difference." By trying to teach the boy language, Itard wanted to reclaim "a creature fallen... into the lowest state of brutishness," but the doctor regrets that he never succeeded in teaching his charge morality. To the last, the Savage could only be motivated by his own *wants*. The boy displayed passion only for nature, the outdoors, and pure water, and he seemed to have some attachment to his *gouvernante*.

Heathcliff's character develops similarly. Even after he acquires education, he lacks conventional morality. Like the wild boy, he can be passionately wild, his motivations are apparently selfish drives to satisfy his own desires, and he develops some feelings for Nelly Dean. Yet the novel mitigates his unredeemed nature by his single-minded love for Cathy.

When François Truffaut documented Itard's reports in film, he invented lovely scenes of the boy's grooming that compare to Nelly's grooming of Heathcliff. In the film, washing the boy transforms the savage into an adorable, sympathetic youth before the viewer's eyes. The camera sees more feeling in the lonely boy than his teacher can. Such pictures of the Wild Boy as actually exist show a human being significantly less cute than the actor who plays his part and engages our sympathies.

The Wild Boy's story is told by Roger Shattuck in *The Forbidden Experiment: The Story of The Wild Boy of Aveyron* (1980). Although

Figure 17. *L'Enfant sauvage (The Wild Child)* Washing the Wild Child in Truffaut's 1970 film. (Photo courtesy *Phototeque*)

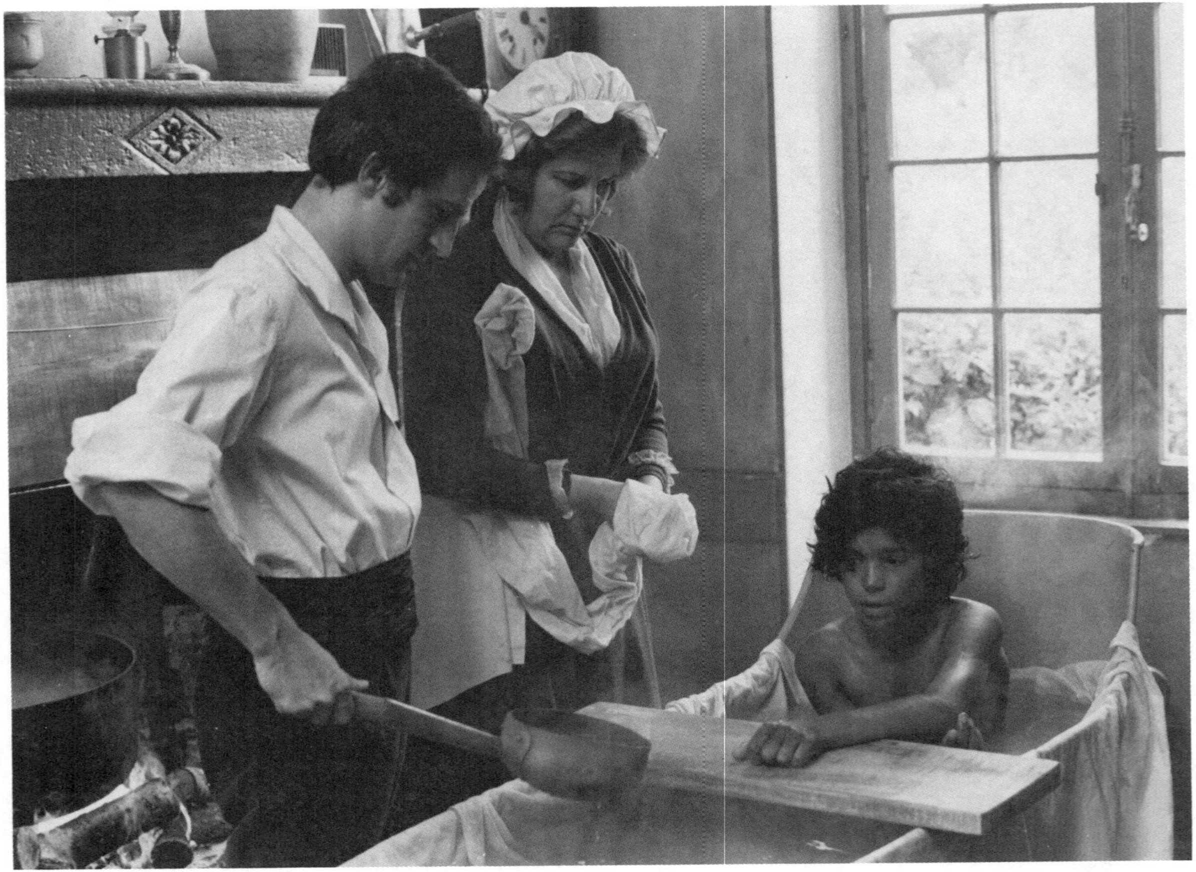

Shattuck's treatment of his subject is uniquely sensitive to the boy's role in nineteenth-century real life drama, the Wild Boy is made the hero, in a manner of speaking, of a twentieth-century narrative history. I quote from Shattuck at some length because the story he tells captures the ambivalences and tensions inherent in both nineteenth- and twentieth-century attitudes toward nature and nurture. It shows how "Beauty and the Beast" made the transitions from fairy tale, to philosophic hypothesis, scientific experiment, and realistic fiction.

Shattuck alerts us to the fact that the Wild Boy, rather than presenting an opportunity to choose between competing theories, was supposed to legitimate a choice that most people had already made:

> In the eighteenth century, naturalists and philosophers were preoccupied by the question of human nature because they believed that the whole subject had to be reformulated and answered afresh. Experimental science, political revolution and "free thinking" philosophy claimed to have over-thrown the dogmas of established religion and the class system of hereditary aristocracy. Man began to be seen not as a special being created in the image of God; he was redefined in terms of his place in the natural world...
> ... In an age seeking the overthrow of old constraints, Rousseau's optimism was more popular than Hobbes' pessimism.[7]

Indeed, the overthrow of old dogmas that the Wild Boy was supposed to verify was sufficiently accomplished to have made this figure identifiable and interesting in the first place. Wild children had turned up earlier in history and had caused considerably less fanfare.

In discussing the reception of the Wild Boy of Aveyron, Shattuck pointedly directs our attention to the names which were conferred upon the child, demonstrating a connection between art and life. Shattuck notices that names are marks of grace and class and that names can direct us to the source of our perceptions of humanity.

Shortly after his capture, the Wild Boy lived, for a time, in an orphanage in Saint-Affrique. Shattuck reports that "during the time that the boy was held in Saint-Affrique, according to one report, the people taking care of him had a name for him: Joseph. It would have been both a convenience and a recognition of his human status, but the name was never recorded or used officially" (pp. 18–19). An investigation into Joseph's history revealed only that the child had turned up once before in 1798 and 1799 in the less cultured town of Lacaune. After quoting from Guiraud's official report, Shattuck speculates that the Wild Boy had a different meaning, and therefore received a different treatment, in the more "advanced" place. Here is Guiraud's description of the boy's reception by the peasants:

During the day, he approached farms, walked familiarly into the houses, and waited quietly and without fear to be given something to eat. The pity he aroused and the hospitable customs of the inhabitants of these mountains produced a kindly welcome. Everywhere, people offered him the things he preferred. Then he went away again and hid in the most isolated spots.... Slowly he became familiar with people and his intellectual faculties developed gradually. (pp. 30-31)

Shattuck comments:

> When taken into custody in Saint-Sernin in January 1800, the boy was neither ferocious nor totally uncivilized. At least during the period after his first escape, he seems to have emerged from a life of complete solitude into a semi-socialized condition. He ceased to fear the sight of other men, and they in turn did not fear him. They helped him and asked for nothing in return except that he not molest them. Though naked, speechless, and filthy, accepting no restraints on his total freedom, he was recognized by the peasants as human. To them he was neither animal nor criminal. The boy in turn seems to have recognized the peasants in their houses as somehow his kind, related more closely to him than the animals. For six months while the autumn of 1799 chilled into winter, the boy and the inhabitants of those distant hills reached an arrangement, a *modus vivendi,* which allowed him to run free among them. He was less domesticated than a dog or a horse, yet unmistakably human. They did not lock him up or insist on clothing him. Most villages had at least one local idiot and took no trouble to hide those cases of flawed humanity. Idiots carried no infection as terrifying to the inhabitants as leprosy or the plague. The boy harmed no one. No one in that sparsely populated countryside took upon himself the responsibility to catch and tame the boy. Thus his "untamed" status achieved temporary social recognition. He had a place in the world. When the boy crossed the border into the Aveyron district, the surprised citizens of Saint-Sernin had no way of knowing that this creature was anything other than a savage, even a monster, and possibly dangerous. In time, they too might have freed him to roam again. But Saint-Sernin was a more cosmopolitan town than Lacaune, though no bigger, and Constans-Saint-Estève came bustling into the commissioner's office aware of his civic and scientific responsibilities. From that time on, the boy never escaped again for long; there were only a few brief escapades in Rodez and Paris. He began to live within civilized society, not on its fringes. (pp. 31-32)

Shattuck adds later that "from many material and moral points of view, he [the Wild Boy] must be seen as better off and better behaved than a child living in the lower depths of a big European city of that era" (p. 63).

After reviewing the history of Aveyron and the effects that the French Revolution had on philosophy, Shattuck explains that unlike the peasants, a growing middle-class populace tempered their readiness to valorize natural man with a corresponding reverence for nurture—for cultured society. Shattuck places Constans's decision in this context:

> He perceived well enough that the boy had survived and might well enough go on living in his wild state. He also perceived that the boy had been deprived of what every parent gives its offspring: the benefits of social exchange and a place in collective life.

> Constans, like all of us, acted on the basis of strong undeclared assumptions. Without even thinking about it, he believed that the experience and rewards of social life exceed those of mere survival as an animal. The peasants around Roquecézière were willing to tolerate what Constans put a stop to—a clear departure from the social order. As Constans saw the situation, total isolation had dispossessed the boy of his birthright as a human being. (p. 65)

In a section called "A Name at Last," Shattuck describes how the child, after months with Itard, was given the name Victor. In a footnote he remarks:

> In choosing the name, Itard was also associating his young charge with the hero of one of the earliest and longest-running melodramas on the Paris stage, *Victor or the Forest's Child,* the work of the young dramatist Pixérécourt, adapted from a popular novel. Because of the success of those two works with the public, the name Victor was there waiting for the real Wild Boy. (p. 110)

The following pages are devoted to describing the impossibility of teaching Victor to speak. Shattuck strikes a wistful note himself: "In recognition of his nascent humanity, Itard gave him a name: Victor. But there had been little of the conqueror about this boy. He had been better served by the humbler name Joseph when he was in Saint-Affrique" (p. 118). The humbler name signified humbler expectations. At puberty, Victor fails to meet his teacher's expectations and when Itard gives up on Victor, the child loses his name—his human status—altogether: "It must have been nearly impossible to distinguish puberty from mere animality in the boy; everyone continued to call him the 'Savage' in French" (p. 135). And finally:

> In 1811, after eleven years inside the institute, Madame Guerin and Victor moved into a house around the corner.... As a boy just entering his teens, Victor Hugo lived only four houses away for two years. It is possible that the occasional references in his novels and poems to a "fabulous monster" refer obliquely to the younger Victor's hearing stories about the Wild Boy of Aveyron—or perhaps encountering him in the streets or back alleys around the institute.... In 1828, at approximately forty, he died.... He was a forgotten man, as Itard had already said twenty years before. He was no longer referred to as Victor after Itard disappeared from his life, simply as the Savage. (p. 176)

The wild child had first caused a great stir and then "faded into the landscape," but the original motivation for training him and his significance as a new character in the landscape did not fade. Victor Hugo is not alone among nineteenth-century writers in depicting fabulous monsters and exploring the relationship between beauty (or ugliness) of the body and beauty of the soul. Significantly, Frankenstein is also a Victor; his monster repulses because it is hideous, but the message of the story is that if it had been properly cared for it would have been loving and good.[8] The theme of nature versus nurture reappears often in Gothic romance. The fairy-tale's foundling prince, frog-prince, and beautiful beast had taken a circuitous route into the tradition of realism; we shall see that the journey left many marks upon him.

From the Wild Boy to Joseph to Victor to Savage, the names conferred upon this being reflect the culture's hope and ultimate disappointment in his promise. Writing about this character, Shattuck betrays a modern appreciation for the resourceful freedom of the boy in the wilderness, a resourcefulness that had apparently made little impression upon the nineteenth-century doctors who were prepared to conclude that Victor was an idiot. At the same time that Shattuck understands why the nineteenth-century scientist felt morally and socially compelled to civilize the boy, he himself waxes nostalgic when he describes the peasants' unenlightened treatment of the child. Throughout his history, Shattuck wavers between an implicit agreement with Victor's teachers that it is better to live as a socialized person than as a "beast" and the critical position that Victor had been deprived of his natural humanity by those who sought to civilize him.

Shattuck, who both respects Itard's liberal views and regrets the experiment motivated by those views, sees no contradiction in his attitudes. In fact, Itard's effort to prove Rousseau's theory may have failed less because of the boy than because Rousseau's theory bases itself upon an internally contradictory assessment of the relationship between nature and nurture. In *Of Grammatology,* Jacques Derrida explains that,

> According to Rousseau, the negativity of evil will always have the form of supplementarity. Evil is exterior to nature, to what is by nature innocent and good. It supervenes upon nature. But always by way of compensation for what *ought* to lack nothing at all in itself. . . .
> It is indeed culture or cultivation that must supplement a deficient nature, a deficiency that cannot by definition be anything but an accident and deviation from Nature.[9]

As a flesh and blood creature, Victor could provide no solution to what was really a problem in logic. While the probability of man's having an animal nature persisted in nineteenth-century thought, it proved only partially acceptable; civilization and nurture could not be altogether abandoned. Itard's diary demonstrates, sometimes painfully, that the fascination with the wild child was expressed as a preoccupation with civilizing him, particularly by teaching him to speak. Rousseau himself offered us both the "noble savage" and *The Education of Emile;* and Freud not only confronted his readers with the power of human nature's dark side, but he also insisted that nurture and civilization were necessary to tame and productively channel animal sexual energy.

The overthrow of old constraints that heralded the Wild Boy had not produced a coherent image of natural man. The entry for 1805 in Shattuck's chronology of Itard and his pupil reads: "Victor's puberty 'crises' disrupts work and discipline; end of regular training" (p. 140). Apparently, the early nineteenth-century doctor was unequipped to deal with the sexuality of man "in a state of nature." Before the end of the century, however, Freud would write *The Sexual Enlightenment of Children* and a case history of "Wolf Man" and Darwin would publish *On the Origin of Species.* While philosophy and science were proving that all men are created equal (a belief from which the middle-class profited), many Victorians feared the new theories of the nature of man and man of nature: a human animal is a ruthless and godless being, to whom sexuality is more important than spirituality.

The Victorian attitude was, at best, ambivalent. If once upon a time the foundling's beauty found its explanation in his royal roots, modern men are all foundlings, people compelled to find and make themselves. Still, the loss of faith in aristocratic entitlement didn't prevent the middle class from desiring aristocratic grace and class themselves. Even equality had its drawbacks; it provided a dangerous rationale for revolution. If men are animals, it was necessary to add that some are more fit and more well trained than others. Thus, if the Wild Boy did not prove anything, neither did he disprove anything. At the time, it was concluded that he was a poor sample; today, we conclude that his teachers were limited.

Victor was a disappointment because he showed no evidence of natural morality, and what we now assume to have been his natural sexuality was then incomprehensible. The name Joseph may have resonated well with Shattuck for reasons beyond his displeasure with the conquering name Victor. The name Joseph reminds us of an ideal of beauty quite the opposite of the new Byronic hero or wolfish man. In preferring the name Joseph, Shattuck prefers the name of one of Western literature's exemplary male beauties, a character notable for his beauty and his sexual restraint.

Henry Fielding's extraordinarily beautiful hero, Joseph Andrews— among other foundlings of eighteenth-century literature—prepared the ground for the reception of the Wild Boy of Aveyron and the creation of the foundling-orphan of nineteenth-century fiction. The title character of *Joseph Andrews* (1742) embodies in his beauty the very contradictions that Derrida points to in Rousseau's thought. At once an exemplar of spirituality and sexuality, this character conflates two traditions of beauty: that of the primitive Daphnis and that of the biblical Joseph. These different models of beauty come to complement each other as literature attempts to accommodate the opposite values that each once represented. By the time Brontë writes *Wuthering Heights,* in the wake of Fielding's parodic treatment of his hero and in the wake of the Wild Boy, she will be able to separate out the strands of these traditions. In the beauty contests in *Wuthering Heights,* natural nobility and natural savagery compete as Brontë represents plausible nineteenth-century versions of the Daphnis figure and the Joseph figure. The preceding tradition had already compromised the beauty and meaning of each type.

Coats and Tales: Joseph in Hebrew Scriptures, Midrash, and Koran

The biblical Joseph is characterized as an instrument of divine will. Singled out equally as an object of love and an object of envy, he resembles Daphnis and other heroes of comic romance whose extraordinary qualities provoke others to deride them and plot against them. Yet Joseph's status as hero is plainly a function of his having been pre-selected for a special role in Genesis' narrative history; while everything in his personal story numbers him among the type of the biblical hero (a beloved son born of a "barren" favored wife; the attempt on his life; the move to a position of political power), Joseph's acts of pride compromise him in the eyes of the reader. This qualification on his perfection is a departure from the pattern of the hero of comic romance just as it fits the pattern of the biblical hero: Joseph, like his father before him and Samson after him, is a complex hero because his human ambitions and faults are necessary to actualize God's plan.

Jacob gives Joseph a fine coat. This detail in the story would seem superfluous, but added to Joseph's dreams of power and to the detail that Joseph tattletales on his brothers, the reader sympathizes with the brothers' jealousy. Even Jacob is slightly annoyed by his favorite son's pretentiousness.[10] Moreover, Jacob encourages Joseph to join his brothers on the very day that the torn and bloodied coat comes back to haunt him as "proof" that his son had been slaughtered by wild beasts. Still, Joseph is more sinned against than sinner, and the narrative is generated by an injustice; the brothers sell Joseph into slavery.

The fact of Joseph's beauty occurs as a single line in the text that serves only to explain why Potiphar's wife lusts after him. Once more Joseph's garment, left behind in his flight from the seductions of Potiphar's wife, is the material sign of a lie: it "proves" that Joseph came "to insult" his lord's wife. Again Joseph is unjustly punished—this time by imprisonment—but once in jail, he has the opportunity to prove himself a reader of dreams. In the context of the false readings of Joseph's clothes, Joseph distinguishes himself as a true interpreter, and eventually earns his release from prison because of his interpretive powers. The day does come when his brothers bow down before him. However extraordinary we may suppose Joseph's beauty to be, Joseph knows his brothers, but they do not recognize him. His identity is withheld for the sake of narrative suspense and the brothers are allowed to prove the fullness of their repentance. Jacob descends to Egypt, and these episodes end happily, God's promises and Joseph's prophesies alike fulfilled.

Although Joseph is God's pawn, his personal heroic qualities are evident: he is wise, chaste, loyal to God, to his own people and to Pharoah; he is a skillful politician (he manipulates both Pharoah and his brothers to get what he wants) and a skillful administrator (he manages Egypt so well that he acquires people and property for his lord, transforming a system of private land ownership into a feudal economy). What is it about the Joseph story that so troubled later readers and made Joseph's beauty—incidental in the Bible—his most remarkable trait?

A rabbinic midrash glosses Genesis 37:2 ("Joseph, being seventeen years old... being still a lad"): "It means, however, that he behaved like a boy, pencilling his eyes, curling his hair and lifting his heel."[11] Joseph, thus rendered immature, effeminate, and vain of his beauty, deserves the treatment that is plainly unjust in the biblical account. Indeed, this comment invents a crime that fits the biblical punishment: Joseph is made guilty of slandering his brothers, claiming that they are lustful. God exacts vengeance by inciting "a bear"—Potiphar's wife—against Joseph himself.

In traditional commentaries and later literature much is made of Joseph's beauty. Jacob loves Joseph best not only "because he was the son of his old age," but also because they share beauty ("his features resembled his"), an interpretation derived from a pun latent in the Hebrew. Other rabbis and the first-century Jewish historian Josephus comment that Joseph inherited great beauty from his mother Rachel.[12]

While, in the Bible, Joseph's beauty is a vehicle to present the lusts of one woman and the chaste virtue of the hero, in one midrash, Joseph's exaggerated beauty provokes all of Egypt's noblewomen to lust, and Joseph's heroic self-control is multiplied exponentially. The "problem" of Joseph's chastity motivates rabbinic expansions in two directions. The first, as we see, is to call Joseph's manhood into question; the second, is to make Potiphar's wife repulsive. We are told in the Midrash Rabbah to Genesis that she "speaks like an animal," that she let Joseph's garments "grow old in her keeping, embracing, kissing, and fondling them," and that she went great lengths in her seductions: "she went as far as to place an iron fork under his neck so that he would have to lift up his eyes and look at her."

In the biblical story, Joseph's innocence of the charges of Potiphar's wife are known only to the reader; Joseph leaves prison because Pharoah needs him. There are midrashim that are less able to tolerate an unjust accusation remaining undiscovered and these suggest that if Potiphar had believed his wife, then Joseph would have been killed rather than imprisoned. Potiphar is given an additional line: "'I know that you are innocent,' he assured him, 'but (I must do this) lest a stigma fall upon my children.'" And Joseph is rewarded with Potiphar's vestures of fine linen, not because he is prepared to save the kingdom, as the Bible has it, but because "his body had not cleaved to sin." For the rabbis, the politics of the body had become more important than the politics of the state.

As much as these midrashim betray the rabbis' uneasiness over Joseph's chastity, others go to great lengths to assure the reader that chastity is a great virtue; in so doing, they protest too much. Joseph's self-control is made to go beyond the lusts of one noblewoman: "The Egyptian women, daughters of kings, desired to gaze upon Joseph's face, yet he would not look upon any of them. He therefore merited both worlds, because he entertained no impure thoughts about them." An alternative reading elaborates: "You find that when Joseph went forth to rule over Egypt, daughters of kings used to look at him through the lattices and throw bracelets, necklets and ear-rings, and fingerrings to him, so that he might lift up his eyes and look at them; yet he did not look at them." Again, just as the rabbis marvel at the self-discipline of their hero, they feel obliged to account for it: "R. Huna said in R. Mattenah's name: He saw his father's face which cooled his blood. R. Menahema said in R. Ammi's name: He saw his mother's face, which cooled his blood."

Writing in first-century Alexandria, the Jewish philospher Philo betrays still greater unease in his treatment of Joseph's character. In Philo's Allegorical Commentary, an exposition of the Bible aimed at Jewish initiates,[13] Philo places Joseph in an allegorical scheme that presents Egypt (a stand-in for contemporary Rome) as the type of the body and its passions. To paint Joseph as wicked, all body and pleasure, Philo omits those biblical episodes and comments uncongenial to his thesis. In *De Josepho,* a work directed to sympathetic Gentile readers, Philo approves of Joseph. In the former account, Philo depicts Joseph as vain and spurious; in the latter, Joseph is lordly. Philo's modern English language editors collect the descriptive language in which Philo depicts Joseph: "prepared to subordinate truth to expediency of falsehood;...eager for vainglory, self-opinionated, presumptuous, swollen-headed with vanity...Joseph is the lover of the body and its passions, the champion of the body and externals, fond of luxury. From his mother he inherited the irrational strain of sense-perception...."[14] A unique passage, *Allegorical Interpretation* (III, 237-42), praises Joseph for controlling himself with Potiphar's wife.

Rabbinic midrash constructs several explanatory fables. In one, a shebear (Potiphar's wife) is arrayed in expensive jewels; the crowd declares that whoever is brave enough to attack her may keep the jewels. The wise man looks at her fangs, not at her attire. In another, a man who is "pencilling his eyes and curling his hair" declares, to the amusement of the crowd, that he is a man. "'If you are a man,' the bystanders retort, 'here is a she-bear, up and attack it.'" If Joseph were a man, he would not apply makeup to his face; if Joseph were a man, he would attack the woman.

These rabbis are clearly troubled by Joseph's chaste beauty, but inasmuch as he is a sacred hero, they fear articulating their doubts too directly. The blunt, less pious phrasing is put in the mouth of a woman: "A matron asked R. Jose: 'Is it possible that Joseph, at seventeen years of age, with all the hot blood of youth could act thus?'" While Rabbi Jose confidently replies that the Bible is clear on the matter, another rabbi finds reason to argue that Joseph's intentions, at least, testify to "hot blood": "On examination he did not find himself a man," and in a footnote, a modern editor explains: "He actually went in to sin, but found himself impotent." Joseph is an ambivalent figure because his beauty and innocence strike the rabbis as unnatural and effeminate; they expand the text in an effort to naturalize the hero.

The Koran, which scorns narrative as a vehicle for religious teaching, chooses to develop but one sustained narrative, Sura 12, "the fairest of stories," the story of Joseph.[15] Intolerant of divine injustice or deception, the Koranic version departs from the biblical account in order to clarify the morality of the story. Allah frequently interrupts himself to make meaning and moral explicit. Western preference for narrative suspense and ambiguity might prejudice us against this version of the story, but the Koran's departures from the Hebrew Bible indicate that Mohammed was no less troubled than the rabbis by Joseph's chaste beauty.

More prophetic than the biblical Jacob, the Koranic Jacob discourages Joseph from telling his dreams lest his brothers "plot against him" (12:5). While the biblical Jacob urges Joseph to follow after his brothers, the Koranic father is more anxious: "a wolf may devour him" (12:13). The coat, designed to justify this fear, is returned to Jacob "with false blood"; no mention is made of its being torn. Seeing the coat whole, Jacob is not deceived by his sons. Later, at the home of Joseph's Egyptian lord, the coat which is dropped in one piece in the Bible is ripped off his back by his master's wife. The tear, displaced from the first coat, is replaced here. Just as the whole coat bore witness to the brothers' lie, the torn one testifies to Joseph's honesty. A witness of the fold explains that because the coat is torn from behind, Joseph speaks the truth (12:26–28).

The Koranic story, otherwise more concise than the biblical version, adds several details: "She verily desired him, and he would have desired her if it had not been that he saw the argument of his lord" (12:24). Thus, Joseph is transformed into a man with natural sexual desires. The Koran sees a double problem: if Joseph's innocence is proved by the torn coat, why is Joseph imprisoned? And if Potiphar's wife is proved guilty, how does she survive the women's gossip in court? The Koran explains:

> 31. And when she heard of their sly talk, she sent to them and prepared for them a cushioned couch (to lie on at the feast) and gave to every one of them a knife and said (to Joseph): Come out unto them! And when they saw him they exalted him and cut their hands, exclaiming: Allah Blameless! This is not a human being. This is no other than some gracious angel.
> 32. She said: This is he on whose account ye blamed me. I asked of him an evil act, but he proved continent, but if he do not my behest he verily shall be imprisoned....

The women see Joseph and bleed. While Potiphar's wife is not vindicated in the eyes of posterity, a silent consensus is reached among the women as Joseph's beauty excuses her lust. Joseph prefers imprisonment to submission and warns Allah: "if Thou send not off their wiles from me, I shall incline unto them and become of the foolish" (12:33). Thus, once more, Joseph's beauty is exaggerated and his natural urges are clarified. "And it seemed good to them (the men-folk) after they had seen the signs (of his innocence) to imprison him for a time" (12:35).

Finally, the Koran adds a third coat to Joseph's wardrobe. Jacob's metaphorical blindness (the prophet does not know what has become of his son) is relieved when Joseph sends his coat home with his brothers. Jacob wipes his eyes with it and his vision is restored. The third coat comes to reveal that which the first coat tried—but failed—to conceal. Thus, the deceptions that motivate the biblical story are not tolerated in the Koran, which makes every sign a readable vehicle for divine justice.

In spite of his simplifying effort to elucidate meaning, Mohammed, like earlier Jewish exegetes, betrays an anxiety over Joseph's masculinity and elaborates upon both Joseph's beauty and the extent to which he must have been tempted. While the Bible shows no concern over either male beauty or "healthy" male sexuality, over time male beauty became suspect if it were not used to seduce women. Vigorous sexuality had become a more important heroic trait than spirituality. The biblical Joseph's chastity leads later interpreters to doubt his masculinity; by exaggerating Joseph's beauty, they virtually deprive him of beauty, imagining an effeminate man who is not a model to emulate.

Joseph and Daphis: Fielding's *Joseph Andrews*

When Fielding comes to write *Joseph Andrews,* his title character is exemplary for his chastity, but like Daphnis, he is bound by a promise to save himself for the woman he loves. Fielding attempts to solve the "problem" of Joseph's beauty by qualifying Joseph's spiritual nature with Daphnis' animal nature. Fielding also draws our attention to the problem of Joseph's chastity.

Joseph Andrews' name refers to two characters notable for their extraordinary beauty: the biblical Joseph, and Samuel Richardson's model of chastity and servant-become-lady, Pamela Andrews. With the progress of Fielding's picaresque novel, we learn that Joseph belongs to the tradition of foundlings (the victim of a switcheroo by the gypsies), but *Joseph Andrews* is still romance enough that, unlike Heathcliff, this foundling will find his real parents and come into a modest inheritance. Significantly, his parents are not royalty but landed gentry, and Joseph is recognized by the mark of birth upon his body, a literal birthmark.

In a parallel story, Joseph's beloved since childhood, Fanny, a foundling raised as a peasant, discovers that her natural parents are the Andrews. Before all of these confusions are untangled, Joseph and Fanny spend some unhappy time fearing that they are blood brother and sister. Like Daphnis and Chloe before them, Rowena and Ivanhoe, and Heathcliff and Catherine after them, Joseph and Fanny love each other because they resemble each other and grew up together. They share nature and nurture. As in Freud's later analysis of the incest taboo, these stories suggest that finding beauty in the other is loving and confirming the beauty of oneself.

In the beauty of these characters, Fielding plays with grace and class and the distinction between nature and nurture as it comes down to him from the romance; he exposes the conventions of the romance plot even as he reproduces this plot, and thereby opens a space for nineteenth-century fiction's more straightfaced considerations.

Fielding wastes no time in attacking the problem of his hero's birth and breeding. Joey is like Pamela, and Fielding pokes fun at Richardson: "I shall only add that this character of male chastity, though doubtless as desirable and becoming in one part of the human species as the other, is almost the only virtue which the great apologist hath not given himself for the sake of giving example to his readers." We learn that Joey—as he is called in the book's first chapters—is "esteemed" to be the son of the Andrews, but that his chronicler has difficulty tracing the line of descent. The narrator adds:

> But suppose for argument's sake, we should admit that he had no ancestors at all, but had sprung up, according to the modern phrase, out of a dunghill, ... would not this *autokopros* have been justly entitled to all the praise arising from his own virtues? Would it not be hard that a man who hath no ancestors should therefore be rendered incapable of acquiring honour, when we see so many who have no virtues enjoying the honour of their forefathers.[16]

The merit of birth alone is not highly regarded by Fielding. Joey is described as "pretty," as the "genteelest young fellow" (the latter from Lady Booby's maid Slipslop) and self-educated. The curate asks "if he did not extremely regret the want of a liberal education, and not having been born of parents who might have indulged his talents and desire for knowledge?" After demonstrating to the reader's satisfaction that he is more learned than anyone with greater pretensions to knowledge, Joey, like Daphnis, declares that he is content with his lot.

Because Joey is "outwardly a pretty fellow... smarter and genteeler than any of the beaux in town," Lady Booby takes him for her "footman," and Fielding forthwith changes his name: "on the seventh day she ordered Joey, whom, for a good reason, we shall hereafter call Joseph, to bring up her teakettle. The lady, being in bed, called Joseph to her..." Like Potiphar's wife, Lady Booby tries, unsuccessfully, to seduce her servant. But Fielding makes Lady Booby undesirable; her only claim to attractiveness is her social rank. At the same time, Fielding understands the temptation of a man both elegant and strong, a man with clear marks of nobility and animalism:

> He was of the highest degree of middle stature. His limbs were put together with great elegance and strength. His legs and thighs were formed in the exactest proportion. His shoulders were broad and brawny, but yet his arms hung so easily that he had all the symptoms of strength without the least clumsiness. His hair was of a nut-brown colour and was displaced in wanton ringlets down his back. His forehead was high, his eyes dark and as full of sweetness as of fire. His nose a little inclined to the Roman. His teeth white and even... and an air which, to those who have not seen many noblemen, would give an idea of nobility. (p. 36)

Fielding's summary line is purposely ambiguous: Joseph's beauty gives the "idea of nobility" because it conforms to a literary convention rather than to an actual appearance. Joseph's beauty is not noble, but it exceeds the beauty of real noblemen. While Joseph's eyes are sweet, "fire," "wanton," and "dark" also describe him. "Fire," metaphorically used to suggest hell, heat, and power and passion, frequently occurs in phrases that describe Catherine and Heathcliff.

Joseph, distressed by "the numberless calamities which attended beauty," is eventually turned out by Lady Booby just as Fanny had been turned out by Slipslop, as the narrator tells us, "on account of her extraordinary beauty— for I could never find any other reason." When we are told what has become of this "poor girl," we are reminded of Daphnis and Chloe:

> ... This young creature (who now lived with a farmer in the parish) had always been beloved by Joseph, and returned his affections... They had been acquainted from infancy, and had conceived a great liking for each other.

Joseph sets out after Fanny. If the reader is left with any doubts that Joseph is a comic revision of the biblical character, Fielding puts those doubts to rest. On his first adventure en route to Fanny, Joseph is attacked by thieves: "They then stripped him entirely naked, threw him into a ditch, and departed with their booty" (p. 47).

Like the other Joseph, Andrews is chaste, and like Daphnis he is true to his beloved in spite of many temptations. Everywhere that Joseph goes, he is set upon by women who take him for a gentleman because of the "whiteness of his skin and the softness of his hands." The adventures of Joseph and Fanny are exaggerated, comic, and otherwise similar to those of Daphnis and Chloe. Like Chloe, Fanny is threatened by rape (more than once) and the conventions of romance ensure that she is saved, always in the nick of time.

Fielding's hero and heroine are explicit attempts to unite the advantages of two competing natures: natural nobility and natural rusticity. Joseph and Fanny are both beautiful because they have the marks of high birth, tempered by the honest sexuality and honest labor that improves character. Fielding's description of Fanny makes just this point:

> She was tall and delicately shaped, but not one of those slender young women who seem rather intended to hang upon the wall of an anatomist than for any other purpose. On the contrary, she was so plump that she seemed to be bursting through her tight stays, especially in the part which confined her swelling breasts. Nor did her hips want the assistance of a hoop to extend them... her arms... were a little reddened by her labour, yet if her sleeve slipped above her elbow... a whiteness appeared which the finest Italian paint would be unable to reach. Her hair was of a chestnut brown, and nature had been extremely lavish to her of it... Her forehead was high... Her eyes black and sparkling; her nose just inclining to the Roman... Her complexion was fair, a little injured by the sun, but overspread with such a bloom that the finest ladies would have exchanged all their white for it... To conclude all, she had a natural gentility superior to the acquisition of art, and which surprised all who beheld her. (pp. 132–33)

In short, with the exception of secondary sexual characteristics, Fanny bears a remarkable resemblance to Joseph.

In the paragraph following this long description, "this lovely creature" is longing for her Joseph, "when her attention was suddenly engaged by a voice" singing. The song begins:

> Say Chloe, where must the swain stray
> Who is by thy beauties undone?

And the second verse begins:

> O rapture unthought of before!
> To be of Chloe thus possessed;

The song plays no role in advancing the story, but Fielding here declares that the model for his heroine derives from pastoral romance.

Fielding also parodies the strategies that the writer of romance typically uses to convey beauty:

> Reader, we would make a simile on this occasion but for two reasons:... the second, and much the greater, reason is that we could find no simile adequate for our purpose, for, indeed, what instance could we bring to set forth before our reader's eyes at once the idea of friendship, courage, youth, beauty, strength, and swiftness, all which blazed in the person of Joseph Andrews. Let those therefore that describe lions and tigers, and heroes fiercer than both, raise their poems or plays with the simile of Joseph Andrews, who is himself above the reach of any simile. (pp. 204–5)

Joseph's and Fanny's adventures are occasioned by their extraordinary beauty, until the mystery of their births is uncovered, and they marry each other. Unlike Daphnis and Chloe, they are not a prince and princess, though Fielding assures us, on the final page of his novel, that they are none the worse for it: "I apprehend Joseph neither envied the noblest duke nor Fanny the finest duchess, that night" (p. 297). How they felt after that night is for the reader to guess.

In the figure of Joseph Andrews, Fielding achieves a good measure of comic effect by combining two models of beauty: that of the natural beauty of romance, exemplified in my analysis by Daphnis, and that of the more refined beauty of the biblical Joseph. By drawing on the model of the Joseph figure, Fielding gets some comic mileage out of the tradition's increasing suspicion of a man who lacks sexual ambition and is vain of his beauty.

Having followed the Joseph character from the Bible through classical medieval retellings to Fielding's novel, we see that Edgar Linton's attractions—he is not man enough for Catherine—had been debased well before Heathcliff's opposing features threatened to supplant the ideal that Linton represents. The rendering of male ugliness—beastliness—into beauty, the noble savage himself, had been prepared for by literature's increasing suspicion of the type of male refinement. To be a real man, we discover, increasingly meant that one had to have something of the animal in him. Today, a man who is called simply "a beast" or "an animal" is not without his attractions.

Joseph Andrews is a step in this direction. Like the aristocratic foundling of Greek romance, Joseph Andrews' beauty and natural grace distinguish him from others who were born into the class in which he was raised. At the same time, however, Fielding's disclaimers when he writes about class, his jibes at the nobility, and his purposeful location of Joseph's origins, not in the nobility but in a middle income family whose virtues are prudence and moderation, expose the conventions of romance. In part these changes derive from the imperatives of realism, but these imperatives themselves derive from the gentry and middle class asserting themselves. Joseph Andrews superficially resembles both Daphnis and the biblical Joseph, but as this member of the gentry is neither a nobleman like Daphnis nor a prophet like Joseph, Andrews' beauty and natural grace are conferred by a more democratic deity.

A democratic trend in literature was recovering the beauty of the man of nature, whose blatant sexuality and lack of a proper human upbringing had become more characteristic of the ugly villain than of the beautiful hero. Just as a feminizing impulse in Romantic literature naturalizes the woman of art by recovering those qualities that had originally made her heroic, so Romanticism, most notably Byron and his heroes, reinvents the man of nature. In both cases, Victorian literature responds by investigating the subversive implications of these trends.

Figure 18. Thomas Phillips, *Portrait of Lord Byron*
A transitional ideal of male beauty.
London, National Portrait Gallery.
(© Snark; Photo courtesy Art Resource)

Beauty in the Beast: *Wuthering Heights*

Through Heathcliff's competition with Edgar Linton, Brontë divides the two traditions that combine in Joseph Andrews. In this novel the ideal of the new wolfish man and that of the frail, fair, and repressed aristocrat both suffer by comparison with one another. *Wuthering Heights* pictures variations on savage nobility and on the noble savage and finds Rousseau's phrase an oxymoron. Heathcliff is distinguished by a ferocious wordlessness characteristic of the wild child, and Brontë calls Catherine's beauty "savage." At the same time, by reminding us, however subtly, of Daphnis and Chloe in her portraits of Heathcliff and Catherine, Brontë impresses us with the distance between modern wild children and those children of nature whose beauty was unqualified and unquestionable. If Brontë invites us to recall that Daphnis and Chloe are literally "noble savages," she also reminds us that Victor, the real Wild Boy, had displayed few signs of morality or nobility.

Like Daphnis and Chloe, Heathcliff and Catherine identify with one another and love one another, but the association of Daphnis' beauty with that of Chloe is openly sexual and innocent, while the identification of Heathcliff and Catherine is part of the supernatural formula of Gothicism. Longus may lavishly describe Daphnis' and Chloe's discovery of the beauty of each other's bodies (long before their marriage); Fanny and Joseph restrain themselves, with some difficulty, until marriage; Brontë's readers would not have tolerated it if she had permitted her characters like pleasures. In *Wuthering Heights*, violent sexuality seethes beneath the surface of its dark characters.

The same political questions are posed by the wild child, the noble savage, and Heathcliff: does a human animal possess enough natural goodness that he can be nurtured into an acceptable social being? To what is the untitled man entitled? Is there beauty in the beast? Q. D. Leavis points out that Mr. Earnshaw resembles the merchant in *Beauty and the Beast*, who brings the Beast (really a "prince in disguise") home to his children.[17] Unlike Daphnis and the Beast, however, Heathcliff lacks the divine right of kings and needs a powerful human champion to legitimate his place in society. After Mr. Earnshaw's death, Heathcliff loses his protector and is continually reminded that he lacks entitlement. Like Itard, Nelly hopes that a good cleaning and a sound moral training will be enough to reenstate the wild child. Both Itard and Nelly will eventually lose faith in their labors and come to agree with the view that such a creature is unredeemable.

Nelly's scrubbing proves as ineffectual as her appeal to youthful fancy. Just as imagining that his lost parents have the power to buy up the Earnshaw and Linton estates gives Heathcliff a claim to neither home, so is the tidied foundling no better fit for (or permitted to fit into) society. Hindley, "irritated at seeing him clean and cheerful," mocks Heathcliff's pretensions to class and threatens "to get hold of those elegant locks" and pull them a bit longer. Master Linton seizes the opportunity to make explicit Heathcliff's resemblance to a wild animal and ventures to observe that "they are long enough already... It's like a colt's mane over his eyes."

By comparing Heathcliff to an animal, Linton would deprive Heathcliff of beauty in Catherine's eyes; Linton characterizes Heathcliff as Dorcon would have liked to characterize Daphnis. While Daphnis may argue that he and Chloe have a type of beauty in common, Heathcliff can make no such claim to Catherine. Yet these children are strangely kin, very likely having been fathered by the same man. In spite of their physical resemblance, Heathcliff and Catherine do not belong to the same class, and Heathcliff's frustration is born out of powerlessness, the lack of a language in which to phrase a convincing response to Linton. Thus, his reaction seems exaggerated, and Linton's punishment seems disproportionate to his crime. Heathcliff responds in the unsocialized manner of the Wild Boy, not verbally, but violently. Because "Heathcliff's violent nature was not prepared to endure the appearance of impertinence from one whom he seemed to hate, even then as a rival," Linton is served with hot applesauce dashed full onto his face and neck, and Heathcliff is banished and beaten. Thus Brontë forces a confrontation between two opposing natures: the aristocratic and verbal nature of Linton and the animal and physical nature of Heathcliff. Each child embodies the power and beauty of something towards which Brontë, as a governess raised on the moors, felt ambivalence.[18] Linton embodies the power and beauty of the monied classes, and Heathcliff—as his name suggests—embodies the uncontained energy and beauty of the wilderness. The tension is clear: inherited wealth was becoming vulnerable to acquisitive natures.

Heathcliff fears that beauty—sexual attractiveness—is indistinguishable from money and entitlement. His fears are not unfounded. As Chloe judged the beauty contest between Dorcon and Daphnis, it is Catherine, of course, who must choose between Linton and Heathcliff. Early in her fateful talk with Nelly Dean, Cathy is asked why she loves Linton. When her first response, "because he is handsome and pleasant to be with," fails to satisfy Nelly, Catherine adds, "and he will be rich, and I shall like to be the greatest woman of the neighborhood" (p. 70). Heathcliff hears Catherine say that marriage to him would degrade her, but he is gone before he can discover that she is more of Chloe's mind than her first remarks suggest. She affirms that she loves Heathcliff "not because he's handsome... but because he's more myself than I am." As it had been for Chloe, the decisive argument for Catherine is that she and Heathcliff are made of the same stuff: "Whatever our souls are made of, his and mine are the same and Linton's is as different as a moonbeam from lightning, or frost from fire." Catherine, like Chloe, has loved her constant companion since childhood best all along. Though her words, "I am Heathcliff" echo in the reader's memory, they come after Heathcliff has effected his escape, and Linton wins Catherine by default.

By suggesting that Heathcliff and Catherine have similar souls as they are similarly ambiguous in their beauty, Brontë explores the effects of their different origins and experiences. Cleanliness, close to grace and godliness, is the novel's metaphor for cultured beauty. In Catherine's childhood, Mr. Earnshaw disliked his daughter's fiery temper and neglected her appearance. At this point in the story, Heathcliff and Catherine are equally dirty clay in the hands of society, and their appeal for readers is not unlike the appeal of the wild child. Readers might wonder if these ungoverned children could learn to rise above their upbringing. As Shattuck writes: "When the Wild Boy of Aveyron was discovered at the end of the century, it was expected that he would provide scientific observers with a special revelation about human nature. Moreover, he was a home-grown native Savage—neither yellow, nor black, nor red, just dirty" (p. 54).

As such we wonder what will become of these ungoverned children. After Mr. Earnshaw's death, Catherine and Heathcliff are discovered snooping at the Lintons and are captured. Heathcliff curses brutishly because Catherine is injured; Heathcliff is therefore evicted while Catherine remains at the Lintons for five weeks. When she returns a "bright, graceful damsel... instead of the rough-headed counterpart of himself," Heathcliff is shamed by the contrast and impressed, for the first time, by their different social positions. Thus, after Heathcliff cleans up for the very Christmas dinner that Hindley intends as a reciprocation for the Lintons' hospitality towards Catherine, Heathcliff's gesture of flinging applesauce is singularly appropriate: Heathcliff takes matters into his own hands and dirties Linton.

Heathcliff's banishment is self-confirming. Alone with Nelly once more, Heathcliff lets the reader know that by rejecting Nelly's romantic notions that virtue will be rewarded in this world, Heathcliff also scorns the next. The humiliated child tells Nelly: "... I'm trying to settle how I shall pay Hindley back. I don't care how long I wait, if I can only do it at last. I hope that he will not die before I do!" Again Heathcliff finds Nelly's rejoinder misplaced: "'For shame, Heathcliff!' I replied. 'It is for God to punish wicked people; we should learn to forgive.'" If there had been a time when God would have insured justice within the bounds of the fiction—as the gods do for Daphnis and Perdita—Heathcliff fears that that time is passed: "'No, God won't have the satisfaction that I shall,' he returned. 'I only wish that I knew the best way! Let me alone, and I'll plan it out: while I'm thinking of that I don't feel pain'" (p. 57).

Heathcliff does, of course, plan it out and return to own Wuthering Heights and Thrushcross Grange together, but not through the means that

Nelly romantically envisioned. Heathcliff, a wild child and a foundling, grows into a self-made man, and thus Brontë demonstrates how the new philosophies serve the interests of an "illegitimate" class without noble roots. In so doing, she calls the qualities of such a man into question, describing him through similes that have contradictory connotations. If the child might have been a prince or a fiend, the adult's beauty is part gentleman and part gypsy. The man whom Lockwood confronts in the novel's first scene has acquired the title "Mister." He is introduced to the reader with the word "but":

> But Mr. Heathcliff forms a singular contrast to his abode and style of living. He is a dark-skinned gypsy in aspect, in dress and manners a gentleman, that is, as much a gentleman as many a country squire: rather slovenly perhaps, yet not looking amiss with his negligence, because he has an erect and handsome figure—and rather morose.

Like the Byronic hero, Heathcliff's qualities of character and appearance are ambiguous because his is the appeal of brute intelligence and sexual power. Catherine's and Heathcliff's beauty is the dark beauty of productivity, energy, and passion, a beauty so alluring that each attracts a fair Linton in spite of acts of capricious cruelty. Once the characters are adults, the beauty contest between Heathcliff and Edgar is repeated and paralleled by a competition between Catherine and Edgar's fair sister, Isabella.

Advised of Heathcliff's return, Linton rehearses the old metaphors: "What, the gipsy—the plough-boy?" but finds himself "at a loss" when he faces the man that Heathcliff had become (p. 83). Nelly compares the two for the reader once more; though Heathcliff seems to have all of the advantages, Nelly does not allow that Heathcliff is definitely the handsomer of the two only because he lacks "the last and noblest part of beauty": grace. Although Heathcliff has all the signs of success, experience, and affluence, Brontë insists upon his primitiveness. That the novel remains ambivalent about commercial success is evident in the description of Heathcliff's beauty. Heathcliff, now bearded and more wolfish than ever, is no prince in disguise. Nelly reports:

> I was amazed, more than ever, to behold the transformation of Heathcliff. He had grown a tall, athletic, well-formed man, beside whom my master seemed quite slender and youthlike. His upright carriage suggested the idea of his having been in the army. His countenance was much older in expression and decision of feature than Mr. Linton's; it looked intelligent, and retained no marks of former degradation. A half-civilized ferocity lurked yet in the depressed brows and eyes full of black fire, but it was subdued; and his manner was dignified, quite divested of roughness, though too stern for grace. (p. 84)

When a midrash criticizes Joseph's character, it takes the biblical comment that Joseph is a "youth" to mean that he appears young and has the faults of a delicate-looking man. Fielding avoids these connotations of youthfulness by emphasizing his Joseph's strength and sexual vigor. And here, Brontë follows Fielding's lead by bringing together what had formerly been an unlikely combination of qualities of beauty; rather than combining these qualities to perfection in one man, however, she juxtaposes the separate ideals in two men and allows the reader to study the deficiencies of each and choose for him or herself.

Catherine apparently wants both. When Nelly hints that Catherine provokes her husband to envy Heathcliff, Catherine once more responds in terms of beauty, referring not to the men, however, but to herself and Isabella: "But does it not show great weakness... I'm not envious: I never feel hurt at the brightness of Isabella's yellow hair and the whiteness of her skin; at her dainty elegance and the fondness all the family exhibit for her" (p. 86). Indeed, it is Isabella who envies Catherine and not vice versa. We are reminded that when Heathcliff and Catherine first lay eyes upon the Linton children, remarked the splendor of their home and their petty troubles, the wild children affirmed that they would not change places "for a thousand lives." It is the Lintons who envy—not Heathcliff's and Catherine's beauty—but their love. Because they love each other and are desired and envied by the Lintons as well, the reader admires the dark beauties over the fair.

Isabella declares her passion for Heathcliff, and Catherine once more prefers her own lot:

> "I wouldn't be you for a kingdom, then!" Catherine declared emphatically—and she seemed to speak sincerely. "Nelly, help me convince her of her madness. Tell her what Heathcliff is—an unreclaimed creature, without refinement, without cultivation; an arid wilderness of furze and whinstone. I'd as soon put that canary into the park on a winter's day as recommend you to bestow your heart on him! It is deplorable ignorance of his character, child, and nothing else, which makes that dream enter your head. Pray don't imagine that he conceals depths of benevolence and affection beneath a stern exterior! He's not a rough diamond—a pearl containing oyster of a rustic; he's a fierce, pitiless, wolfish man. (pp. 90-91)

Catherine's description of Heathcliff is of a man of nature who lacks the benefits of nurture; each metaphor reenforces the one before, that Heathcliff possesses the dangerous allure of wildness, untamed and unrefined. Catherine never cared to believe that Heathcliff was a "prince in disguise," and Heathcliff and Catherine are great Romantic figures precisely because they have ceased believing in romance. Isabella is destroyed because, like the members of the leisured classes, an unrealistic fantasy retains a hold on her; unable to perceive the threat to her position, she mistakenly believes that the new wolfish man is a benevolent Daphnis.[19]

Isabella's confusion is shared by the reader because Heathcliff at once fits into the tradition of the beautiful foundling and refuses to fulfill our expectations of his redemption. With the progress of the novel, both Heathcliff and Catherine become more attractive and more uncultured.

Shortly before her death, Catherine looks into the mirror and refuses to believe that what she sees is a reflection of herself; she is so altered that her image terrifies her (p. 106). During this illness, Heathcliff holds Catherine in his arms, but he is no longer described as a transformed gentleman; instead, Nelly refers to him as a "mad dog" and remarks that "I did not feel as if I were in the company of a creature of my own species" (p. 134). The marvel of Heathcliff, like that of the wild child, is that his humanity consists in his animalism.

The questions remain: Does nature or nurture have priority in the creation of character, in the production of beauty and goodness? Everything in *Wuthering Heights* conspires to conceal the source of evil. Does Hindley's rough treatment of Heathcliff toughen a potentially beautiful child into an evil (and deceptively handsome) man, or does Heathcliff possess an unredeemable brutish nature that is ever reflected in his fiery, black, demonic eyes? Is Linton exemplary of the goodness and loveliness of civilized man, or is he an exemplar of the weakness of the landed gentry? Are Heathcliff and Catherine vindicated by the greatness of their passions and the deprivations of their youth or is the taunting Joseph—a rustic chorus throughout the novel—right that they are unnatural godless children? As J. Hillis Miller observes, the repetitions in the novel, the double narrative and the unreliability of the two narrators all reenforce ambivalence and ambiguity.[20] The beauty of the characters, far from being an exception, encodes the opposing values that generate ambiguity.

The man of nature and the woman of art reappear in nineteenth-century literature as heroes and heroines of ambiguous beauty because both have those dangerous qualities that are necessary for survival in the commercial world. Like Becky Sharp, Heathcliff is a dark beauty who may or may not deserve the power that he acquires. Indeed, the subject of *Wuthering Heights* is the rights to money and property. What are the consequences of allowing people of brute intelligence to displace generations of established families? Alternatively, does a man whose wolfish cunning is a condition of his survival triumph justly over men whose claims to wealth are based on a false view of their natural entitlement? By taking us through a second generation, Brontë tries, unsuccessfully, to settle these questions.

Using family resemblance, Brontë toys with the relationship between heredity and environment and tries new combinations of nature and nurture in her descriptive language. The repetition of names is the key to her enterprise. Heathcliff and Isabella's son, Linton Heathcliff, is, as his name implies, an impossible being. Ill and peevish from infancy, he has Linton weakness without the benefit of a careful upbringing. He dies without offspring, but not before he marries Catherine's daughter, the younger Catherine Linton. Cathy is equally an Earnshaw and Linton; she has her mother's beauty but her father's flaxen hair and gentle grace. Cathy's life

Figure 19. Merle Oberon as Cathy and Laurence Olivier as Heathcliff in *Wuthering Heights* (United Artists, 1938) *(Photo courtesy Phototeque)*

reverses the pattern of that of her mother: while the older Catherine is raised wild and becomes a cultured Linton with marriage, much is made of the care with which the younger Cathy is raised in protected isolation at the Lintons, and then she is removed to Heathcliff's uncivilized space in young adulthood.

Finally, there is Hareton Earnshaw, upon whom Heathcliff wreaks his vengeance by raising him as Heathcliff himself had been raised. Isabella describes him as "a ruffianly child, strong in limb and dirty in garb, with a look of Catherine in his eyes and about his mouth" (p. 116). Because Heathcliff raises Hareton as he himself had been raised, in Hareton, Brontë represents the combination of Earnshaw nature and absence of nurture. Hareton is the only child who is not named after a character in the fiction, though his is a family name that appears on the gates to the Heights, "Hareton Earnshaw" with the year "1500" beside it. Hareton is another noble savage, but unlike Heathcliff, his origins are not only known but his lineage is well-established. Because he shares a name with the Heights' original owner, his rights to property are clear, and this savage will be tamed. The novel closes with Cathy, appropriately enough, schooling Hareton, and this couple inherits the world of the fiction.

Of the three characters in this second generation, only Linton Heathcliff is unlovely. One would expect Cathy and Hareton to be more beautiful than their parents because, as legitimate heirs who have weathered the trials of homelessness, they combine nobility and savagery in good moderation. Indeed, they are unambiguously beautiful, but they also lack the vitality, interest (and therefore value) of their parents and Heathcliff. They are not hero and heroine because the novel comes to a close before their predictable story is told. While Brontë strikes a balance for the middle-class reader, the balance is at best precarious. Sexual passion (incestuous passion) and energy—the beauty of free wild children—are at once destroyed and mourned by the novel. Heathcliff and Catherine haunt the reader as they haunt the moors. As the voices of memory, Nelly Dean and the servant Joseph are not silenced.

Brontë's characterizations, as they are developed in the beauty of her principal figures, refuse to champion a set of values. Instead, they open a problematic articulated along the nature-nurture axis. Class, in all of its senses, is at issue, and the perspective that the characters have on each other is class-bound. Only Nelly Dean, a servant, can afford to imagine that Heathcliff is a prince in disguise; when Isabella ventures a similar assumption, she forfeits her rights and happiness.

146   *Grace: The Birth of Breeding*

Wild in the Third Story: *Jane Eyre*

The rights of heirs and orphans is as much the subject of Charlotte Brontë's *Jane Eyre* (1847) as it is a compelling concern in her sister's novel. In both cases, the questions of nature and nurture and the paradoxes of grace and class are expressed through the variety of perspectives on the characters' beauty. Rochester resembles Heathcliff. He is "of middle height and considerable breadth of chest. He had a dark face with stern features and a heavy brow." When Jane first sees him, "his eyes and gathered eyebrows looked ireful and thwarted." Jane concludes that he is not handsome or heroic looking and while she has a "theoretical reverence and homage for beauty, elegance and gallantry," confronting this ill-humoured stranger she concludes that she has not "met those qualities incarnate in masculine shape." If she had, she says, "I should have known instinctively that they neither had nor could have sympathy with anything in me, and should have shunned them as one would fire, lightning, or anything else that is bright but antipathetic."[21] Jane sounds something like Catherine here as she associates herself with Rochester because they both lack beauty. One also senses, however, that Jane is proud of her discrimination, as if conventional good looks are not worth having or admiring. When Rochester sits before her in his parlour and surprises her with the question, "Do you think me handsome?" she says "No" before she can muster a more polite response (p. 115).

Mrs. Gaskell records that "Charlotte determined to make her heroine small, plain and unattractive in defiance of the accepted canon."[22] While Brontë is as deliberate in her effort to render an unattractive Rochester as she is to render a plain Jane, Brontë's intention to make Rochester and Jane hero and heroine subverts her intention to make them unattractive. The early reviewer Elizabeth Rigby is, therefore, suitably confused. She writes that "the hero and heroine are beings so singularly unattractive that the reader feels that they have no vocation in the novel but to be brought together..." but goes on to lament their popularity: "in these days of extravagant adoration of all that bears the stamp of novelty and originality, sheer rudeness and vulgarity have come in for a most mistaken worship." She concludes that the book is an "anti-Christian composition."[23]

Rochester has all the appeal of a Byronic hero; he is wild, dark, rootless, troubled and brooding. In *The Madwoman in the Attic,* Gilbert and Gubar convincingly argue that Jane has shades of Byronism in her character.[24] In fact, Jane, an unwanted orphan raised through charity and continually reminded of her lack of entitlement, is more like Heathcliff than is Rochester. But Heathcliff and Rochester sport the same kind of brutal beauty that was coming into popularity in the early decades of the century. By making Jane, the orphan and the self-made woman, marry Rochester, a savage nobleman,

Figure 20. Joan Fontaine as Jane and Orson Welles as Rochester in *Jane Eyre* (Twentieth Century-Fox, 1944)
However much the author insists upon her plainness, for the reader, Jane acquires beauty.
(Photo courtesy Phototeque)

Brontë succeeds where her sister fails: *Jane Eyre* transforms these characters with extraordinary appearances into middle-class ideals. To effect this physical and spiritual transfiguration, Brontë appeals to the literary tradition to sanction their beauty and to undermine the beauty of her conventionally attractive, but unappealing, characters.

The foundling figure appears in Greek literature not only as a type of beautiful Daphnis, but also as the tragic and unlovely Oedipus. Maimed as he is at the novel's end, Rochester justly reminds readers of Oedipus. In *The Hero,* Lord Raglan identifies twenty-two typical stages in the life of "a hero," and while Daphnis would earn high marks had he been included as an example, Oedipus is given a perfect score.[25] Raglan gives the biblical Joseph twelve points. Jesus, another divinely selected hero of humble upbringing, would have done much better had Raglan not decided to exclude him in a vain attempt to avoid charges of heresy. Though Raglan does not make this point, in the stories that he compares beauty inheres to Nature's chosen characters.

The story of the foundling surrounded by tokens of nobility and raised by peasants at once served the common man's fantasy and justified the nobleman's authority: any one of us may be a misplaced prince or princess, but princely qualities will make themselves apparent wherever they are hidden. Indecipherable as the foundling's beauty is, it is doubly authorized by Nature because not only is this character born with the beauty of a prince or princess, but his or her royal qualities manifest themselves in a pastoral setting where they are unsupplemented by cosmetics, courtly affectations, or finery. The handsome prince is attracted to Snow White though she is isolated in a mountaintop coffin; the prince recognizes and can revive a princess when he sees one. The power of such stories rests in fantasy, wish fulfillment, and their justification of things as they are.

The character who learns the truth of his birth too late, after he has murdered his father and slept with his mother, seems to us a blameless victim of fortune because we no longer imagine that appearance is fully legible. We find Oedipus' story rich in other ways: Freud uses it as a basis to construct the family romance. Like the foundling of comic romance, Oedipus is a marked man; but he is marked not by his beauty but by the disfigurement that is his punishment. Blind and maimed, he wanders aimlessly and homelessly, a victim of what Freud will call "symbolic castration." While Daphnis refuses Dorcon's reading of his beauty, Oedipus' crime is that he does not know who he is; he cannot read the signs that Nature stamped upon him. Not only doesn't he know that his strength and wisdom could not have been produced by the parents who claim him, but he fails to recognize his natural parents when he sees them. Not to know royalty when one sees it is dangerous, and Oedipus' crime, as the story makes clear, is against the social order.

It is the very social order that associates strength, wisdom, and beauty with high birth that Charlotte Brontë would overturn when she maims

Rochester on the model of Oedipus. Brontë initially disarms her readers by making Jane and Rochester of unenviable appearance, but with the progress of the novel both Jane and Rochester acquire beauty. Their appearances are not so much altered as we are made to reassess our criteria for appreciating beauty.

Rochester competes with only two other men, Jane's two cousins named John, John Reed and St. John Rivers. The first John is excessively violent and savage; he tries to destroy Jane, but succeeds only in destroying himself. While St. John Rivers is handsome, he is excessively spiritual, and Jane must refuse his proposal of marriage, a proposal to sacrifice her body to her soul. This John, without a sense of physical self-preservation, destroys himself as well. As Rochester is educated by the novel into a caring man whose excessive sexuality is tempered by suffering, he becomes the most desirable man of all. Moreover, because Rochester loves Jane in spite of her plainness and social status, and because he rejects the lovely, but unlovable, Miss Ingram, the reader comes to admire the rough edges of his beauty. Noble as he is, the suggestion of wolfishness redeems Rochester in our eyes as we too are supposed to have learned that the polish which money puts on beauty conceals either the mad beastliness of a Bertha or the worldly greediness of a Miss Ingram.

The reader reassesses Jane in like fashion. Her sense of self in the novel's earliest scenes is of an unlovely (and consequently unloved) child, and she speculates that if she had been pretty, she might have received better treatment at the hands of her aunt. Her rival for affection is Georgiana Reed, who is so spoiled and vain, however, that the reader hardly wishes Jane to have been her likeness. Such beauty occurs at the expense of virtue, and both Reed sisters grow to become unhappy unworthy adults.

Before Jane and Rochester become engaged for the first time, Jane faces two rivals, only one of whom is known to her. Miss Ingram's beauty is a symptom of vanity and love of money; as her character is so seriously deficient, the reader neither admires her nor believes her beauty to be genuine. Jane supposes that Rochester means to marry Miss Ingram, and Jane and Rochester have a parting scene that results in their engagement to one another. Jane announces that she plans to leave Thornfield:

> "Where do you see the necessity?" he asked suddenly.
> "Where? You sir, have placed it before me."
> "In what shape?"
> "In the shape of Miss Ingram; a noble and beautiful woman—your bride."

Although Jane utters the word "noble" as if to qualify Miss Ingram's beauty, she declares to the reader that "if God had gifted me with some beauty and much wealth," she would make Rochester feel some of her pain. At God's feet, she says aloud, "we are equals!"

Rochester summons Jane as his wife. Little does Jane realize how right she is when she says, "Your bride stands between us." Rochester answers: "My bride is here... because my equal is here, and my likeness. Jane, will you marry me?" Jane is incredulous and Rochester repeats: "You—poor and obscure, and small and plain as you are—I entreat you to accept me as a husband." Jane consents. She turns to her lover: "And if I loved him less I should have thought his accent and look of exultation savage" (pp. 222-24).

In the coming weeks, Rochester behaves as if the woman he had fallen in love with were not small and plain. Jane objects to his ordering jewels:

> "Jewels for Jane Eyre sounds unnatural and strange: I would rather not have them."
> "I will myself put the diamond chain round your neck, and the circlet on your forehead,— which it will become: for nature, at least, has stamped her patent of nobility on this brow, Jane; and I will clasp the bracelets on these fine wrists..."

Hence we learn that Jane looks noble, but she is no woman of art, and she objects to manacles and chains, even if they are made of diamonds:

> "No, no, sir! Think of other subjects, and speak of other things, and in another strain. Don't address me as if I were a beauty; I am your plain Quakerish governess."
> "You are a beauty in my eyes; and a beauty just after the desire of my heart—delicate and aerial... I will make the world acknowledge you a beauty too... I will attire my Jane in satin and lace, and she shall have roses in her hair; and I will cover the head I love best with a priceless veil." (p. 227)

While Rochester gives the reader to understand that the world would take Jane for a beauty if only she had expensive clothes and gems, Jane is positively insulted; she would rather look Quakerish. She persuades Rochester to forget the gems, reminding him of "Samson and Hercules with their charmers." Jane's beauty is the beauty of plainness, plain good sense and plain good looks, and by now, the reader is sufficiently won over that we believe Jane to be better off without the expensive ornaments.[26] Though the real obstacle to this marriage is still a mystery to us, we are nonetheless uncomfortable with the engagement because their difference in rank entitles Rochester to treat Jane as a plaything. The servant, Mrs. Fairfax, is disapproving and we are moved by her arguments, though Jane herself is indignant: "'Why?'" she asks, "'am I a monster?'" Mrs. Fairfax replies, "'No: you are very well; and much improved of late....'" Jane has grown more beautiful even to Mrs. Fairfax, but "a monster" does stand between Jane and the "one Jane Rochester" whom she sees in the mirror on her wedding day as a figure so unlike "my usual self that it seemed almost the image of a stranger" (p. 257). The monster is, of course, Mrs. Bertha Rochester.

Just as Catherine Earnshaw Linton looks in the mirror and is terrified by the image she sees, so too does Jane look into her mirror—twice in the novel—

and fall unconscious with terror. The first time Jane is in the Red Room and faints when she imagines herself to be an imp. Jane recalls this event on the second occasion when she is awakened in the night and sees from behind "a woman, tall and large, with thick hair hanging down her back." Jane sees the woman's face reflected when the woman turns to the mirror, and Jane later tells Rochester that "it was a savage face," blackened, with black eyebrows raised over bloodshot eyes. This woman symbolically claims her prior right to Rochester; she puts on Jane's wedding veil herself, removes it, tears it in half, and tramples upon it (p. 249). Miss Ingram's beauty is a symptom of moral emptiness, and Bertha Mason's natural beauty has degenerated into an ugly beastliness—the physical manifestation of mental derangement. These are Jane's rivals. Jane, the object of male desire, is clearly the most beautiful of all.

Charlotte Brontë develops the "Beauty and the Beast" theme in a female version. Gilbert and Gubar argue that the madwoman is Jane's oversized powerful self, the savage repressed in each woman. But the madwoman is also an alien, culturally and naturally. At once the savage in man and woman, she is also a beast whose "moral insanity" marks her as less than human. In *Wuthering Heights*, the beast becomes the self-made man; in *Jane Eyre*, the plain orphan is a self-made woman, and when the beast destroys herself, Jane survives. Nature and nurture combine to create middle-class beauty because the novel raises Jane, by educating her and granting her a modest inheritance, into a beauty, and debases Rochester, punishing him by maiming him and depriving him of some of his wealth, into a man who is Jane's equal—finally, in the eyes of man and God. Their first born inherits Rochester's eyes as they had been; they are described with adjectives that suit Heathcliff as well: "large, brilliant and black."

Thornfield Hall maps the society of which the novel is a critique. The first floor on which people socialize is the place of high society, of parties for rich beautiful women. The "third story" houses the madwoman, and the floor which mediates between the two is domestic; there Jane schools Adèle and there people sleep. When the inhabitants of these "stories" leave their places, they disturb. The madwoman burns beds and tears veils on the second floor, and Jane, the governess, is unwelcome and derided in the parlour. By the novel's end, Thornfield Hall is destroyed, and Jane, a plain, high-spirited beauty with the virtues of modesty and prudence, lives with her husband, a tamed Byronic hero, in a single-storied middle-class dwelling.[27]

Jane and Rochester combine the qualities of grace and class because their beauty is not the splendid beauty of high society, but a middle-class ideal. Jane herself resembles Medina in Book II of Spenser's *The Faerie Queene*, and in Miss Ingram and Bertha Mason, Brontë surrounds Jane with her versions of Elissa and Perissa. In both cases, the only real beauty is the middle beauty, the "golden mean," of the middle story, deservedly and happily loved. Savage and noble are both destroyed to open a space for a heroine and hero, neither savage nor noble, but an apparent compromise between the two.

As Gilbert and Gubar, among others, have shown, *Jane Eyre* is also a kind of Cinderella. Because her parents formed a financially unequal match, she is left with a family that mistreats her and calls it charity. Unadorned and orphaned, her ugliness and unworthiness are taken for granted by the Reed family. In this home, Jane, a stepchild flanked by Eliza and Georgiana, has a pair of wicked stepsisters and a wicked stepmother herself. In the fairy tale, wickedness is equivalent to ugliness and the reader, registering Jane's position as an unlucky Cinderella, may already expect this romantic heroine to eventually be discovered by her handsome prince. Trained as we are, we cannot help but think of the vain and selfish sisters as ugly. The same scenario is repeated in Thornfield Hall where Jane's presence is apparently erased by the Ingram sisters and their mother and, more violently, by Bertha Mason. In all of these cases, the effort expended to suppress the anomalous figure indicates that she is not innocuous. Jane and Cinderella pose a threat to their benefactors; their power is the power to expose the mask of beauty that looks like, but is not, benevolence. After these homes, Jane lives for a while with cousins from her poorer parent's side of the family. The Rivers sisters are modestly beautiful, good, and kind. This happy domestic scene, so obviously a mirror reversal of the Reed family—two sisters and a brother John—reenforces our suspicion that the wealthy are blind to real value and overestimate their own attractions.

The moral of Brontë's novel, like the moral of the Cinderella story, is that virtue is ultimately rewarded by domestic happiness. In both cases, Nature works to preserve her heroines. In nature, Jane finds a fairy godmother, a cooperative creation that leads her, when she wanders cold and starving through the woods, to the home of generous relations. While *Wuthering Heights* seems more fantastically Gothic than does *Jane Eyre, Jane Eyre* is more optimistic and, as Heathcliff might add, more romantic. In *Jane Eyre,* wishing does make it so.

A reader who shares Heathcliff's cynicism might also notice that although Jane is temporarily kept in ignorance of her claims to a moderate income, her claims to happiness are, in fact, backed by money. Jane, the orphan, becomes an heiress. Rochester, savage as he may seem, is a diminished "prince in disguise." He succeeds in acquiring his beloved without recourse to Heathcliff's savage violence because nature and supernature cooperate with Rochester. Thus, while Charlotte Brontë invites us to imagine new domesticated ideals of beauty, the price her story pays is loss of social realism. "Plain beauty," Charlotte Brontë's effort to create a realistic heroine, is as much at odds with itself as is "noble savagery"; this revised construct is internally contradictory. The "plain beauty" is a variation on the "noble savage"; both phrases remain oxymorons.

Foundling of Low Birth: *Great Expectations*

The process that I have been charting is the democratization of the character of beauty. Charles Dickens, who raised himself out of the poverty of his youth, is a novelist of democracy because he insists that our virtues and beauty are acquired rather than inherited. In *Great Expectations* (1861), Pip's expectations are embodied in the beautiful and apparently regal Estella. Dickens translates those conventions of beauty that are particularly Gothic (dark savage characters) in the Brontës' novels into features that distinctly, but falsely, mark social strata.

Pip is yet another hero of obscure origins. He assumes incorrectly that the money for his education, the money that is supposed to make him a gentleman, comes from Miss Havisham, a source he can respect. Pip is ashamed when he learns that it comes from a grateful convict. While Magwitch, a vital, sincere, if frightening, victim of social inequality, loves Pip and comes to be loved by the reader, Pip would prefer to have been receiving charity from the decaying old lady who had changed neither her routine nor her dress since the unhappy day on which she was to be married. Pip assumes that Miss Havisham is grooming him for Estella, and Miss Havisham, ornamented by Estella, needs no further recommendation as far as Pip is concerned.

Estella, seen through Pip's eyes, is an unparalleled beauty. Her name, "star," recalls Sidney's Stella, and Pip, an Astrophel—star-lover—himself, admires her in Sidney's terms; she seems to him noble and angelic, though she has been raised to be cruel and treats him brutally. The flaw in Pip's character is that he reaches for stars. By the novel's end, Dickens hopes that the reader has grown up with Pip and learned that the noble star is without real light. The novel strips high-class glamour of beauty to teach Pip that Estella was not designed for him by either Miss Havisham or his creator.

While Magwitch wished to transfigure Pip into a gentleman, the experience transforms Pip into a hero. As Pip's perspective on Magwitch changes, we see a beast, a repugnant member of society's anti-social class, become a beauty. And while everyone assumes that Estella is a natural and noble beauty, it turns out that Magwitch is her natural father and that Miss Havisham has played the part of an unnatural mother. Making Magwitch both the natural father of Estella and the father of Pip's social ambitions betrays Dickens' effort to reverse the traditional authorities of beauty and virtue. On the one hand, Magwitch's role as nurturing parent to Pip proves more important than his role as Estella's natural one; the detail seems just a bit of irony. On the other hand, while Dickens would deprive noble beauty of value, Estella is not noble; she was raised out of her class, and her natural parents are from the lowest classes. The balance between nature and nurture is unstable because, reversing the romantic formula, Pip's angelic princess is a foundling in disguise.

Dickens' ambitious enterprise is to overturn the expectations of readers long accustomed to romance plots. In the original ending for the novel, Pip is quite certain that he does not regret the loss of Estella. He realizes that he never loved her for who she was, but only for what she seemed to be. When Pip and Estella accidentally meet, she says, "I am greatly changed, I know," and the reader is given to understand that if she is no longer the beauty she once was, suffering has improved her character. But Edward Bulwer Lytton persuaded Dickens to unite Pip and Estella. Angus Calder, a modern editor of *Great Expectations,* writes:

> The cancelled ending has only once been preferred to its successor by the editor of a printed text. George Bernard Shaw, with his familiar iconoclasm, used it in a limited edition of the novel, published in 1927, for which he wrote a most interesting preface. He argued with Shavian perversity, that the first ending, "was, in fact, the truly happy ending."[28]

Shaw is perverse only if Estella deserves Pip. After all, if her father had been a beast with beauty, Estella has been a beautiful beast. In pastoral romance, to be raised by the goats signified selection by the gods; beast and beauty were one and the same. In Gothic romance, the possibility of a noble savage is left an open question; the beast's beauty is unclear. Dickens' two endings to *Great Expectations* are the difference between fairy tale and realism, and it is the original ending that anticipates the modern point of view. If nineteenth-century readers could not tolerate an ending that fails to unite beautiful hero and heroine, my guess is that many twentieth-century readers are in sympathy with Shaw's "perversity."

The stories of such beautiful heroes as Daphnis and Joseph (in all of his incarnations) may have led people to expect more of the Wild Boy, Heathcliff, and Estella than was any longer possible in the nineteenth century. The heroes of pastoral romance and the Bible remind us of the time when culture was close to nature; its activity was restricted to the soil. Beauty had little to do with nurture as it was conferred solely by divine selection. The wellborn enjoyed a monopoly on Nature's bounty and the miracles of biblical and classical narratives are the result of Nature's intervention on behalf of the beauties whom she favored. By the age of the nineteenth-century novel, however, the mind and body had lost their figurative status as tilling grounds, and people were as easily cultivated as crops. Nurture began to produce beauty as well as nature because nature became distinct from, even opposed to, culture.

If culture was not invented in the nineteenth century, its advantages and disadvantages were newly scrutinized as Victorians developed strict codes of cultured conduct, confronted foreign cultures and sent anthropologists to compare cultures. Several of nineteenth-century fiction's most popular genres attest to a simultaneous fascination with and suspicion of both foreign and high culture.

The novel of manners and the silver fork novel address the rising middle class, at once parodying the affectations of a decaying aristocracy and teaching the nouveau riche how to behave naturally in cultured circles. The *Bildungsroman,* which describes the procedure by which heroes and heroines become worthy adults, lays bare both the dangers of a lax upbringing and the advantages of a principled education. The nineteenth-century novel widens the divide between nature and culture already evident in Fielding; for the benefit of its middle-class readership, it assumes that breeding rather than birth provides for such qualities as beauty, wealth and virtue. Heroes, like our political leaders, are groomed rather than born for positions of power. But Nature always recovers her authority, and nurture itself has become naturalized. We call first nurture "maternal instinct," the "natural" urge to nurture; we call well-trained leaders "born leaders," and we insist that beautiful people display that which remains "the last and noblest part of beauty," natural grace.

7

Delicacy: The Flower of Health

> *You lie, in faith, for you are call'd plain Kate,*
> *And bonny Kate, and sometimes Kate the curst;*
> *But Kate, the prettiest Kate in Christendom,*
> *Kate of Kate-Hall, my super-dainty Kate,*
> *For dainties are all Kates, and therefore, Kate,*
> *Take this of me, Kate of my consolation—*
> *Hearing thy mildness prais'd in every town,*
> *Thy virtues spoke of, and thy beauty sounded,*
> *Yet not so deeply as to thee belongs,*
> *Myself am mov'd to woo thee for my wife.*
>   Shakespeare, *The Taming of the Shrew*

Petruchio's opening speech to Katherina has the force of a riddled prophesy and magician's spell. He finds in Katherina a "cate," as dainty foods and ladies were sometimes called, a "deli*cate*," a "delicacy." Here is the Kate who names and surpasses all others, the "super-dainty Kate." By his wit, Petruchio turns the outside in and the inside out in order to subdue the world. In control of language and naming, Petruchio controls all. And the "mad marriage" of Petruchio and Katherina, of "devil" and "devil's dam," proves to be the exemplary marriage in a madcap world. Katherina is tamed by the sense of Petruchio's nonsense, for Petruchio, she learns, can and will make everyone see in her, "the prettiest Kate in Christendom," a Kate whose "mildness" will indeed be "praised in every town," her "virtues spoke of" and her "beauty sounded." In Katherina, Petruchio has found a worthy apprentice, and in Petruchio, Katherina has found a worthy mate.

    When Katherina denies that she is "Kate," Petruchio begins his lesson in verbal trickery by saying "you lie, in faith." To lie in truth is the source of his power. Calling her Kate, he gives her a name that allows her to be one thing and its contradiction; he shows her that, by assuming that name, she becomes simply Kate and beautiful Kate, at once "plain" and "bonny." In becoming Kate, Katherina acquires the art of self-transformation. Petruchio's lessons are about language and masquerade: Katherina learns that the rich man may be married in the guise of a pauper and heretic, that delicacies, if they be called tough, will not feed her, and that beautiful dresses, if they be called rags, will not clothe her. By the time that Kate and Petruchio travel back to her father's house, she will mimic him in his art, calling the sun the moon and an old man a maid. And when Petruchio bids her right the world and call the sun the sun and the old man an old man, she does so, earning for herself delicacies, dresses, an admiring husband, and all else that she could desire. Together, this couple assumes superiority over braggart husbands and insipid wives. As Petruchio pockets the sums that have been wagered on Kate's disobedience, Kate herself truimphs. With the apparently submissive but forceful speech that closes the play, she humbles the others and achieves victory. Petruchio calls himself "the winner," and the audience is now convinced that Kate is (as she has probably always been) the prize among the women, Petruchio's "consolation," "the prettiest Kate in Christendom."

By renaming Katherina Kate and by punning on its sense as "delicate" ("for dainties are all Kates"), Shakespeare attributes to Kate a quality of beauty that does her justice in both her lustily shrewish and graciously obedient aspects. "Delicacy," in a sense that is today obsolete, meant voluptuous, luxurious, and addicted to sensual pleasure and delights. One who was "delicate" appreciated delicacies and was likely to be a robust glutton. The senses of delicacy with opposite connotations have proven more durable. Delicacy names features of beauty notable for their refinement. According to the *OED*, delicacy may mean "exquisite fineness of texture, substance, finish, etc.; graceful slightness, slenderness, or softness; soft or tender beauty." A person with delicacy is sensitive, and to handle something with delicacy is to apply exacting skill in a sensitive situation.

Once upon a time, "a delicate" given to luxury and pleasure may well have been scorned for sumptuous gluttony and envied for the wealth that facilitated a life of idle indulgence. Thus, delicate as she becomes, one is not likely to imagine Shakespeare's Kate as a particularly frail or weak beauty; she is simply "cate" enough to be domesticated. Before the nineteenth century, however, robust health had ceased to be a sign of wealth. Aristocratic beauty could be defined with the ambiguously valued terms that the *OED* uses to define delicacy: "tender, sensitive, dainty, frail, and fine," a beauty often marked by "weakness of constitution or health; want of strength or robustness; susceptibility to injury or disease." The money that backed aristocratic delicacy was enviable, but people were learning that in the changing economic order only healthy and rugged travellers survived the climb upward. Upholding the values of delicacy was for women. As we have seen in the preceding chapter, the Joseph figure's beauty therefore came to seem unnatural, effeminate. While one result of the Darwinian revolution was

Figure 21. Claude Monet, *Les femmes au jardin*
Flowers signified both the bloom of health and the beauty of frailty.
Paris, Louvre.
(©*Giraudon; Photo courtesy Art Resource*)

that health became a prerequisite of male beauty and heroism, femininity, defined in opposition to masculinity, did not have to be physically strong.

While beautiful women could be delicate, for men and women alike, delicacy and nervous sensitivity increasingly lost appeal. Poor health seemed to be first the aristocrat's and later the working man's curse. In *Wuthering Heights,* Catherine Earnshaw must choose between the rugged individual and the delicate aristocrat. Victorian men faced similar choices as the delicate health that had once clearly signified feminine beauty and virtue became increasingly "lamentable." This ambivalence has survived the Victorian age. When we speak of a delicate woman, we mean either that she is dainty and lovely, or it is a polite way of saying that she is weak of mind and body, nervous and unfit.

Delicate Beauty Goes Out: George Eliot's *Adam Bede*

Through her descriptions of her female characters' beauty in *Adam Bede* (1859), George Eliot not only frees the delicate heroine to go out without subjecting her to risks that the delicate heroine typically faces, risks of rape or death, but Eliot also attempts to create healthy delicacy, a beauty both spiritual and sexual. In so doing, this novel records a transition in the Victorian evaluation of health.

Eliot revises the connotations of delicate beauty by doubling and exchanging the Poysers' beautiful nieces for one another; Hetty Sorrel and Dinah Morris displace one another not only in the novel's economy and structure of desire but also as meaningful figures of beauty. Eliot changes the tradition of the delicate heroine by recovering senses of delicacy hidden in the word's linguistic history. In Dinah's and Hetty's names, in the adjectives applied to each, and in the objects with which each is associated, Eliot alludes to a code of delicacy. Among the images in that code are the flower, the pet, the bird, the Medusa, and the corpse. These images express both the beauty and dangers of delicacy: the passion of the red rose is made to contrast with the purity and fragility of the white lily.

Adam Bede presents the positive value of delicate health: Dinah is as morally strong as she is physically frail, Hetty as weak willed as she is robust. Illness seems to be redemptive: the guilty lovers, Hetty and Arthur, are each recovered in the eyes of the reader as they grow morally stronger in illness. One critic accordingly observes that "in Eliot's novels those unacquainted with infirmity... tend to have short memories and little imagination."[1] Eliot will, however, exchange these religious values for naturalistic ones by challenging the oppositions of sexuality and spirituality, delicacy and health.

Shortly before *Adam Bede* begins, Dinah Morris, a Methodist preacher who lives among the poor in Snowfield, comes to visit her Aunt and Uncle

Figure 22. Rembrandt van Rijn (Style of), *Old Woman Cutting Her Nails*
"Paint no yet oftener a madonna... but do not impose on us any aesthetic rules which shall banish from the region of Art those old women scraping carrots"—Eliot, *Adam Bede*.
(© The Metropolitan Museum of Art, Bequest of Benjamin Altman, 1913; Photo courtesy Art Resource)

Poyser in the relatively comfortable village of Hayslope. She had come to recover her health, which, we are told, is naturally frail. Within the novel's first pages, her delicate beauty is the talk of the carpentry shop, where the men tease Seth Bede for his affections, but the indelicacy of a young woman preaching is equally the buzz of the village.

That evening the reader sees Dinah first through the eyes of a stranger who, because he is familiar only with ecstatic and bilious Methodists, is unprepared for Dinah Morris:

> She seemed above the middle height of women, though in reality she did not exceed it—an effect which was due to the slimness of her figure and the simple line of her black stuff dress. The stranger was struck... not so much at the feminine delicacy of her appearance, as at the total absence of self-consciousness in her demeanour.... There was no keenness in the eyes; they seemed rather to be shedding love than making observations; they had the liquid look which tells that the mind is full of what it has to give out, rather than impressed by external objects. She stood with her left hand towards the descending sun, the leafy boughs screened her from its rays; but in this sober light, the delicate colouring of her face seemed to gather a calm vividness, like flowers at evening. It was a small oval face, of a uniform transparent whiteness, with an egglike line of cheek and chin, a full but firm mouth, a delicate nostril... surmounted by a rising arch of parting between smooth locks of pale reddish hair. The hair was drawn straight back... and covered... by a net Quaker cap.... It was one of those faces that make one think of white flowers with light touches of colour in their pure petals.[2]

In the novel's first description of Dinah, the references to the white flower connect Dinah to Richardson's languishing heroine Clarissa. The passage evokes an ethereal figure, "transparent," thrice "delicate," "pale," "egglike" in its fragility, a pure white flower in Quaker dress, unconscious of her beauty because hers is the beauty of the spirit that requires no attention to the flesh. As Dinah preaches, she takes on the look of Clarissa in her agitated mode, the lily threatened with harm:

> ... The pause seemed to be filled with agitating thoughts that showed themselves on her features.
> Her face became paler; the circles under her eyes deepened, as they did when tears half-gather without falling....
> But now she entered into a new current of feeling. Her manner became less calm, her utterance more rapid and agitated. (p. 38)

Bessy Cranage, inattentive as Dinah preaches, is the first to phrase the question of beauty, and she contrasts two traditional types. As Dinah speaks, Bessy is

> lost in puzzling speculation as to what pleasure and satisfaction there can be in life to a young woman who wore a cap like Dinah's. Giving up this inquiry in despair, she took to

studying Dinah's nose, eyes, mouth, and hair, and wondering whether it was better to have such a sort of pale face as that, or fat red cheeks and round black eyes like her own. (p. 39)

Bessy gives up her first inquiry in despair because she cannot imagine the pleasures and satisfactions of self-effacement. But even small-minded Bessy has a vague notion that types of beauty are meaningful and legible, and she cannot settle upon which is the "better sort of beauty." Putting the issue of Dinah's cap aside, Bessy wonders if the look of frailty may not surpass in beauty the look of robust health. In this frame of mind, Bessy throws down her earrings and, greatly overcome, repents of her vanity.

The local Reverend Irwine correctly predicts that Bessy will not remain long affected, yet he suggests to Captain Donnithorne that they pay a visit to Dinah Morris. Donnithorne remembers, with some surprise, his first impression of her:

"Oh, By Jove!" said Captain Donnithorne, laughing. "Why, she looks as quiet as a mouse. There's something rather striking about her, though. I positively felt quite bashful the first time I saw her.... It's a type of face one rarely sees among our common people." (p. 71)

The reader enters Hall Farm in advance of Irwine and Donnithorne, and finds Hetty gazing at her own reflection in the polished dishes while the narrator gazes at Dinah: "the rays... lit up her pale red hair to auburn, as she bent over the heavy household linen which she was mending for her aunt." Robust Hetty is inactive, while frail Dinah undertakes chores, significantly, tasks of needlework.[3] Turning her eyes to Mrs. Poyser, the narrator remarks "the family likeness between her and her niece Dinah Morris, with the contrast between her keenness and Dinah's seraphic gentleness of expression, might have served a painter as an excellent suggestion for a Martha and Mary" (p. 81). Dinah is now specifically identified as a painterly model for the Virgin Mother.

The Poysers are concerned both for their niece's frail health and her public displays, and Mrs. Poyser fears that she will be duly chastised when the Reverend and Arthur Donnithorne pay this unexpected visit. Instead, the Reverend is so impressed that he concludes to himself, "He must be a miserable prig who would act the pedagogue here," by discouraging her public preaching. When he asks aloud, "And you never feel any embarrassment from the sense of your youth—that you are a lovely young woman on whom men's eyes are fixed?" Dinah replies, "... I've preached to as rough ignorant people as can be in the villages about Snowfield—men that looked very hard and wild—but they never said an uncivil word to me..." (pp. 97-98).

By convincing the learned Reverend that only "a miserable prig" would disapprove of Dinah Morris and by twice emphasizing that Dinah Morris goes among "rough, hard and wild men" without provoking disrespect, Eliot undermines a tradition within literature that long associated the beauty of female delicacy with domestic confinement. The reader, after all, would not wish to be characterized as a "miserable prig." Betrayed in the question that the Reverend asks of Dinah is the concern that exposing her beauty may lead to some harm. Eliot has another Dinah in mind, and Irwine's question may be motivated by his own recollection of the Dinah he would have read about in Genesis 34.

Lilies Exposed: Dinah and Susanna in Hebrew Scriptures, Apocrypha, and Midrash

Dinah, only daughter born to the matriarchs and patriarchs, is sister to our delicate hero Joseph, though she is not much of a heroine. We are told only that she "went out to visit the women of the land; and when Shechem... the prince of the land saw her, he seized her and lay with her and humbled her" (vv. 1-2). Shechem is so taken with his victim, however, that he determines to marry her and asks leave of Jacob to do so. The biblical narrator offers only one moralizing sentence: "The sons of Jacob came in from the field when they heard of it; and the men were indignant and very angry, because he had wrought folly in Israel by lying with Jacob's daughter, for such a thing ought not to be done" (v. 7).

Leah's sons devise a plot. They agree to the marriage and to dwell as neighbors among Shechem's people on the condition that the Hivite men agree to be circumcised. On the third day following the operation, when the men would have been most sore, Simeon and Levi slaughter them and take "Dinah out of Shechem's house" (v. 26). When Jacob declares that his sons' deviousness has jeopardized his position in the land, they protest: "Should he treat our sister as a harlot?"

In contemporary biblical criticism, the story is understood first and foremost as a political and historical parable that "portrays, in the guise of individuals, relations between the Canaanite city and the early Hebrew tribes."[4] It accounts for, among other things, the decline of the tribes of Simeon and Levi. Although Dinah seems to function as the innocent victim of a rape for whose sake her brothers take misguided and excessive revenge, classical commentaries derive lessons from the story that imply a more aggressive female actress. Commenting on the creation myth of Adam and Eve, one midrashist—remembering Dinah—understands why man must subdue woman: "man must master his wife, that she go not into the market place, for every woman who goes out into the market place will eventually come to grief. Whence do we know it? From Dinah, as it is written, And Dinah... went out, etc."[5] "To go out," in an age when women acted within the boundaries of the tent, is not an innocent activity. Just as Jael's "going out"

(Judges 4:18) is understood to contain the meaning that a beautiful and over-ornamented woman goes out with intent to seduce, so is Dinah's action interpreted.

If Dinah's brothers are loathe to have her treated as a harlot, the rabbis have no such qualms. Because Job says that his wife speaks as a "vile woman," one rabbi concludes that his wife is none other than Dinah. Moreover, several rabbis imagine that Dinah is violated to punish Jacob for refusing to wed her to Esau and for his other acts of pride. In their view, not only is Dinah a harlot, but, by extension, so is her mother, Leah: "A woman is not immoral until her daughter is immoral." To the rabbi who expresses reluctance to call the matriarch a whore, Rav Kahana replies, "Even so... because it says *Leah went out to meet him* (Gen. 30: 16), which means that she went out to meet him adorned like a harlot." Dinah, therefore, simply follows in her mother's footsteps. Each and every consequent disaster is blamed upon Dinah's "going out," which proves that in spite of God's best efforts to make women modest, women are "frivolous," "coquettish," "gossiping" and "wanton." Rabbi Samuel, son of Nahman, explains that when Dinah went out "her arm became exposed," and that this display of her beauty was a conscious provocation. Given Dinah's designs, the rabbis do not interpret Simeon and Levi's recapturing of Dinah as the welcome rescue that it seems to be in the biblical account; her brothers must drag her by force from Shechem's house because "when a woman is intimate with an uncircumcised person, she finds it hard to tear herself away." For Jacob's sake, one rabbi wishes that Dinah had never been born, and while the Bible makes the point that the rapist did "what ought not to have been done," and that Dinah's brothers behaved rashly, from the Midrash Rabbah one concludes that the moral of the Biblical account is that a woman should never "go out."

The literary tradition offers another sample of womanhood, the power of whose beauty tempts even noble and respected men to lust. An apocryphal addition to the Book of Daniel, the story of Susanna and the Elders has become a favorite subject of visual representation. Susanna—whose name means lily[6]—is described as "a very beautiful woman who feared the Lord." Two elders who regularly visit her husband are overcome with lust for this flower in Israel, and the elders try to overcome Susanna at her bath. They offer her the alternative of acting the harlot with them or being convicted of harlotry on the strength of their testimony as witnesses. Susanna, "hemmed in on every side" (Susanna 1:22), chooses against sin. At her trial, Susanna, "a woman of great refinement and beautiful in appearance" (v. 31), is suitably veiled. As we have seen in Scott's *Ivanhoe*, unveiling the veiled beauty serves a double purpose: it rekindles lust in the wicked and moves the clear-sighted to see truth where there is so much beauty. The narrator of "Susanna" explains that "the wicked men ordered her to be unveiled that they might feast upon her

Figure 23. Rembrandt van Rijn, *Susanna at Her Bath*
"A very beautiful woman who feared the Lord"—an opportunity to display the female nude.
(©*Scala; Photo courtesy Art Resource*)

beauty. But her family and friends and all who saw her wept." In spite of the general weeping, Susanna is convicted and sentenced to death. Here, an otherwise realistic story takes a fantastic turn. Daniel, inspired by God, exposes the false witnesses and Susanna is vindicated. Whether or not we are familiar with the midrashic reading of the Dinah story per se, paintings of Susanna at her bath, rape accounts in Hebrew Scriptures, Susanna, Richardson's *Clarissa,* tales of rape or false accusations of harlotry convey the double message that delicate beauty is vulnerable, especially vulnerable when exposed, and susceptible to blame. As a careless delicate beauty or a beauty who acts indelicately risks either rape or accusation of harlotry, a man's duty is to safeguard his wife, and, as the descendants of Richardson's *Clarissa* know, a virgin's duty is to safeguard herself.

Crimson Rose: Hetty Sorrel

While Dinah Morris' friends have full confidence in her virtue, it is not surprising that they fear for her reputation. Working against this literary tradition of delicate heroines, Eliot takes special pains to demonstrate that Dinah's purity is uncompromised and that she invites no sexual harassment. The forbearance of the Reverend in a competing church is a strong indication to the reader that accusations of indelicacy are inappropriate. Thus, Eliot allows her model of frail, refined and angelic beauty to take uncharacteristic liberties. At the same time, Hetty Sorrel's consciousness of her charms tempts others to take liberties with her. A woman of strong character, no matter how weak her constitution, may safely go out among the roughest people. Although Eliot allows her model of frail beauty to take uncharacteristic liberties, Dinah's friends wish her to stay comfortably at home.

As matters turn out, real reason for concern lies elsewhere, with the Poysers' other niece, Hetty. While Dinah charms the Reverend by her unself-conscious beauty, Hetty is self-consciously charming the squire. The result will be tragic. Concern and desire are misplaced in the novel, and Eliot will effect several reversals in order to set matters right.

While Dinah is engaged in her conversation with Mr. Irwine, the young squire Arthur Donnithorne goes into the dairy to watch Hetty,

> a distractingly pretty girl of seventeen, standing on little pattens and rounding her dimpled arm to lift a pound of butter out of the scale.
> Hetty blushed a deep rose-colour when Captain Donnithorne entered the dairy and spoke to her; but it was not at all a distressed blush, for it was inwreathed with smiles and dimples, and with sparkles from under long, curled, dark eyelashes.... Hetty tossed and patted her pound of butter with quite a self-possessed, coquettish air, slyly conscious that no turn of her head was lost.

> There are various orders of beauty, causing men to make fools of themselves in various styles, from the desperate to the sheepish; but there is one order of beauty which seems made to turn the heads not only of men, but of all intelligent mammals, even of women. It is a beauty like that of kittens, or... babies just beginning to toddle and to engage in conscious mischief—a beauty with which you can never be angry, but that you feel ready to crush for inability to comprehend the state of mind into which it throws you. Hetty Sorrel's was that kind of beauty. Her aunt, Mrs. Poyser, who professed to despise all personal attractions... continually gazed at Hetty's charms on the sly, fascinated in spite of herself, and after administering such a scolding as naturally flowed from her anxiety to do well by her husband's niece—who had no mother of her own to scold her, poor thing!—she would often confess to her husband, when they were safe out of hearing, that she firmly believed, "the naughtier the little huzzy behaved, the prettier she looked."
>
> It is of little use for me to tell you that Hetty's cheek was like a rose-petal, that dimples played about her pouting lips, that her large dark eyes hid a soft roguishness under their long lashes....

Eliot continues at some length to tell what it is "of little use to tell," concluding,

> of little use, unless you have seen a woman who affected you as Hetty affected her beholders, for otherwise, though you might conjure up the image of a lovely woman, she would not in the least resemble that distracting kitten-like maiden.... Hetty's was a springtide beauty; it was the beauty of young frisking things, round-limbed, gambolling, circumventing you by a false air of innocence—the innocence of a star-browed calf, for example, that... leads you a severe steeplechase over hedge and ditch, and only comes to a stand in the middle of a bog. (pp. 89-91)

Everything in this description adds up to a beauty that is "charming," "rosy," "round," "distracting," "kittenish," falsely innocent and otherwise deceptive, a beauty that leads its beholder into a bog. If the reader has not been led astray by false beauty, the narrator insists that her description would fail to conjure up Hetty and that we would imagine "a lovely woman," not in the least like this distracting maiden. By this point in the novel, Dinah and Hetty are both fully described: both women are distractingly pretty, but Dinah distracts attention from the body and Hetty distracts attention from the soul. Dinah elevates; Hetty debases. Dinah clarifies; Hetty obscures.

As frail preacher and rosy farm girl, Dinah and Hetty are exaggerated antithetical types. Dinah, pure and with "airs from heaven," may safely go out among rough men in these early episodes without incurring any disapproval from the narrator, and Hetty cannot safely go out among even the most refined gentry. It is only after Eliot fixes in our minds the virtue of the one and the wickedness of the other that she will temper her own commentary on each and humanize them both. Eliot's struggle is to untangle a tradition that sees evil in any beautiful woman who goes out unprotected.

Scarlet Rose: Hester Prynne

The suffering of Nathaniel Hawthorne's Hester Prynne exemplifies, for Eliot, the treatment of such heroines. If Dinah takes her name from the biblical character, Hetty and Arthur Donnithorne take their names from characters in *The Scarlet Letter* (1850). In his foreword to *Adam Bede*, F. R. Leavis writes that though *Adam Bede*'s subject is one of characteristic interest to Eliot,

> even here one can see her indebted, at least for stimulus and suggestion (of kinds that matter immensely to an artist engaged in self-discovery as George Eliot was), to a great and noble predecessor. This time it was not the genial Scott, but the novelist of Puritan New England. George Eliot had read *The Scarlet Letter* when it came out, and (what doesn't surprise us) expressed a great admiration for Hawthorne. The idea that Hawthorne's influence can be discovered in *Adam Bede* was prompted, as it came to me, by the name of Hetty. Once one thinks of Hester Prynne, the effect of the suggestion has its compelling significance, even if one is at first inclined to dismiss the echo as mere chance. The treatment of the agonized conscience in Arthur Donnithorne convinces one before long that in the treatment of the seduction theme *The Scarlet Letter* has told significance. This real affinity (for all the difference of temperament and art between the two authors) brings home to one, in fact, that the association of the names was more than a chance clue. One notes, further, that Hawthorne's male sinner is also Arthur—Arthur Dimmesdale for George Eliot's Arthur Donnithorne. (pp. ix-x)

Hawthorne's treatment of his hero and heroine is complex and ambivalent. The reader is left to decide if Hester, an extraordinary beauty and character, acts on good or evil impulses when she goes out alone into the New World and has a child born of an adulterous liaison with the Reverend Dimmesdale. Hester and her daughter Pearl are each models of delicacy and indelicacy; both are associated with symbols that the novel creates to stand for, paradoxically, both aggressive ostentation and human frailty: the scarlet letter and the scarlet rose. Because *The Scarlet Letter* is set in seventeenth-century Salem, Hawthorne exploits his readers' distance from the events he describes to alternately criticize and draw us into sympathy with Puritan values.

The novel is presented to the reader together with a wild rose plucked from the bush outside the prison ("the black flower of civilized society") in the hope that the story will "symbolize some sweet moral blossom ... to relieve the darkening close of a tale of human frailty and sorrow." We are asked to imagine that the "delicate gems" on the rosebush offer "their fragrance and fragile beauty" to the criminal "in token that the deep heart of Nature could pity and be kind to him."[7] Thus, from the novel's onset, fragile beauty and human frailty (both symbolized in the flower) walk companions. The red rose appears relentlessly as a symbol with ambiguous connotations in this fiction.

Delicacy: The Flower of Health

As the narrator equivocates and responds to frailty with a mixture of severity and compassion, he presents his fiction as if he were a model historian. However much Hester suffers in his hands, he seems objective and judicious. Puritan society appears to be at once severe and kind; Hester sports beauty and is without beauty; she is guilty and innocent, tormented and above suffering. The scarlet letter too is an appropriately shifting symbol of ambiguity, as the "A" stands first for Adultery, then for Angel, and finally for Able.

The narrator's ambivalent stance is evident when Hester is first described. As Hester emerges from the prison, Hawthorne emphasizes the difference between her large healthy perfection and the "delicate, evanescent... grace" that is idealized in his own time. It is unclear which character of beauty the narrator prefers:

> The young woman was tall, with a figure of perfect elegance on a large scale. She had dark and abundant hair, so glossy that it threw off the sunshine with a gleam, and a face which, besides being beautiful from regularity of feature and richness of complexion, had the impressiveness belonging to a marked brow and deep black eyes. She was lady-like too, after the manner of the feminine gentility of those days; characterized by a certain state and dignity, rather than by the delicate, evanescent, and indescribable grace, which is now recognized as its indication. And never had Hester Prynne appeared more lady-like, in the antique interpretation of the term, than as she issued from the prison. Those who had before known her, and had expected to behold her dimmed and obscured by a disastrous cloud, were astonished, and even startled, to perceive how her beauty shone out, and made a halo of the misfortune and ignominy in which she was enveloped. It may be true, that, to a sensitive observer, there was something exquisitely painful in it. Her attire, which, indeed, she had wrought for the occasion, in prison, and had modelled much after her own fancy, seemed to express the attitude of her spirit, the desperate recklessness of her mood, by its wild and picturesque peculiarity. But the point which drew all eyes, and, as it were, transfigured the wearer,—so that both men and women, who had been familiarly acquainted with Hester Prynne, were now impressed as if they beheld her for the first time,—was that SCARLET LETTER, so fantastically embroidered and illuminated upon her bosom. It had the effect of a spell, taking her out of the ordinary relations with humanity, and enclosing her in a sphere by herself. (pp. 50–51)

By remembering the ideal of delicate beauty that was larger and stronger than the ideal of frail delicacy, Hawthorne both reflects and encourages the trend that was again beginning to value larger-bodied and healthier women.

Hawthorne is interested to paint this exemplary woman as an indistinguishable blend of divinity and sinfulness:

> Had there been a Papist among the crowd of Puritans, he might have seen in this beautiful woman, so picturesque in her attire and mien, and with the infant at her bosom, an object to remind him of the image of Divine Maternity, which so many illustrious painters have vied with one another to represent; something which should remind him, indeed, but only by contrast, of that sacred image of sinless motherhood, whose infant was to redeem the world.

> Here, there was the taint of deepest sin in the most sacred quality of human life, working such effect, that the world was only darker for this woman's beauty, and the more lost for the infant she had borne. (p. 53)

Hawthorne effects the reversal in this passage by contrasting the suggestion of Hester as Madonna (again the reference is to a tradition in the visual arts) with the truth of her sin; the narrator does not clarify for the reader whether we are to believe that the world is truly "darker for this woman's beauty."

In like fashion, the principal male characters are introduced through the contradiction between their appearances and their roles. Hester's husband, Chillingworth, the man who has been most wronged, is described as a kind of sexual monster: his gaze becomes "keen and penetrative," as "a writhing horror twisted across his features like a snake." Dimmesdale, Hester's fellow sinner, and doubly culpable for his silence, is described in contrast to the demonic Chillingworth, as a "pale young man,"

> a person of very striking aspect, with a white, lofty, and impending brow, large, brown, melancholy eyes, and mouth which, unless when he forcibly compressed it, was apt to be tremulous, expressing both nervous sensibility and a vast power of self-restraint. Notwithstanding his high native gifts and scholar-like attainments, there was an air about this young minister,—an apprehensive, a startled, a half-frightened look,—as of a being who felt himself quite astray and at a loss in the pathway of human existence, and could only be at ease in some seclusion of his own. Therefore, so far as his duties would permit, he trod in the shadowy by-paths, and thus kept himself simple and childlike; coming forth, when occasion was, with a freshness, and fragrance, and dewy purity of thought, which, as many people said, affected them like the speech of an angel. (p. 62)

Like Hester, Dimmesdale's beauty is divine; he is a "divine"—literally and figuratively—and a half-frightened creature who has been led astray.

In spite of her apparently defiant strength, Hester is mortified by the crowd and swoons under its gaze. She finds herself alone with Chillingworth, who blames himself for her fall. Not only should he not have left her alone unprotected, but he explains that he should have known better than to marry her: "Misshapen from my birth-hour, how could I delude myself with the idea that intellectual gifts might veil physical deformity in a younger girl's eyes." He adds that, "Mine was the first wrong, when I betrayed thy budding youth into a false and unnatural relation with my decay" (p. 69).

In this dialogue, the floral metaphor connotes youth and innocence, though it is used to account for Hester's guilt. Hester herself becomes a symbol:

> for the accumulating days and added years, would pile up their misery upon the heap of shame. Throughout them all, giving up her individuality, she would become the general symbol at which the preacher and moralist might point, and in which they might vivify and embody their images of woman's frailty and sinful passion.

Hester, uniquely beautiful, is reduced to a Theophrastan type. She stays among people where "she must needs be the type of shame" (p. 73).

While Hester dresses herself in the most austere and self-effacing attire, she dresses Pearl in exquisite clothes that, like the Scarlet A, advertise Hester's skill at embroidery, an occupation that the narrator presents as a special female pleasure: "Women derive a pleasure, incomprehensible to the other sex, from the delicate toil of the needle." Hester, in particular, "had in her nature a rich, voluptuous, Oriental characteristic,—a taste for the gorgeously beautiful, which, save in the exquisite productions of her needle, found nothing else... to exercise itself upon" (p. 77). Hawthorne simultaneously punishes and rewards Hester by forcing this lover of gorgeousness into Puritan dress and by allowing her a remarkable skill in an art that she uses most lavishly first to make her letter and then to clothe her child. As both the letter and Pearl embody Hester's crime, Hester's pleasure is intricately woven into her pain. Pearl and the letter are constant sources of comfort and distress to Hester.

On Pearl especially, Hawthorne spares no language of description. She is "a lovely and immortal flower," the beauty of which "became every day more brilliant" (p. 81). The child is of supernatural beauty, the picture of innocence and guilt:

> Certainly, there was no physical defect. By its perfect shape, its vigor, and its natural dexterity in the use of all its untried limbs, the infant was worthy to have been brought forth in Eden; worthy to have been left there, to be the plaything of the angels, after the world's first parents were driven out. The child had a native grace which does not invariably coexist with faultless beauty, its attire, however simple, always impressed the beholder as if it were the very garb that precisely became it best. But little Pearl was not clad in rustic weeds. Her mother, with a morbid purpose, that may be better understood hereafter, had bought the richest tissues that could be procured, and allowed her imaginative faculty its full play in the arrangement and decoration of the dresses which the child wore, before the public eye. So magnificent was the small figure, when thus arrayed, and such was the splendor of Pearl's own proper beauty, shining through the gorgeous robes which might have extinguished a paler loveliness, that there was an absolute circle of radiance around her, on the darksome cottage floor. And yet a russet gown, torn and soiled with the child's rude play, made a picture of her just as perfect. Pearl's aspect was imbued with a spell of infinite variety; in this one child there were many children, comprehending the full scope between the wild-flower prettiness of a peasant baby, and the pomp, in little, of an infant princess. Throughout all, however, there was a trait of passion, a certain depth of hue, which she never lost; and if, in any of her changes, she had grown fainter or paler, she would have ceased to be herself,—it would have been no longer Pearl. (pp. 82–83)

Pearl's beauty—of peasant and princess, of angel and fiend—is a tormenting puzzle, such that "Hester could not help questioning... whether Pearl were a human child. She seemed rather an airy sprite..." (p. 84), who uses sticks, rags and flowers as the "puppets" of her "witchcraft." "Fiendlike,"

Pearl throws flowers at her mother's breast as the narrator returns obsessively to the double meaning of the girl's beauty and attire. She is the white pearl of innocence and the red rose of passion, a frail flower that is, nevertheless, as invulnerable as a supernatural sprite.

At the Governor's home where Hester pleads to be allowed to keep Pearl, the child's similarity to the letter, in its double function as protection and punishment, is an argument in Hester's favor. When Pearl announces her name, the old minister says that "Red Rose" would be a more appropriate appellation, and spying the ornamented child, the Governor says that "such a child's mother must needs be a scarlet woman, and a worthy type of her of Babylon!" (p. 101). Hester, who has already been mistaken for a Madonna, is now mistaken for her antithesis, the Whore. Hester combines both and is neither.

In spite of the fact that Pearl has been well-schooled in the Catechism, the imp replies to the minister's first question, "that she had not been made at all, but had been plucked by her mother off the bush of wild roses that grew by the prison door" (p. 103). Hester raves: "She is my happiness!—she is my torture... she is the scarlet letter" (p. 104). As much as Pearl is happiness and torture, so the torture of the letter has become a happiness to Hester; the symbol transfigures. The sign of sin becomes a religious symbol that "had the effect of the cross on a nun's bosom. It imparted to the wearer a kind of sacredness, which enabled her to walk safely amid all peril. Had she fallen among thieves, it would have kept her safe" (p. 149).

Wearing the letter, Hester may now safely "go out." Although the symbols in *The Scarlet Letter* shift, outer beauty is a faithful representation of inner beauty. Chillingworth becomes increasingly demonic in appearance as he undertakes "the devil's office"; the A on Dimmesdale's heart imprints itself on his breast, and the changes in Hester's beauty correspond to the changes in her character:

> All the light and graceful foliage of her character had been withered up by this red-hot brand, and had long ago fallen away, leaving a bare and harsh outline, which might have been repulsive, had she possessed friends or companions to be repelled by it. Even the attractiveness of her person had undergone a similar change. It might be partly owing to the studied austerity of her dress, and partly to the lack of demonstration in her manners. It was a sad transformation, too, that her rich and luxuriant hair had either been cut off, or was so completely hidden in her cap, that not a shining lock of it ever once gushed into the sunshine. It was due in part to all of these causes, but still more to something else, that there seemed to be no longer anything in Hester's face for Love to dwell upon; nothing in Hester's form, though majestic and statue-like, that Passion would ever dream of clasping in its embrace; nothing in Hester's bosom, to make it ever again the pillow of Affection. Some attribute had departed from her, the permanence of which had been essential to keep her a woman. Such is frequently the fate, and such the stern development, of the feminine character and person, when the woman has encountered, and lived through, an experience

of peculiar severity. If she be all tenderness, she will die. If she survive, the tenderness will either be crushed out of her, or,—and the outward semblance is the same—crushed so deeply into her heart that it can never show itself more. The latter is perhaps the truest theory. She who had once been a woman and ceased to be so, might at any moment become a woman again if there were only the magic touch to effect the transfiguration. We shall see whether Hester Prynne were ever afterwards so touched, and so transfigured. (p. 150)

Hester, who had been a model of feminine delicacy in its antique sense, a lover of the luxurious and a tender beauty, has been punished for her act of indelicacy with loss of her beauty and womanhood. A woman is here defined by the tenderness which makes her desirable; should she succumb to passion, however, and remain tender, she would die. Hawthorne, aware of the fate of the Victorian angel, suggests that his plot could have gone another way: perhaps we would better appreciate Hester's virtue if she had been a delicate, evanescent victimized beauty who dies. But Hester is not, as Hawthorne made clear, a Victorian beauty; she is too strong and staunchly Puritanical. Meeting the condition for life—the repression of any appearance of delicacy—means ceasing to meet the first condition of womanhood. Singularly beautiful and womanly, Hester had been especially vulnerable to "Love," "Passion," and "Affection"; without tenderness, however, Hester is without beauty, "almost repulsive," without womanhood, and, therefore, utterly invulnerable. Because no one would want such a woman, Hester is now safe.

When Hester meets the man whom she loves once more, she does, of course, undergo the radical transfiguration that the narrator had anticipated. As the pair confront each other, the narrator declares: "Each a ghost, and awe-stricken at the other ghost!" (p. 174). Hester comforts Dimmesdale, takes him to her breast (the letter) and then tears the letter off:

> Oh, exquisite relief! She had not known the weight, until she felt the freedom! By another impulse, she took off the formal cap that confined her hair; and down it fell upon her shoulders, dark and rich, with at once a shadow and a light in its abundance, and imparting the charm of softness to her features. There played around her mouth, and beamed out of her eyes, a radiant and tender smile, that seemed to be gushing from the very heart of womanhood. A crimson flush was glowing on her cheek, that had been long so pale. Her sex, her youth, and the whole richness of her beauty, came back from what men call the irrevocable past, and clustered themselves, with her maiden hope, and a happiness before unknown, within the magic circle of this hour. And, as if the gloom of the earth and sky had been but the effluence of these two mortal hearts, it vanished with their sorrow. All at once, as with a sudden smile of heaven, forth burst the sunshine pouring a very flood into the obscure forest, gladdening each green leaf, transmuting the yellow fallen ones to gold, and gleaming adown the gray trunks of the solemn trees.... (p. 186)

Hester, who had lost the essential quality of womanhood, now derives her beauty from the very heart of womanhood itself. But in spite of her remarkable transfiguration, when Hester resumes the letter, her face becomes again "like a mask; or like the frozen aspect of a dead woman's features." In Hawthorne's imagery, she is corpse and angel; a woman of the flesh and a womanless being of the spirit; Medusa and Madonna; Whore of Babylon and nun. In the spirit of the times in which he writes, Hawthorne unsettles the opposition between sexuality and spirituality. By combining the features of the tradition's antithetical types of womanhood in a single figure, Hawthorne succeeds in producing a healthy heroine. Hester pays the price in suffering isolation.

It is within Dimmesdale's power to rescue Hester and Pearl from the contradictions of their existence. When Pearl, who had been a torment as imp and divinity, kisses her father's lips after his public avowal (bringing that which had been inside out), "a spell was broken." Pearl grows up and leads a happy life, and Hester, whose life is characterized by good works, becomes "Able," the exemplary woman of purposeful labor.

Hawthorne expresses at best a guarded admiration for Hester's tender beauty as he raises her to the status of angel while condemning her to years of misery for the crime of "going out." Eliot responds to this fiction and the implication that unprotected tender women provoke lust in the best of men. To do so, she first reestablishes the distinction between sexual and spiritual beauty that Hawthorne rejects. Eliot adopts the metaphor of the flower and applies it variously to both Hetty and Dinah. Hetty, a rose like Hester, inherits Hester's strength, luxurious beauty and love of luxury; like Hester, Hetty is sexually vulnerable. Dinah, a white lily like Susanna and Clarissa, is physically more tender and delicate than Hester; Dinah inherits Hester's angelic, Madonna, and death-like qualities, her spirituality and commitment to good works. But Eliot knows as well as Hawthorne the fates endured by delicate heroines, literature's virtuous victims; she follows Hawthorne's lead in preserving her heroine in health, though she is unwilling to compromise her heroine's virtue or happiness.

Lily is Rose: Dinah and Hetty

That which Van Ghent calls the "leisurely pace" of *Adam Bede* affords Eliot the opportunity to describe both Dinah and Hetty at great length.[8] Eliot is emphatic and redundant; she repeats the phrases that capture each woman's beauty so often that the reader comes to visualize faces and bodies engraved with meaning.

Dinah is a lily, a bird—which is a favorite Christian icon of the spirit used by the Romantics—an angel, a sublime corpse. Like Clarissa, Hester Prynne in her aspect of death, and Little Nell Trent, Dinah seems to belong on that familiar list of Victorian types who are most beautiful in death. But Eliot qualifies the image. When Dinah first comes to Lisbeth Bede, Lisbeth mistakes Dinah for her sister's spirit "come back from the dead." Her second guess is that this must be an angel: "she saw nothing at first but a pale face—a pure pale face, with loving gray eyes, and it was quite unknown to her. Her wonder increased; perhaps it was an angel." Lisbeth is brought down to earth, however, when she notices that Dinah's hands bear "traces of labour"; Dinah cannot be an angel because she is "a workin' woman." But Lisbeth persists: "ye comed in so light, like the shadow on the wall, an spoke i' my ear, as I thought ye might be a sperrit. Ye've got a'most the face o' one as is a-sittin' on the grave i' Adam's new Bible" (pp. 113-14). At the novel's end, this picture will open Adam's eyes to the reality of Dinah.

Adam hears a female voice in the house, and hoping against hope that Dinah is Hetty, his illusion is shattered: "But now her slim figure, her plain black gown, and her pale serene face impressed him with all the force that belongs to a reality contrasted with a preoccupying fancy" (p. 120). While Adam loves Hetty, he understands Seth's love for Dinah: "I don't wonder at thee for loving her, Seth. She's got a face like a lily."

Book One ends with a series of thematically paired chapters: "Dinah Visits Lisbeth" and "In the Cottage"; "In the Wood" and "Evening in the Wood"; "The Return Home" and "The Two Bed-Chambers"; and a summary, "Links," that structurally enforce Eliot's twinning of her heroine and villainess. The first two of these chapters belong to Dinah, and they begin as she first encounters Adam. Readers who are surprised by Adam's marriage to Dinah at the end of the novel miss the impact of the lines that follow Adam's rude surprise, as Eliot subtly portrays Dinah's sexual awakening:

> For the first moment or two he made no answer, but looked at her with the concentrated examining glance which a man gives to an object in which he has suddenly begun to be interested. Dinah, for the first time in her life, felt a painful self-consciousness; there was something in the dark penetrating glance of the strong man so different from the mildness and timidity of his brother Seth. A faint blush came, which deepened as she wondered at it. The blush recalled Adam from his forgetfulness. (p. 120)

Seth's mildness and timidity, his Joseph-like chastity, do not compare favorably with Adam's more obvious masculinity. Dinah is explicitly, but only symbolically, penetrated by Adam, while Hetty's literal penetration (which took place at the same moment) passes unremarked.

The next two chapters are the chapters of Hetty's sexual awakening, her first kiss with Arthur and the beginning of their clandestine affair. Two chapters follow which belong to Hetty and Dinah together. As the women return home, they meet one another en route. Dinah selflessly speaks on behalf of the man who affected her so mysteriously, but Hetty is preoccupied with fantasies of a future life with Arthur: "and it made a strange contrast to see the sparkling self-engrossed loveliness looked at by Dinah's calm pitying face" (p. 142).

Dinah and Hetty, both motherless girls, the former a niece to Mrs. Poyser, the latter a niece to Mr. Poyser, occupy symmetrical positions in the social structure of the novel's world, though Hetty desires to live above their station and Dinah desires to live below it. Each is adamant, and each is wrong. They return home to occupy adjoining bed-chambers.

"The Two Bed-Chambers" first pictures Hetty worshipping her image in the mirror, remembering her meeting with Arthur, adorning herself in earrings and a lace scarf, and finally prancing about her room. The narrator speaks sarcastically of physiognomists:

> How pretty the little puss looks in that old dress! It would be the easiest folly in the world to fall in love with her: there is such a sweet babylike roundness about her face and figure; the delicate dark rings of hair lie so charmingly about her ears and neck; her great dark eyes with their long eyelashes touch one so strangely, as if an imprisoned frisky Sprite looked out of them....
>
> The dear, young, round, soft flexible thing! Her heart must be just as soft, her temper just as free from angles, her character just as pliant.... Every man under such circumstances is conscious of being a great physiognomist....
>
> It was very much in this way that our friend Adam Bede thought about Hetty;... Before you despise Adam as deficient in penetration, pray ask yourself if you were ever predisposed to believe evil of any pretty woman—if you *could*... believe evil of the one supremely pretty woman who has bewitched you. (p. 153)

For several pages the narrator waxes philosophical on the subject of beauty and its effects, all the while adding phrases to capture Hetty's extraordinary beauty.

At the same time that Hetty imagines herself a stately and magnificent bride to Arthur, Dinah enjoys the view from her window, prays, and thinks of the unfortunate people of Snowfield. Startled out of her reverie by a noise in Hetty's room, Dinah—who has a vision of Hetty as a "poor thing struggling torn and bleeding"—determines to give her divine direction. The narrator marvels:

> What a strange contrast the two figures made, visible enough in that mingled twilight and moonlight! Hetty, her cheeks flushed and her eyes glistening from her imaginary drama, her beautiful neck and arms bare, her hair hanging in a curly tangle down her back, and the baubles in her ears. Dinah, covered with her long white dress, her pale face full of subdued emotion, almost like a lovely corpse into which the soul has returned charged with sublimer secrets and a sublimer love. They were nearly of the same height.... (p. 159)

Eliot might be describing the body and the soul doing battle, as in a metaphysical psychomachia. The crux of this juxtaposition, like the paradox of the psychomachia, is that neither body nor soul exists as an image of earthly beauty without the other. Dinah's resemblance to a corpse again encodes her spirituality, and the scene ends with Hetty pale and crying, while Dinah departs yet again "like a ghost."

At this point in the story, Dinah leaves Hayslope, but not before reasserting her self-image of nun-like sexless spirituality; she assures Seth that she plans never to marry. The reader has been fully impressed with the contrasting beauties and characters of Dinah and Hetty: Dinah, who is slim, pale and modest, does not seem to attract Adam's, Arthur's, or the common men's sexual notice, while Hetty, who is round, rosy, and vain, does. Comparing the beauty of her two nieces in the very terms that Bessy compared her own looks to those of Dinah, Mrs. Poyser remarks that "If Dinah had a bit o' colour in her cheeks an' didn't stick that Methodist cap on her head... folks 'ud think her as pretty as Hetty." But Mr. Poyser knows better: "The men 'ud never run after Dinah as they would after Hetty." Indeed, Mrs. Poyser is willing to admit that Dinah has character traits that prevent her from equalling Hetty in beauty: "But as for Dinah, poor child, she's niver likely to be buxom as long as she'll make her dinner o' cake and water, for the sake o' giving to them as want" (p. 187). Quoting no less an authority than Scripture, Mrs. Poyser argues that "one must love your neighbor as yourself." Eliot agrees with Mrs. Poyser and will bring Dinah to believe that God did not mean for her to neglect her own happiness and well-being.

In one of the many conversations on the subject of beauty in *Adam Bede*, the wealthy notables sit on high and chat lightly about the relative beauty of Hayslope's farm girls. Their discussion concerns delicacy, as Mrs. Irwine begins by remarking that Hetty Sorrel's beauty could not be appreciated by the indelicate class to which she belongs:

"... She's a perfect beauty! I've never seen anything so pretty since my young days. What a pity such beauty as that should be thrown away among the farmers, when it's wanted so terribly among the good families without fortune! I daresay, now, she'll marry a man who would have thought her just as pretty if she had round eyes and red hair."

Arthur dared not turn his eyes towards Hetty while Mrs. Irwine was speaking of her. He feigned not to hear, and to be occupied with something on the opposite side. But he saw her plainly enough without looking; saw her in heightened beauty, because he had heard her beauty praised—for other men's opinion, you know, was like a native climate to Arthur's feelings: it was the air on which they thrived the best, and grew strong. Yes! She *was* enough to turn any man's head: any man in his place would have done and felt the same....

"No, Mother," said Mr. Irwine, replying to her last words; "I can't agree with you there. The common people are not quite so stupid as you imagine. The commonest man, who has his ounce of sense and feeling, is conscious of the difference between a lovely, delicate woman and a coarse one. Even a dog feels a difference in their presence. The man may be no better able than the dog to explain the influence the more refined beauty has on him, but he feels it."

"Bless me, Dauphin, what does an old bachelor like you know about it?"

"Oh, that is one of the matters in which old bachelors are wiser than married men, because they have time for more general contemplation.... But as an example of what I am saying, that pretty Methodist preacher I mentioned just now told me that she had preached to the roughest miners and had never been treated with anything but the utmost respect and kindness by them. The reason is—though she doesn't know it—that there's so much tenderness, refinement and purity about her. Such a woman as that brings with her 'airs from heaven' that the coarsest fellow is not insensible to."

"Here's a delicate bit of womanhood, or girlhood, coming to receive a prize, I suppose," said Mr. Gawaine....

The "bit of womanhood" was our old acquaintance Bessy Cranage, otherwise Chad's Bess, whose large red cheeks and blowsy person had undergone an exaggeration of color, which, if she had happened to be a heavenly body, would have made her sublime. Bessy, I am sorry to say, had taken to her ear-rings again since Dinah's departure, and was otherwise decked out in such small finery as she could muster. Any one who could have looked into Bessy's heart would have seen a striking resemblance between her little hopes and anxieties and Hetty's. The advantage, perhaps, would have been on Bessy's side in the matter of feeling. But then, you see, they were so different outside! You would have been inclined to box Bessy's ears, and you would have longed to kiss Hetty. (pp. 265-66)

Eliot accomplishes a great deal of characterization in this casual dialogue, not only of the three young women under discussion but also of the self-styled connoisseurs. Hetty and Bessy are likened to one another as vain fanciful creatures and are contrasted for the various degrees of their beauties, and Dinah is distinguished as a "delicate," "tender," "pure," "refined," and "pretty" woman. While Mrs. Irwine has pointed to Hetty as an exemplary beauty, her son responds by speaking not of Hetty but of Dinah, conjuring her up as the model Victorian angel with "airs from heaven" and power over man and beast. Irwine's serious catalogue of Dinah's advantages is cut short by Mr. Gawaine, who picks up on the description of Dinah's delicacy and applies the word to Bessy, though Mr. Gawaine, remarking upon the "delicate bit of womanhood," undoubtedly uses "delicate" in its more rarified form: his lighthearted words are meant to convey that Bessy, in her country finery, clearly loves delights. Eliot gives the reader to understand that when it comes to "bits of womanhood," there is delicate and then there is delicate.

More importantly, the judges are seen in their true lights. Mrs. Irwine, "a beautifully aged brunette... erect as a statue of Ceres," shows herself to be a snob; Arthur's better-natured pride and folly are also exposed as he avoids the eyes of the beautiful girl whom he has seduced, and Mr. Irwine emerges as Eliot's touchstone of moral rectitude, offering up an example of truly delicate beauty, the beauty of the absent young Methodist, Dinah Morris.

Significantly, Mrs. Irwine has the dark "face of a fortune teller," and her "hands are laden with pearls, diamonds and torquises." Her snobbishness extends to her own invalid daughter, Anne, for whom she has no patience. Anne's only place in the story is to be a "poor sufferer" who may "once have been pretty," and who finds sympathy only from her brother. We learn again that Reverend Irwine feels singular compassion for feminine frailty.

Interwoven throughout *Adam Bede* is an extended essay on female beauty and the faults of male beholders. In a chapter entitled, "In Which the Story Pauses a Little," Eliot takes time to make her point explicit:

> All honour and reverence to the divine beauty of form! Let us cultivate it to the utmost in men, women, and children.... But let us love that other beauty too, which lies in no secret of proportion, but in the secret of human sympathy. Paint us an angel, if you can, with a floating violet robe, and a face paled by the celestial light; paint us yet oftener a Madonna...; but do not impose on us any aesthetic rules which shall banish from the region of Art those old women scraping carrots.... (p. 177)

As in Brontë's effort to create a "plain Jane," Eliot also seems to subscribe to the aesthetic of the ordinary that is characteristic of middle-class fiction.[9] But Eliot, though she gives us Mary Burge and Mary Garth (a worthy ordinary sinner whom Rembrandt would be pleased to paint), Dinah and Dorothea are the real Marys, as both heroines are likened to Madonnas and angels. Eliot's ideals are not ordinary.

At the party for Arthur, Eliot contrasts two readings of Hetty's face to show again that character is difficult to read when signs of beauty contradict signs of behavior. While the sensible woman is less easily fooled than the sensible man by beauty, Mary is fooled about Adam's thoughts:

> Quiet Mary Burge, who sat near enough to see that Hetty was cross and that Adam's eyes were fixed on her, thought that so sensible a man as Adam must be reflecting on the small value of beauty in a woman whose temper was bad.... And it was true that if Hetty had been plain, she would have looked very ugly and unamiable at that moment, and no one's moral judgment would have been in the least beguiled. But really there was something quite charming in her pettishness.... Adam felt no movement of disapprobation; he only felt a sort of amused pity, as if he had seen a kitten setting up its back. (p. 255)

Adam is continually confused by the mixed messages of Hetty's face: "it was impossible to come to any but fluctuating conclusions about Hetty's feelings. She was like a kitten, and had the same distractingly pretty looks, that meant nothing, for everybody that came near her" (p. 205).

Bewitched as Adam is, he is sensitive to the symptoms of Hetty's vanity and disapproves of her love of finery. As Hetty sticks a flower in her hair, Adam tells her, "Why, Dinah Morris looks very nice, for all she wears such a plain cap and gown. It seems to me as a woman's face doesna want flowers; it's almost like a flower itself. I'm sure yours is" (p. 218). Adam, who had said that Dinah has the face of a lily, associates Dinah and Hetty through the metaphor of the flower. This remark provokes the most broadly comic scene in the novel, in which Hetty puts on Dinah's clothes and frightens Mrs. Poyser (who thinks that she sees a ghost); as a result, jugs drop and break and the children roar with laughter. As the novel moves from comedy and the light trials of farm-life romance to genuine tragedy, Hetty's appearance slowly changes, and her masquerade in Dinah's clothes reverberates. Adam remarks the changes in Hetty's eyes: "something harder, older, less child-like" (p. 337), and the narrator asks us to forgive his misguided pity. The tone is first sarcastic:

> Possibly you think that Adam was not at all sagacious in his interpretation... falling in love with a girl who really had nothing more than her beauty to recommend her.... Of course, I know that as a rule, sensible men fall in love with the most sensible women of their acquaintance, see through all the pretty deceits of coquettish beauty....

But the tone shifts as Eliot makes a virtue of Adam's tendency to see goodness where he sees beauty:

> Beauty has an expression beyond and far above the one woman's soul it clothes.... The noblest nature sees the most of this impersonal expression in beauty, ... and for this reason, the noblest nature is often the most blinded to the character of the woman's soul that beauty clothes. (p. 339)

The corruption in Hetty's soul begins to take a toll on her body, but suffering, and ultimately remorse, improve Hetty's appearance in Eliot's eyes; Hetty takes on that frail ill health that had formerly characterized only the spiritual Dinah. When Hetty faints among strangers in her troubles, losing the rosy bloom that had typified the farm girl, the narrator uses the phrase that she had formerly applied to Dinah: Hetty is said to look "like a beautiful corpse" (p. 360). Describing Hetty's "journey in despair," the narrator watches Hetty become more deathly and more deadly; the kitten becomes a tiger, and then a monster, as the narrator registers the paradox of literature's *femme fatale*, the passionate passionlessness of the Medusa:

> the face was sadly different from that which had smiled at itself in the old speckled glass.... A hard and even fierce look had come in the eyes, though their lashes were as long as ever, and they had all their dark brightness. And the cheek was never dimpled with smiles now. It had the same rounded, pouting, childish prettiness, but with all love and belief in love departed from it—the sadder for its beauty, like the wondrous Medusa-face, with the passionate passionless lips. (p. 367)

The echo of *The Scarlet Letter* is unmistakeable. Hetty, in this unnatural aspect, looks as Hester Prynne had looked when the signs of Love disappear from her face, but Hetty, who is of weaker character than Hester, does determine to die; she twice attempts suicide, but finds herself unequal to the task. Not a victimized *femme mourante*, Hetty becomes the ultimate *femme fatale* and commits the most unnatural crime imaginable in the world of this novel: Hetty is guilty of infanticide.

After her baby's death, however, Hetty more and more takes on the air of the delicate Romantic heroine that had formerly characterized Dinah. The letter which identifies Hetty to Mr. Irwine contains a description that corresponds to Hetty "but that she is said to look very pale and ill." And the narrator, who had spared no sarcasm in her earlier descriptions of Hetty, is now moved to great pity for this "wild woman," this "hunted wounded brute," and emotionally declares, "my heart bleeds for her as I see her" (p. 371).

The identification of the two women is made explicit during the process of trying to identify the silent criminal. Mr. Irwine tells Hetty's betrothed, Adam Bede,

> "She will not confess her name or where she comes from; but I fear, I fear, there can be no doubt it is Hetty. The description of her person corresponds, only that she is said to look very pale and ill. She had a small red-leather pocketbook in her pocket with two names written on it—one at the beginning, 'Hetty Sorrel, Hayslope,' and the other near the end, 'Dinah Morris, Snowfield.' She will not say which is her own name...." (p. 389)

Eliot devotes most of the novel to contrasting Hetty and Dinah only to bring them into an embrace. Dinah, in her unassuming loveliness, acquires power only in the presence of the lost soul, and Hetty, whose vanity and immoderate beauty have proven her destruction, needs Dinah for spiritual survival. At the heart of *Adam Bede* is the quickening of Hetty's weak spirit and the fortification of Dinah's weak body. The two women cling to one another in a scene for the sake of which *Adam Bede* was written. Eliot wrote in a letter that Hetty's confession to Dinah provided the starting point for the novel. It was a moment that had been described to Eliot twenty-five years earlier by her aunt.[10]

In the prison scene, Dinah Morris and Hetty Sorrel face one another and reflect one another's faces; both young aspects are pale and readable, though the meanings they convey are contrary:

> The two pale faces were looking at each other; the one with a wild despair in it, the other full of sad yearning love. Dinah unconsciously opened her arms and stretched them out....
> Hetty kept her eyes fixed on Dinah's face—at first like an animal that gazes, and gazes, and keeps aloof.
> "I'm come to be with you, Hetty—not to leave you—to stay with you—to be your sister to the last."
> Slowly, while Dinah was speaking, Hetty rose, took a step forward, and was clasped in Dinah's arms.

And so the two beauties remain inseparable, as Dinah, a woman of the spirit, works to save the soul of a woman of the flesh. Their need for one another is overwhelming.

The crowd of onlookers who line the streets as the criminal is brought to justice have a double motivation in this case:

> All of Stoniton had heard of Dinah Morris, the young Methodist woman who had brought the obstinate criminal to confess, and there was as much eagerness to see her as to see the wretched Hetty.

> But Dinah was hardly conscious of the multitude. When Hetty had caught sight of the vast crowd in the distance, she had clutched Dinah convulsively....
> And in a low voice, as the cart went slowly along through the midst of the gathering crowd, she poured forth her soul with the wrestling intensity of a last pleading for the creature that clung to her and clutched her as the only visible sign of love and pity. (p. 437)

The voyeuristic crowd sees two women bound up in one another, savior and condemned, both beautiful in their wretched pallor.

Before the guilty verdict was read, the reader had been afforded Adam's unique perspective on the "statue" that Hetty had become:

> Why did they say that she was so changed? In the corpse we love, it is the likeness we see.... There they were—the sweet face and neck, with the dark tendrils of hair...—pale and thin, yes, but like Hetty, and only Hetty. Others thought she looked as if some demon had cast a blighting glance on her....to Adam, this pale, hard-looking culprit was the Hetty who had smiled at him in the garden under the apple-tree boughs—she was that Hetty's corpse....

Describing Adam's tender feelings for his fallen Eve, Eliot's imagery associates the "demon" and the "corpse."[11]

Hetty's weakening into a different model of beauty functions to justify the transformation by which Dinah ceases to be a frail heroine. If Hetty pales to the point that she resembles her own corpse, Dinah, in Adam's presence, becomes so rosy that she bears only a family resemblance to herself: she blushed "a deep rose colour. She looked as if she were only a sister to Dinah" (p. 475). Lily and rose have exchanged places, and Dinah, once a sublime corpse, is vitalized by the realization of her own sexuality. Persuaded that God does not mean for her to remain self-denying, Dinah chooses to leave the poor people of Snowfield in order to marry Adam and live more comfortably herself. When we see Dinah in the novel's epilogue, she has acquired the only attribute of beauty that Mrs. Poyser thought she was wanting, a little extra fleshiness: "We can see the sweet pale face quite well now: it is scarcely altered—only a little fuller, to correspond to her more matronly figure, which still seems light and active enough in the plain black dress" (p. 504). Hetty dies in exile and Dinah marries the man who loved them both. As Fisher writes, "what we see in *Adam Bede* involves a withering of extremes and a surge of new life from the center."[12]

The characterizations of the Poysers' nieces is accomplished through a procedure of doubling: Hetty and Dinah are the two halves of the nineteenth-century's Janus-faced woman, until Eliot produces beauty out of the synthesis of the healthy (but fatal) Medusa and the virtuous (but sickly) angel. Adam Bede, who loves first one woman and then the other, stands in for the reader. The narrator takes every opportunity to ask us to identify with Adam's motivations, feelings, and actions, however misguided they may be.

Admirable as Adam is, we are repeatedly told that he behaves typically of men in general when he misreads female beauty. Through Adam, therefore, Eliot educates the reader.

As a romantic heroine who sacrifices some of her delicacy for health, Dinah is Eliot's response to the Victorian angel. Like Hawthorne, Eliot persuades us that a healthy heroine can be more virtuous than a frail beauty because she has a body strong enough for purposeful labor (an ideology for the middle class). Dinah is no angel, as Lisbeth immediately realized, because she is a "working woman." Hetty's flawed character is epitomized in her dislike of work and fantasies of idleness, though her strength is needed on the farm. Her punishment is fitting: by the novel's end, Hetty cannot stand on her own feet.

In like fashion, Adam and his brother Seth are contrasted in terms of their beauty and characters, in spite of the fact that they are "similarly featured." Adam is, by all accounts, the most handsome man in Hayslope. The reader first encounters the Bede brothers at work: Seth is more frail and less able, more absentminded because more spiritual. While their fellow laborers prefer Seth for his mild temper, Eliot, like the boys' mother, seems to prefer Adam. We are repeatedly offered samples of Adam's industry and Seth's religion. "Spirited" and "spiritual" characters divide throughout this novel, as Adam pursues Hetty, who cannot return his love, and as Seth pursues Dinah, who cannot return *his* love. Lisbeth tells Dinah: "Thee couldstna put up wi' Seth.... He isna cliver enough for thee.... But happen, thee'dst like a husband better as isna the cut o'thysen: the runnin' brook isna athirst for rain. Adam 'ud ha' done for thee." Eliot draws a chiasmus to connect Adam and Dinah. In so doing, she creates the kind of union that the century favored: the spirited, strong, healthy, self-made man, and the spiritual, frail, slight woman. But Eliot modifies these types, correcting Adam's rash temper, and weakening Dinah's spirituality by strengthening her body.

To create such a union, Eliot, unlike Hawthorne, is guilty of some purposeful anachronism. In 1799, the year in which *Adam Bede* is set, a noblewoman like Mrs. Irwine would not have been at all likely to select Hetty as the "perfect beauty." Hetty sports too much peasant "rude health." In 1859, however, the year in which both *Adam Bede* and Darwin's *On the Origin of Species* were published, Hetty was an ideal, and "lovely frailty" as a concept had almost ceased to exist. Eliot and Darwin are writing at a time when commercial competition led people to see man as a creature struggling for survival, the stronger the better. In an era when only wealthy women could afford the luxury of debility, the lower classes were easily, and negatively, marked by "rude health."[13] With urbanization, however, poverty among the city populace bred disease, and the rising middle class could distinguish itself by bodily vigor. No one would have scorned Adam Bede.

In 1799, however, Adam Bede would not have cut an ideal figure; he lacks exquisite aristocratic refinement. His timid brother Seth would have been a more likely hero. Thus, the nostalgic memory of simple healthy peasant life provided the model for middle-class beauty sixty years later. Dinah, who would truly have been a 1799 beauty, a frail woman of powerful faith and angelic spirituality, was of a type which was being regularly challenged, as we have seen, by such representations as those of Amelia Sedley and Isabella Linton. Thus, Adam and Hetty are viable ideals in the time of the novel's appearance, while Dinah is an ideal of the time about which Eliot is writing. When Mrs. Irwine regrets that Hetty's beauty is wasted on the farmers when it is needed among "better families without fortune," she addresses one problem faced by the declining aristocracy as ideals of beauty changed to suit the middle class.

Written for an 1859 readership, Dinah and Adam are the industrious and able-bodied hero and heroine who meet the needs of the changing times. But having transformed both characters by their experiences, Eliot is not entirely satisfied with the compromises that the conventions of realism forced upon her novel. It is for this reason that the narrator interrupts herself to qualify her conclusions. Eliot regrets the loss of certain of those values that would have made Seth and the thinner paler Dinah a satisfying couple in 1799. Forced to choose between healthy sexuality and the freedom of asexual spirituality as criteria for beauty, Eliot—not without some hesitation—chooses health.

Eliot's decision to model Dinah on the delicate heroine and to undermine that tradition by supplying Dinah with a healthy body compels Eliot to impose a conventional morality on her. Mrs. Poyser is thereby proven right on another score. Eliot puts a stop to Dinah's objectionable preaching. Bound by the conventions of realism, Eliot is only able to free the frail woman to go out. Once Dinah is transfigured into a sexual being, a wife and mother, the fiction is compelled to carry her to safety indoors. Thus, it is significant that the novel closes with a discussion of women preaching. Adam, who has been cured of his naive trust in beauty by his experience with Hetty, has the last word on the subject. When Seth argues, "if Dinah had seen as I did, we'd ha' left the Wesleyans and joined a body that 'ud put no bonds on Christian liberty," Adam approves his wife's decision to submit to the new ruling against women preachers:

> "Nay, lad, nay," said Adam, "she was right and thee was wrong. There's no rule so wise but it's a pity for somebody or other. Most o' the women do more harm nor good with their preaching—they've not got Dinah's gift nor her sperrit—and she's seen that, and she thought it right to set th' example o' submitting, for she's not held from other sorts o' teaching. And I agree with her, and approve o' what she did." (p. 506)

Eliot had been very deliberate in her effort to lead the reader into believing that Dinah should be free to preach. By the novel's end, however, Dinah assumes her place beside the hearths of the needy, the only place where her ministrations had ever been effectual anyway. While Eliot tried to create a delicate woman who could both go out and not die to prove her virtue, she ends by concluding that some unspecified harm does indeed come of a woman's going out to preach. Irwine had intimated as much in his first meeting with Dinah. The truly virtuous woman must set the example for those less gifted than she by staying at home herself. Adam catches the author's resignation when he says that there is no rule that is not a pity for somebody.

The characters in *Middlemarch* revise the types in *Adam Bede*. Another "Rose," Rosamund Vincy, like Hetty, is pictured as a pretty and beguiling kitten gazing in her mirror. While Hetty and Rosamund are described through the same images and by the same adjectives, Dorothea rises above Dinah Morris and other women "of middle height." Dorothea tries to be like Dinah, wearing Quaker dress and initially disdainful of ornament, but Eliot does not allow her to remain so. As Eliot increases the stature of her heroine, she also diminishes the stature of her hero. Ladislaw is no Adam Bede. As one who is curiously unconscious of sexual roles, Ladislaw is more like Seth than Adam; neither man is deluded by the charms of such kittens as Rosamund and Hetty and neither has visions of protecting frail beauty.[14] But for the same reasons that Dinah prefers Adam to Seth, readers of *Middlemarch* persist in favoring Lydgate's qualities of male strength and ambition. We forgive the strong man's having been beguiled by the charmer, the Rose. In Eliot's fictions, however, the stronger the heroine in physical terms, the weaker her mate becomes.

As heroines became healthier and stronger, they became less compatible with the ideal of rugged manhood whose principal function was to protect the delicate domestic angel, the frail vessel of virtue. Because we value health, it is difficult to appreciate the ways in which women were, and are, encouraged to foster debility, to suffer for beauty. Medical truths sometimes follow rather than dictate social truths (as in the fluctuation of "ideal" weights, or the prescription of the corset to support weak backs). The "new woman" emerged with force in England, seeking equal rights, in the 1890s, when the surplus population of women—women without partners and without ready means of self-support—found voice. The new woman's fashions and values rebelled against delicacy as a standard of beauty in dress, complexion, physique and manners. She had to go out and she wanted an image of beauty that was healthy and reputable. In the 1890s, establishing health as a minimalist criterion for beauty and virtue became as vexing a problem of characterization as it was of vital interest to a growing class of women.

The Certain Beauty of Health: Gissing's *The Odd Women*

Rhoda Nunn, the heroine of George Gissing's *The Odd Women* (1893) is a new woman. When we first meet her, as a dinner guest of the Madden family, she is described equivocally:

> Tall, thin, eager-looking, but with the promise of bodily vigour... she had a good head, in both senses of the phrase, might or might not develop a certain beauty, but would assuredly put forth the fruits of intellect.[15]

At this early point in the novel, the reader knows neither if Rhoda is heroine nor if she is beautiful. Gissing does, however, establish health as a criterion for beauty. Rhoda may be too tall, too thin, and too eager-looking, but "if the promise of bodily vigour" is fulfilled, she may yet "develop a certain beauty." At the same time, Gissing establishes a potential opposition between beauty and brains. Rhoda has a "good head," both worthy of sculpture and intelligent, but while her intelligence will certainly bear fruit, her potential for beauty may not be realized.

Gissing's novel is a polemic championing the rights of a particular category of new women: "odd women." They are odd both because they are unmatched and because they are unusual. Beauty is a vexing problem of characterization in this novel because conventionally beautiful women may hope to attract husbands, and the reader must be made to appreciate the beauty and value of unconventional types if we are to sympathize with them in their difficult situation. To faithfully represent an odd woman and to also make her appealing to readers, Gissing is left with the problem of creating a heroine who, at one and the same time, is and is not attractive. Gissing's novel struggles, therefore, against the Romance plot.

All but one of the Madden sisters are candidates for a life of loveless misery. The father who might have supported them dies and leaves them without money. When we first see them, they form a happy family. The oldest, Alice, is nineteen: a "plain, shy, gentle-mannered girl, short of stature, and in movement something less than graceful" (p. 1).

> Next in age to Alice came Virginia, a pretty but delicate girl of seventeen. Gertrude, Martha, and Isabel, ranging from fourteen to ten, had no physical charm but that of youthfulness; Isabel surpassed her eldest sister in downright plainness of feature. The youngest, Monica, was a bonny little maiden only just five years old, dark and bright-eyed. (p. 2)

Writing that Virginia is pretty *but* for her delicacy, Gissing invites the reader to assume that delicacy is not a quality of beauty. Monica, the only girl with clear potential for conventional beauty, is carried over from Romantic novels; she provides a counterpoint to her sisters and Rhoda Nunn.

The novel summarily passes over the next decade and a half. Gertrude and Martha sicken and die before the reader comes to know or care about them. By lavishing no sentiment upon these women in death, Gissing undermines the Victorian angel and presents, through silence, the unsentimental anonymity of working-class women's suffering. Alice, who had been a "plain, shy girl," a potential Jane Eyre, is more fully described when Gissing returns to the thirty-five-year-old woman. She

> tended to corpulence, the result of a sedentary life; she had round shoulders and very short legs. Her face would not have been disagreeable but for its spoilt complexion; the homely features, if health had but rounded and coloured them, would have expressed pleasantly enough the gentleness and sincerity of her character. Her cheeks were loose, puffy and permanently of the hue which is produced by cold; her forehead generally had a few pimples; her shapeless chin lost itself in two or three fleshy fissures. (p. 9)

Alice's face would not be disagreeable and her homely features would have pleasantly expressed gentleness and sincerity if only poverty had not deprived her of health and healthy color. Alice's unappealing looks fail to reflect her qualities of character. The description implicitly contrasts Alice as she is with Alice as she might have been. Alice might have been, but is no longer, material for a heroine. Forced upon the reader in the fullness of a description that does not omit mention of pimples, is the message that social injustice creates unhealthy environments for spinsters and that unhealthy women do not earn our sympathy because they are unlovely.

The reader still wonders who will emerge as the novel's heroine. Gissing turns to the next sister. Virginia, who had been a pretty if delicate girl, is described now in a way that eliminates her as a candidate for heroism. Like Alice, Virginia

> had also an unhealthy look, but the poverty, or vitiation, of her blood manifested itself in less unsightly forms. One saw that she had been comely, and from certain points of view her countenance still had a grace, a sweetness, all the more noticeable because of its threatened extinction. For she was rapidly aging; her lax lips grew laxer, with emphasis of a characteristic one would rather not have perceived there; her eyes sank into deeper hollows; wrinkles extended their network; the flesh of her neck wore away. Her tall meagre body did not seem strong enough to hold itself upright. (p. 9)

Virginia, ostensibly prettier than Alice still, is described so graphically in terms of beauty's decay that she is ultimately less appealing to the reader than Alice. Alice is better on the inside than she seems, but Virginia's character, like her appearance, is in a hopeless decline.

Before Gissing returns to the woman with the "good head" whose story will indeed command the reader's attention, Gissing traces the fates of three variously featured women, contrasting the beautiful Monica, the once pretty Virginia, and the downright plain Isabel:

Delicacy: The Flower of Health   189

> Virginia could scarce hope that her faded prettiness, her health damaged by attendance upon an exacting invalid and in profitless study when she ought to have been sleeping, would attract a man in search of a wife. Poor Isabel was so extremely plain. Monica, if her promise were fulfilled would be by far the best looking, as well as the sprightliest, of the family. She must marry.... Her sisters gladdened at the thought.
>
> Isabel was soon worked into illness... the poor hard-featured girl drowned herself in a bath. (pp. 11–12)

Once more Gissing establishes that spirited health is the first requirement of beauty. It is Isabel's illness, compounded with her ugliness, that drives her to drown herself. Virginia, whose loss of health is lamented as the cause of her lost beauty, would find no place in an Austen novel: "Virginia could scarce hope to... attract a man in search of a wife." Upon Monica, the prettiest and sprightliest of the sisters, the others may pin their hopes.

Like the sisters, the reader invests her hopes in Monica, "who so notably surpassed them in beauty" (p. 12), though she "had no aptitude for anything but being a pretty, cheerful, engaging girl" (p. 11). As beauty encodes meaning, Monica's dainty beauty signifies spirituality, but Gissing makes the same point about our experience of conventions that Eliot makes with respect to both Hetty Sorrel and Rosamund Vincy:

> Monica's face was a recognized type of prettiness; a pure oval; from the smooth forehead to the dimpled little chin all its lines were soft and graceful. Her lack of colour, by heightening the effect of black eyebrows and darkly lustrous eyes, gave her at present a more spiritual cast than her character justified; but a thoughtful firmness was native to her lips, and no possibility of smirk or simper lurked in her attractive features. The slim figure was well fitted in a costume of pale blue, cheap but becoming; a modest little hat rested on her black hair; her gloves and her sunshade completed the dainty picture. (p. 26)

Monica marries the first man she attracts, but as she is like Hetty Sorrel ("a woman with nothing but her beauty to recommend her"), Monica's marriage and subsequent acts of indelicacy become the source of her own and her sisters' greater unhappiness.

While Monica is pretty as a picture, Rhoda retains in adulthood the "interesting," if less beautiful, qualities that might have intrigued a sculptor. Rhoda's promise of bodily vigor has been fulfilled, but Gissing does not insist upon her beauty. Instead, when the reader next meets Rhoda, Gissing emphasizes the masculine qualities of her beauty and character, redeeming her features by suggesting that femininity lurks beneath them. Although hers is not the kind of beauty that the delicate sex would admire, a "male connoisseur" might be able to see through to (or release) Rhoda's subtle feminine forces. Moreover, while Alice's appearance has ceased to reflect her character and while Monica's appearance falsely reflects her character, Rhoda's face is legible:

190   *Delicacy: The Flower of Health*

> She had a clear though pale skin, a vigorous frame, a brisk movement—all the signs of a fairly good health. Whether or not she could be called a comely woman might have furnished matter for male discussion; the prevailing voice of her own sex would have denied her charm of feature. At first view the countenance seemed masculine, its expression somewhat aggressive—eyes shrewdly observant and lips consciously impregnable. But the connoisseur delayed his verdict. It was a face that invited, that compelled, study. Self-confidence, intellectual keenness, a bright humour, frank courage, were traits legible enough; and when the lips parted to show their warmth, their fullness, when the eyelids dropped a little in meditation, one became aware of a suggestiveness directed not solely to the intellect, of something like an unfamiliar sexual type, remote indeed from voluptuousness, but hinting a possibility of subtle feminine forces that might be released by circumstance. (p. 20)

If Monica's is "a recognized type of prettiness," Rhoda is described by contrast to Monica as having the potential beauty of "an unfamiliar sexual type." As such, she is like Hester Prynne during the loveless years when she suppressed her tenderness; like Hester, Rhoda has "subtle feminine forces that might be released by circumstance."

Without apparent beauty, Rhoda does not imagine that her vocation is to attract a husband. Like Dinah Morris and Hester Prynne, Rhoda therefore devotes herself to good works. But Rhoda chooses no traditional feminine charity; she embraces the task of establishing a place in the labor force for "odd women." As her sexless appearance, her "consciously impregnable lips," as well as her name suggest, Rhoda is a kind of modern nun, a sister.

Gissing's novel continues to strain against the romance plot as he works to develop Rhoda into a fit heroine for his story. Everard Barfoot is introduced as the necessary "connoisseur" of beauty who will evaluate Rhoda's character for the reader. Devilishly handsome himself, Everard devotes his energies to assessing female charms. When Rhoda meets him, she is dressed in black, "without ornament . . . likening herself to the suggestion of her name, by the excessive plainness with which she arranged her hair." Everard considers Rhoda's face and determines for us that it has indeed developed a certain beauty, a "certain beauty" which is sufficiently uncertain that its possessor remains ungoverned by it. Like Dinah Morris, Rhoda's unconsciousness of having feminine beauty makes it possible for her to go out as men do without concern for delicacy:

> It was doubtful whether she regarded any subject as improper for discussion between mature and serious people. Part of the cause for this, perhaps, was her calm consciousness that she had not a beautiful face. No, it was not beautiful; yet even at first meeting it did not repel him. Studying her features, he saw how fine was their expression. The prominent forehead, with its little unevenness that meant brains; the straight eyebrows, strongly marked, with deep vertical furrows generally drawn between them; the chest-nut brown eyes, with long lashes; the high-bridged nose, thin and delicate; the intellectual lips, a protrusion of the lower one, though very slight, marking itself when he caught her in profile; the big strong chin; the shapely neck—why, after all, it was a kind of beauty. The head might have been sculptured with fine effect. And she had a well-built frame. (pp. 101-2)

Gissing forces Rhoda through the hoops of the romance plot in order that she may acquire the status of a heroine in the reader's eyes by acquiring beauty in the eyes of a lover. For Everard,

> Rhoda was beginning to class with women who are attractive both physically and mentally. Strange how her face had altered in his perception since their first meeting. He smiled now when he beheld it—smiled as a man does when his senses are pleasantly affected. He was getting to know it so well, to be prepared for its constant changes, to watch for certain movements of brows or lips when he said certain things. (p. 142)

When it comes to the matter of Rhoda's beauty, Everard is becoming the sort of man of whom Eliot would approve: "Beauty in the academic sense he no longer demanded; enough that her face spoke eloquently, that the limbs were vigorous. Let beauty perish if it cannot ally itself with mind" (p. 176).

Everard seems to admire Rhoda for her strength of character, but when Rhoda and Everard quarrel, the hero is ready to give up his lover rather than meet her demands. He becomes a strangely detached spectator; it seems almost as if he cannot enter with any force into the novel's milieu of women. Inasmuch as we have learned to see Rhoda through Everard's eyes, however, Rhoda's place as heroine depends upon his vision. While Gissing means to suggest that Everard is unworthy of Rhoda, it is Rhoda who comes up the loser. As Rhoda begins to realize that something is skewed in Everard's expectations of her, Gissing robs her of beauty:

> At a stage in life when she had sternly reconciled herself never to know a man's love, this love had sought her with a passionate persistency of which even a beautiful young girl might feel proud. She had no beauty; she was loved for her mind, her very self. But must not Everard's conception of her have suffered? In winning her had he obtained the woman of his desire? (p. 296)

Rhoda and Everard do not marry, and the reader is left to wonder if Rhoda's strength and intelligence have not proved her undoing.

Everard's cousin, Miss Barfoot, represents an alternative ideal. Miss Barfoot is depicted as an unmarried woman sufficiently pretty and wealthy that one would mistake her for a married woman:

> She was handsome, and her carriage occasionally betrayed a consciousness of the fact. According to circumstances, she bore herself as a lady of aristocratic tastes, as a genial woman of the world, or as a fervid prophetess of female emancipation, and each character was supported with a spontaneity, a good-natured confidence, which inspired liking and respect. A brilliant complexion and eyes that sparkled with habitual cheerfulness gave her the benefit of the doubt when her age was in question; her style of dress, gracefully ornate, would have led a stranger to presume her a wedded lady of some distinction. (p. 50)

While Gissing would thereby invest an odd woman with a clear beauty that corresponds to her strength of person and character, he undercuts his own message because the most noble, virtuous and upright of his odd women is also the most beautiful, wealthy and marriageable. The reader is left to wonder why she is not married. The suggestion of a long passed and unhappy romance with Everard is weak and unconvincing.

The Odd Women ends poignantly with the surviving Madden sisters and Rhoda at the side of Monica's deathbed. Monica's infant daughter functions both as promise and warning, as Monica's fate reverses that of Hetty Sorrel; Monica does not kill, but is killed by, her child. Rhoda holds the baby murmuring "poor little child," but it is Rhoda and Monica who are the "poor girls," victims of failed romances.

In Gissing's novel, the reader is asked to use health as a criterion for assessing female beauty. At the same time, the health and intelligence that Gissing means to use as proof of his heroine's unusual beauty make her fit for the market place but unfit for "happily ever after." Rather than persuade the reader that Rhoda is a worthy model of beauty and behavior, Gissing betrays his conviction that marriage to a worthy man would indeed have been the happiest ending for Rhoda if only there had been such a man in the novel, if only there were enough such men in England.

The private desires of Gissing's readers and the models of beauty they would emulate derive, as Gissing clearly assumes, from the Victorian romance, complete with its angel heroine at the hearth. Although Gissing presupposes the romance and kills the romantic heroine, he is unable to solve the narrative problem that he poses for himself. From the biblical Dinah and the Apocrypha's Susanna through Hester Prynne and Dinah Morris, the text enforces an act of renunciation upon its heroine that the narrative validates when and if it recovers the heroine's beauty and virtue. Gissing's novel, strains against, but is limited by, romance's conventions of character and plot. Gissing does produce a heroine of renunciation, but as Gissing is unwilling to validate this self-effacement, he throws his heroine, rather than the romance plot, into doubt. In the attempt to represent faithfully the lower strata of the class structure, Gissing's narrative achieves some open-endedness, but finally defeats itself by defeating its principal characters.

In *The Political Unconscious,* Fredric Jameson describes the problem in other terms. Alerting us first to Gissing's reliance upon Dickensian and melodramatic paradigms in his early fiction, Jameson sees the richer and more sophisticated solutions of Gissing's mature novels as developments from his first fictional experiments.

> The quest for an income is therefore never commodity desire in Gissing, but something like a predesire, a precondition for desiring which has been systematically devalued in advance, so that neither success... nor failure casts the melodramatic shadows of high naturalism. In his later work the inevitability of frustration has been secretly bracketed and suspended by the essential pettiness and worthlessness of what could never be any more than a means to an end in the first place: the indispensible prerequisite to a self-realization

that never comes, fatally condemning all these characters to preoccupations and anxieties which are distractions from and substitutes for some true and ideal (private) life. The dialectic of desire is thus in Gissing something like the negation of a negation. Since his characters never reach the point of being in a position to desire, it is as though the whole system of success and failure has been undermined from the outset by a narrative strategy which may thus be read as something like the final form of *ressentiment* itself.... it is now generalized into global refusal of commodity desire itself.[16]

Repeatedly insisting on the importance of health, however, Gissing indicates that his sense of frustration is not complete. Although the "global refusal of commodity desire itself" is expressed on one level as a refusal to imagine beauty (a singularly valuable commodity for women), Gissing qualifies his "global refusal" with the unique positive assertion that health is a criterion for value, a requisite quality of the beauty that he cannot describe. Like Everard Barfoot, Gissing does not demand "beauty in the academic sense," but his persistent concern for his heroine's health through the novel's conclusion is a placement of value, a commitment that contrasts with the novel's many refusals, to health as a measure of worth.

The Delicacy of Health: Hardy's *Jude the Obscure*

Jameson argues that Gissing saves his fictions from the melodrama of high naturalism by devaluing the quest for an income ("the precondition for desiring"). But by leaving the reader with health as a criterion of value, Gissing anticipates, rather than supercedes, the melodrama of high naturalism. Hardy's *Jude the Obsure* (1895), a naturalist fiction that concerns itself explicitly with social Darwinism, depicts no beauty that is not destructive. Rhoda Nunn's good health leaves open the possibility that she will succeed, if not in love, then at least in the market place. As her success would be at no one's expense, and as her virtue is intact, there is an optimistic strain here. For Hardy, the health that is a precondition for one man's survival means overcoming someone weaker. Inasmuch as scarcity prevails in the competitive world of *Jude,* each value (that which is worth having or being) necessitates someone else's deprivation.

Like Gissing, Hardy describes his beautiful characters with reference to the tradition of delicate heroes and heroines. Unlike Gissing's characters, however, Hardy's characters are exemplary beauties. In his delicate hero and heroine, Hardy demonstrates that the value of such beauty is illusory; it ensures that its possessor will be defeated by those who are less frail. At the same time, in *Jude* health is, at best, of ambiguous value: indelicacy, flagrant violation of social rules, strength and bodily vigor guarantee survival but are the character traits of those who live selfishly. The beauty of Hardy's delicate characters (delicate in all of the word's senses) is inevitably undermined such that the reader is left admiring no one in an unqualified way.

Hardy's refusal to identify value is evident in the mixed responses of readers to the heroines of *Jude*. Is Arabella or Sue the truer beauty? D. H. Lawrence, in his *Study of Thomas Hardy,* assumes that she is Arabella, but Lawrence's own bias favors the sexual over spiritual.[17] Most readers favor Sue, sensing that the novel prefers the spiritual beauty in spite of the narrator's protestations to the contrary.

Susanna Bridehead, as her name suggests, first appears to Jude as the embodiment of chaste spirituality. Like the Apocrypha's Susanna, Sue has the kind of beauty that tempts men to lust, though she refuses to indulge them in their "gross" desires. At the same time, Sue insists that she is like Dinah Morris, that she may flaunt conventions of delicacy because she is that type of woman whom no man would molest. Sue's behavior ultimately contradicts the essence of her character: she hints that withholding herself from the "young undergraduate" who loved her contributed to his death; she marries Phillotson and will not share his bed; she runs away from her husband and takes refuge with her cousin Jude, with whom she has children out of wedlock.

Jude finds in Sue a tender beauty, the "Spirit of Intellectual Beauty." At the same time, she is a *femme fatale;* she does bring death. Following a description of Sue, Albert J. Guerard writes: "So summarized, Sue Bridehead may seem a monstrously unpleasant person.... But she is, as it happens, one of Hardy's most appealing heroines." Although Sue suffers the worst torments and losses in the course of the novel, Guerard observes that "she is not alive as a victim."[18] Sue seems a far cry from Rhoda Nunn, but as Robert Gittings writes, she was "seized on by critics of the 1890s as representing the 'New Woman' of that era, restless intellectual and in some ways unfeminine."[19] While the large-bodied new woman like Rhoda is represented as masculine, the slight unhealthy new woman is unfeminine because intellectual. Gittings argues that Sue is a heroine more typical of the 1860s, and certainly then her beauty, if not her ideas, had been fashionable.

Hardy presents Arabella Donn as Sue's antithesis in beauty and character. While Sue looks the part of an angel, Arabella looks the part of an animal. Sue seems to be all spirit, a sexual neurotic; Arabella seems to be all flesh, a creature of sexuality. The hero, first beguiled by Arabella, comes to despise those impulses in himself that draw him towards her. Although Jude does not respect the values that Arabella embodies and reveres those values that Sue embodies, the narrative casts Jude in the role of an inept evaluator. Insofar as we sympathize with Jude, we believe in Sue's beauty. Insofar as we comprehend the lessons that bring Jude to destruction, we are asked to appreciate Arabella's qualities.

One hesitates to call Jude, who is named for the patron saint of lost causes, a hero. He lacks the masculine strength that, by the 1890s, had become an important criterion for male beauty. Jude is a failure, who begins as a slight boy with his nose in his books. A kind of Heathcliff, a poor, orphaned, unwanted boy who is forced to labor in order to make his way in the world, Jude might have become successful in his businesses and exemplified the self-made individual. But labor is merely Jude's stepping-stone to loftier spiritual goals, and like Seth Bede, Jude is easily distracted from his work because he is busy contemplating matters of the mind. In the Darwinian universe of Jude, the fundamental opposition is between strength and weakness, and Jude is pathetically weak.

Urged by his schoolmaster Phillotson "to be kind to the animals and the birds, and read all you can,"[20] Jude is taught the outdated lessons of Christianity which assign priority to spiritual over physical survival. When Jude is hired as a scarecrow by Mr. Troutham (whose name, part fish and part pig, carries the novel's central symbols of fertility and sexuality), Jude feeds the "birdies," the spirits. Jude is not much of a man; he won't tread on the earth worms, "could scarcely bear to see the trees cut down," and is pained by "the perception that what was good for God's birds was bad for God's gardeners." Instead of beating away the birds, Jude earns a thrashing for himself. In the novel's first pages, the narrator predicts Jude's future on the basis of his character and anticipates his story: "this weakness of character, as it may be called, suggested that he was the sort of man who was born to ache a good deal before the fall of the curtain on his unnecessary life should signify that all was well with him again."

Phillotson's failure also predicts Jude's failure as the older man overvalues labors of the mind, studies dead languages, prefers a university city populated with "ghosts" to rural England, and comes to nothing. Jude is offered the opportunity to forego a life like that of Phillotson. The opportunity presents itself while he walks, distracted, on the country roads and is recalled from his dreams when "the characteristic part of a barrow-pig" is thrown in his face. Jude is awakened to,

> a fine dark-eyed girl, not exactly handsome, but capable of passing as such at a little distance, despite some coarseness of skin and fibre. She had a round and prominent bosom, full lips, perfect teeth, and the rich complexion of a Cochin hen's egg. She was a complete and substantial female animal—no more, no less....

Passably beautiful turns out to be beautiful enough. Arabella is a mistress of artifice and deception. After trapping Jude into marriage, Arabella chills her husband on their wedding night: "A long tail of hair, which Arabella wore twisted up in an enormous knob at the back of her head, was deliberately unfastened, stroked out, and hung upon the looking glass...." Arabella's dimples as well as her hair are manufactured. A mere mockery of country simplicity and modesty, Arabella practices her arts in order to capture a man who will ensure her an income. The narrator does not regard these machinations as unnatural, however, arguing that artifice is part of humanity's animal nature. Arabella is one of those women who have "an instinct towards artificiality in their very blood, and became adepts in counterfeiting at the first glimpse of it" (p. 50).

Disillusioned as Jude is, it is Arabella who leaves him when she discovers that he is inept as a provider. Always at his books, Jude has too much heart to properly bleed the pig they must kill to live on, and in a symbolic gesture Arabella tosses Jude's books to the floor, her hands greasy with lard. Jude then fixes his love on an angelic bodiless ideal of womanhood, "the photograph of a pretty girlish face, in a broad hat with radiating folds under the brim like the rays of a halo" (p. 63). In spite of the narrator's cynicism, the reader recognizes homage to the spiritual ideal when Jude kisses the pasteboard and places it on his mantlepiece so that Sue's image "seemed to look down and preside over his tea." Mocking Jude's preference for art over life, when Jude lays eyes on the living woman, the narrator comments that Jude finds her "suspiciously like the original in the portrait" (p. 72).

Jude lacks the courage to approach his idol, and the narrator uses strongly critical words to impress upon the reader how excessive Jude's sentimentality is: "she remained more or less an ideal character, about whose form he began to weave curious and fantastic daydreams" (p. 73). Jude's perceptions are shaped by art and distorted by his romantic tendencies, so that when Sue is first described, Hardy makes a point of saying that he reports not what Sue's beauty does convey, but what it seems to convey to Jude: "She looked right into his face with liquid, untranslatable eyes, that combined, or seemed to him to combine, keenness with tenderness, and mystery with both...." Jude is powerfully affected: "His closeness to her was so suggestive that he trembled and turned his face away with a shy instinct...."

Jude is so unaggressive that he leaves Sue to retain her place in his fantasies. While the narrator shares Jude's private contemplation upon Sue's "general mould and build" with the reader, we are told once more that that which Jude admires may not be everyone's idea of beauty:

> He could perceive that though she was a country-girl at bottom, a latter girlhood of some years in London, and a womanhood here, had taken all rawness out of her.... He remembered that she was not a large figure, that she was light and slight, of the type dubbed elegant...that was about all he had seen. There was nothing statuesque in her; all was nervous motion. She was mobile, living, yet a painter might not have called her handsome or beautiful. But the much that she was surprised him. (pp. 73–74)

Hardy parodies Jude's Romantic image of Sue: "So she would be to him a kindly star, an elevating power; a companion in Anglican worship, a tender friend" (p. 74); Jude's vision does not carry the force of reality: "To be sure she was an ideality to him still" (p. 80). Without having exchanged a word with his ideality, Jude extrapolates her character from her beauty, and the narrator of this anti-romance both deflates Jude's perceptions of Sue and suggests that however much Jude persuades himself of the purity of his intentions, he is self-deceiving. As a human animal, Jude may be convinced that his longing is spiritual, but his attraction to Sue is nothing if not sexual:

> "I can see she is exceptionally bright; and it is partly a wish for intellectual sympathy, and a craving for lovingkindness in my solitude." Thus he went on adoring her, fearing to realize that it was human perversity. For whatever Sue's virtues, talents or ecclesiastical situation, it was certain that those items were not at all the cause of his affection for her. (p. 80)

Sue's self-image also derives from the tradition of the delicate heroine. Sue feels the same freedom that Dinah Morris and Rhoda Nunn feel to go out among men and participate in traditionally male occupations. While Sue Bridehead insists that she too is an androgynous type of beauty, the story of her life—man after man painfully yearning for her—belies her own testimony. Sue tells Jude:

> "My life has been entirely shaped by what people call a peculiarity in me. I have no fear of men, as such, nor of their books. I have mixed with them—one or two of them particularly—almost as one of their own sex. I mean I have not felt about them as most women are taught to feel—to be on their guard against attacks on their virtue; for no average man—no man short of sensual savage—will molest a woman by day or night, at home or abroad, unless she invites him. Until she says with a look 'Come on' he is always afraid to, and if you never say it, or look it, he never comes." (p. 118)

In this speech, Susanna Bridehead, articulating a prevalent belief of the 1890s that has survived until today, convicts the Apocrypha's Susanna of seducing the elders. Jude has mixed feelings. Although he is pleased that Sue "remained as she began," he "felt much depressed; she seemed to get further and further away from him with her strange ways and curious unconsciousness of gender" (p. 119).

In his portrait of Sue, Hardy also valorizes and undermines the figure of the tomboy, whose popularity is attested in the success of such novels as Mrs. Southworth's *The Hidden Hand*.[21] The peculiar appeal of the tomboy in literature and fashion is that this look afforded women certain freedoms without threatening the grown man's prerogatives; she was a miniature man, a boy, an asexual creature like the Angel, sturdy and brave, but cute and childlike. This ideal was a compromise between delicacy and health.

The widow who attends Jude's aunt paints an image of Sue in her youth that prefigures the grown woman, a little girl who is at once the most delicate beauty and the most indelicate in her behavior. Among the schoolchildren, Sue had been "the smallest of them all, 'in her little white frock and shoes, and pink sash.'" At the same time,

"She was not exactly a tomboy, but she could do things that only boys do, as a rule. I've seen her hit in and steer down the long slide on yonder pond, with her little curls blowing.... All boys except herself, and then they'd cheer her, and then she'd say, 'Don't be saucy, boys,' and suddenly run indoors. They'd try to coax her out again. But 'a wouldn't come."

Jude's aunt remembers Sue's behavior with less tolerance for her coquettish impertinence and tells a story from her own memories: "Why, one day she was walking into the pond with her shoes and stockings off, and her petticoats pulled above her knees, afore I could cry out for shame, she said: 'Move on, aunty! This is no sight for modest eyes.'"

Sue repeats this gesture in adulthood, fleeing from her boarding school to Jude by wading through the river. The school authorities cannot conceive of how she escaped given the barrier of water; a young lady would not be so indelicate. By soaking his heroine, however, Hardy takes the opportunity to impress us with another kind of delicacy. Frail as she is, Sue risks illness. After Jude strengthens his delicate friend with some revivifying brandy (Phillotson later revives the shaken Sue with the same remedy), and puts her in his dry clothes, Sue falls to sleep. Jude sees not a brazen woman, but a tender beauty:

> He softly went nearer to her and observed that a warm flush now rose to her hitherto blue cheeks, and felt that her hanging hand was no longer cold. Then he stood with his back to the fire regarding her, and saw in her almost a divinity. (p. 116)

When Sue awakens, this "divinity" speaks like a traitor to the tradition that associates woman's beauty with religious purity. She tells Jude that it is absurd to treat the sexual female in the "Song of Solomon" as an emblem of the Church. Jude's reply is not to the point: "You know you are the fairest among women to me, come to that" (pp. 122–23). In so saying, Jude associates Sue with the Rose of Sharon and the lily of the valley. Sue falls back to sleep and the narrator conjures up an alternative image of her: "She slept on inside his great coat, looking warm as a new bun and boyish as a Ganymedes."

The novel contrasts these varieties of beauty with that of Arabella, and the two women compete for Jude. When Sue wants to know how she compares to his wife, she is more interested in Arabella's beauty than in her character: "I suppose she—your wife—is a very pretty woman, even if she's wicked." Jude replies, "She's pretty enough, as far as that goes"; Sue persists: "Prettier than I am, no doubt!" But Jude does not comfort Sue because he finds no basis for comparison: "You are not in the least alike."

The two women pull Jude apart. All the while that Sue remains at a distance, Arabella retains her hold on Jude. Jude's excessive adoration of Sue makes him ashamed of his desires and behavior with respect to Arabella. While Arabella calls to Jude's body, Sue embodies Jude's intellectual and spiritual ambitions. Sue, like those ambitions, is a fashioning of Jude's imagination. In the presence of Sue's airy beauty, Jude therefore finds the subject of his relations with Arabella too indelicate for Sue's ears:

> Looking at his loved one as she appeared to him now, in his tender thought the sweetest and most disinterested comrade that he had ever had, living largely in vivid imaginings, so ethereal a creature that her spirit could be seen trembling through her limbs, he felt heartily ashamed of his earthiness in spending the hours he had spent in Arabella's company. There was something rude and immoral in thrusting these recent facts of his life upon the mind of one who, to him, was so uncarnate as to seem at times impossible as a human wife to any average man.

From these thoughts Jude's eye turns to comparing Sue's body with that of Arabella: "He regarded the delicate lines of her profile, and the small tight apple-like convexities of her bodice, so different from Arabella's amplitudes. Though she knew that he was looking at her, she did not turn to him" (p. 150).

When Sue flees from Phillotson, in another ironic twist, Jude and Sue are at the very hotel and in the very room where he spent the night with Arabella. (Jude is doomed to visit each place with each woman.) Jude's intention to protect Sue from knowing about that encounter is foiled by a gossipy barmaid. She tells Sue that she remembers Jude's having been there with a lady "that wasn't you by no manner of means," but "a handsome, full-figured woman." How, he asks her, does she expect him to stay away from Arabella when she won't allow him to have her? Jude's argument is defeated by Sue's tears.

> "Never mind!" he said. "So that I am near you, I am comparatively happy. It is more than this earthy wretch called Me deserves—you spirit, you disembodied creature, you dear, sweet, tantalizing phantom—hardly flesh at all; so that when I put my arms round you I almost expect them to pass through you as through air! Forgive me for being gross, as you call it!"

Sue's self-image derives from Romantic poetry, and she begs Jude to recite lines from Shelley's "Epipsychidion" as if they referred to her. Jude agrees that the words about a disembodied spirit, "too gentle to be human/ Veiling beneath that radiant form of woman" apply to Sue. Sue appears to delight in denying her body (pp. 195-96).

When Arabella reappears, however, Sue thinks better of her decision to withhold herself. For a space of time over which the novel passes relatively quickly, Jude and Sue are happy in spite of their poverty and migratory existence. The events of the novel then make a mockery of their romantic love. In a grotesque and symbolic gesture, Arabella's son kills Sue's children, leaving a note that shows that he has something of his mother in him, a note that shows his understanding of scarcity. The child writes, "Done because we are too menny." Grieved, Sue embraces a perverse Christianity and sacrifices herself to Phillotson, abandoning Jude to Arabella and ultimately to death. Although Sue shudders in disgust, Phillotson "gloomily considered her thin and fragile form a moment longer as she crouched before him in her nightclothes," and then takes the "complaisant spirit" into his arms. The widow Edlin comments, "weddings be funerals 'a b'lieve nowadays."

Only Arabella, robust and alive, survives the ordeals of the novel. Jude dies alone, reciting a lament from *Job,* while his wife enjoys herself at the games. Mrs. Edlin and Arabella attend to the body of the thirty-year-old hero and the widow remarks, "How beautiful he is!" Arabella agrees that "he's a 'andsome corpse," but she is unsentimental, sturdy and unmoved. The tone of her final remarks is triumphant. Mrs. Edlin says that Sue has come to look "tired and miserable... years and years older," and Arabella speaks as one who has been victorious in the competition with Sue: "She's never found peace since she left his arms, and never will again till she's as he is now!"

Hardy's vision is a tragic one. His delicate heroine cannot survive. Sue's beauty derives from her frailty but the values and spirituality she embodies bring on her misery and her lover's and children's deaths. The healthy large woman, self-conscious of her charms, an unabashed Hetty Sorrel, an animal in a Darwinian world, emerges triumphant, but to the reader, Arabella has no real beauty. She is beautiful only at a distance, coarse and unrefined at close inspection. Delicacy of body, an educated mind and refinement of manner—the traits that once marked an aristocrat—do not survive beside the crude healthy farmgirl who has not had the instincts of survival processed out of her by books and religion. The quality of health that becomes so valuable in *Adam Bede* and *The Odd Women* proves to be an ugly necessity in Hardy's world of gross sexuality. *Jude* at once celebrates that sexuality and laments the loss of spiritual beauty and romantic love. The novel admires, mocks, and defeats its hero and heroine. In Arabella, the reader finds "a delicate" in the antique interpretation of the term, a lover of the sensual, but in *Jude,* gross sensuality, bound up as it is with survival, does not have the positive connotations of beauty.

8

Conclusions: Beauty beyond Description

> *Those who find ugly meanings in beautiful things are corrupt without being charming. This is a fault.*
> *Those who find beautiful meanings in beautiful things are the cultivated. For these there is hope.*
> *They are the elect to whom beautiful things means only Beauty....*
>
> *The nineteenth-century dislike of Realism is the rage of Caliban seeing its own face in a glass.*
> *The nineteenth-century dislike of Romanticism is the rage of Caliban not seeing his own face in a glass.*
>
> Oscar Wilde, preface to *The Picture of Dorian Gray*

Basing myself on the assumption that the human subject is constituted, at least in part, in the language of physical description, I have tried to expose the character of beauty, to discover how characters in nineteenth-century fiction are made worthy of appreciation and what cultural values are challenged or reenforced as a text works to establish its own standard of loveliness. Characterization and beauty are each large subjects; each has received much scholarly and critical attention. We have looked at the place where beauty and characterization meet. My hope is that this work responds to a need that Gérard Genette articulates in "Principles of Pure Criticism." Genette writes that [from analyses of Emile Benveniste],

> and from those that could follow from them, extending the example, the very least that emerges is that narrative, even in its most elementary forms, and even from the purely grammatical point of view, delineates a very particular use of language, akin to what Valéry called, in relation to poetry "language within language," and any study of the great works of narrative (epic, novel, etc.) ought to at least take this fact into account, just as any study of the great works of poetry ought to begin by considering what was recently called the "structure of poetic language." The same goes, of course, for all the other forms of literary

expression and, to take an example, it is rather strange that no one has even thought (to my knowledge at least) to study for itself, in the system of its specific resourses and constraints, so fundamental a type of discourse as description. This kind of study, which has still hardly begun, and then only on the fringes of the official framework of literary teaching, might be dubbed with the very old and somewhat discredited name of rhetoric.[1]

Beauty—defiant and transcendent—scorns any medium that dares try to pin it down. The power of the beautiful image derives more from its suggestiveness than from its actualization. A study of ugliness or of the grotesque might therefore have better met the need that Genette expresses. One could catalogue the tropes, examine the metaphors, list the adjectives, scrutinize the syntactic patterns, focus on the repertory of words that writers use in the genre of the novel to describe people and things, correlate appearance with significance, and thereby systematically determine the resources and constraints of this lexical system.

Beauty is, however, another matter, because as the commonplace has it: "beauty defies description." While both the ugly and the ordinary are imaginable and describable, the beautiful is described by means of another rhetoric, a rhetoric that works to undermine description itself through its insistence that words do no justice to that which is unimaginably, indescribably lovely. By limiting my subject to subjects of beauty, I tried, therefore, less to produce a rhetoric of description, than to investigate the rhetoric which conveys beauty's ineffability. Any rhetoric, as Genette suggests, will have an element of predictability, but "the system of its specific resources and constraints" is, in this case, peculiarly self-effacing. Texts recognize varieties of ugliness and ordinariness and help the reader to visualize things and people by focusing on details. Beauty is recognizable as such only insofar as it is both unique and like other things beautiful. Thus, descriptions of the beautiful are conspiratorial; they imply shared standards and suggest that the example at hand surpasses the standard. Beauty, like language, is a sign system; we learn its rules without lessons because beauty is a matter of cultural consensus, and its meanings are agreed upon by silent social consent.

My central premise has been that although we speak of beauty as if it were natural and universal, we know that beauty is culturally defined. Our culture teaches us what to value for its beauty and how to express that appreciation appropriately. In a consumer society, beauty is a valuable commodity, and, from the museum to the modelling agency, beauty commands a high price. By asking what constitutes beauty in our heroes and heroines, we ask about the values assigned to that beauty and into what we, as readers, are making an investment.

Elaborate physical description is a convention of realism. As characters are invested with materiality and acquire physical traits through detailed descriptions commensurate with descriptions of social and natural settings, literature reflects, and creates, the cultural consensus that assigns meaning to types of beauty. Descriptions of beauty rely upon our acceptance of conventional ideals; conventions are, by definition, repeated, and that which is repeated often enough takes on the appearance of truth. Because the cultural consensus on that which is worthy of appreciation is reached in silence, beauty seems self-evident. As a result, the meanings assigned to beauty are concealed by the fact of beauty itself.

Textual reproduction results in family resemblance; physical traits, features of appearance are inherited by a character from his or her literary ancestors: Daphnis, Rebecca, Joseph, the Madonna, Alice in Wonderland, Clarissa Harlowe, or any of the other figures who exemplify a type of beauty in our shared cultural imagination. Because each such figure is associated with characteristic qualities, every figure of beauty resonates with meaning and is value-laden.[2] At the same time, the values encoded in a type of beauty are not static. The beautiful type is not a stereotype;[3] each type of beauty changes in appearance and meaning as he or she is reintroduced into new literary and social contexts. In fiction, characters are never identical to, but merely share a family resemblance with, their literary ancestors. Out of the array of available images from the past, features are selected and recombined to form new and original configurations. It is in these variations that readers can discover their own society's reassessment of time-honored convictions about beauty and its attendant truths.

Novelistic presentations of character are characters *re*presented; every literary production relies upon the reader's familiarity with any number of literary conventions.[4] Conventions of beauty are no different. In the effort to make their reproductions original, writers subtly modify traditional images of beauty and the values they embody. The relationship between tradition and innovation is significant because each modification is an adaptation, a literary response to changes in the social, political, and economic orders.

Tradition and innovation both contribute to a text's effort to establish its own symbol of beauty and fix that emblem to a value standard. In so doing—in the act of describing the hero and heroine—writers may at once reenforce and challenge prevailing ideals. Because they inevitably depend upon the ideals of the past, descriptions of beauty are conservative. Innovation mitigates against the conservative pull of the tradition by modifying conventions. As social artifacts, literary texts contain the tensions of the age in which they are produced, recording values in transition. In great works of art, these tensions are well concealed because the more well-crafted the art the more coherent new constructs seem.

In *Art and Illusion,* E. H. Gombrich compares the evolution of conventions in the realist tradition of painting to biological evolution.[5] I have been pursuing a similar analogy here. By reproducing the familiar, texts are able to naturalize beauty's mutations, enforcing the reader's conviction that the values of a particular time and place are transcendent, timeless, and universal. In the most well-crafted texts, modifications are seamlessly woven into traditional images of beauty, and thus, beauty seems to be, but is not, innocent. In the process of biological selection, those random mutations that best adapt the species to changed environments become standard (naturalized); the writer, who operates more like a sentient Creator than a haphazard Nature, adopts a procedure of textual selection that is not random but deliberate, motivated by an interest in influencing or accommodating the social environment.

At any historical moment more than one ideal of beauty is available to image makers. Models featured in contemporary advertisements illustrate this procedure. By their example models of beauty dictate a range of options to society concerning everything from the height of heels and width of skirts to the roundness of arms and redness of cheeks. At the same time, a society idealizes those figures who embody qualities that it chooses—for various underlying social and political reasons—to admire and emulate. The Ivory Girl of soap ads does more than reflect a population's preference for clear skin, sneakers, and ponytails; her style of beauty reflects the premium that our culture places on youth and vigor. And this beauty suggests a series of characteristic qualities and personal virtues. She is like Pygmalion's Galatea, an ivory girl too; both are chaste and pure. These adjectives are then displaced to define the product itself: "pure as Ivory Soap." Here we see the adjective's power to point inside and outside simultaneously: an unblemished face becomes identified with an unblemished, unspotted, "virginal" character. Thus, modern images still associate feminine goodness with inexperience even if they do not seem to do so; the arbitrary association of female virginity and morality finds reenforcement in the linguistic construction of the Ivory Girl's beauty.

Competing with the Ivory Girl is the smartly clad businesswoman or the seductive ingénue. Both of these latter types wear clothes that restrict their movements; their skirts are tighter, heels higher, and makeup thicker than that of the sportswoman. A model in a black low-cut evening dress who wears a diamond tiara invites us to consider her characteristic qualities of quiet poise, sophistication, and elegance; her height suggests power, but her immobilizing attire suggests the virtue of keeping her powers in check, and her tastefully worn jewelry implies that the rewards for such behavior are nothing less than money and love. When we see these models in popular culture, we recognize, consciously or unconsciously, that they are drawn from the high tradition of oil painting and literature.[6] Thus, our most valued traditions sanction and validate the messages of advertisers. While a range of beauties and attendant virtues are available for us to admire out of the repertoire of the past, a larger range is excluded. In America today no model figure is likely to be as fleshy as Rubens' model or as fragile as Little Nell. Moreover, criteria for beauty are peculiar to particular cultures. In certain contexts, for example, freckles connote cuteness, but in India, a woman is disfigured by freckles much as a Parisian woman's beauty would be compromised by pimples.

Within a culture's own boundaries, the exemplary character of beauty may be situated in relation to other characters, both historical and contemporary. Insofar as he or she is modelled on one traditional type rather than on another, the values embodied in that type are preferred over those embodied in other types. Insofar as this character departs even from the traditional image on which he or she is based, the values embodied in the chosen ideal are modified. Thus, each character of beauty registers a double protest: one against a contemporary set of values and another against a traditional set of values.

These protests show up in the uses of descriptive language. When a writer effectively creates in language an original image of beauty—an image that departs from some conventional ideal—the connotations of descriptive vocabulary change. For example, if smallness and pallor were once criteria of a kind of beauty that implied a pious character, the heroine who is tall and rosy challenges the value of piety itself. Because adjectives are shifting and can refer to the inside and outside simultaneously, a text can subtly exploit these associations: a dull complexion becomes a dull personality; the small woman may be characterized as having a small mind. And if the time was when a heroine's beauty had little to do with worldly intelligence, the idealization of larger women introduced vitality as a potential quality of beauty. Larger heroines had larger minds and more expansive spirits; rosy heroines were livelier. Thus, the word vitality acquired positive connotations in the nineteenth century, just as it became possible to imagine that a woman could be too pious, *too* religiously narrowminded. Not surprisingly, vitality (physical strength and a healthier complexion) rose in value during the period in history when industrialization depended upon robust individuals outside of the lower classes. Similarly, piety lost some of its absolute value when society was not only rethinking its religious convictions in the light of such intellectual challenges as Darwinism but was also feeling the need to free the rising bourgeoisie from some of the doctrinal strictures that interfered with comfortable entry into a commercial and competitive marketplace.

I do not mean to suggest that the tall heroine won a victory over the small heroine in the nineteenth century. There have always been heroines both tall and small. But, rather, I am suggesting that when a writer such as George Eliot places Dorothea Brooke in the tradition of the statuesque woman, she adds associations to height which accommodate a set of nineteenth-century values.

At the same time, she devalues those physical attributes that are associated with character traits for which she does not care. A fictional situation informed by a more traditional or religious vision may respond by depicting a delicate heroine whose beauty is associated with delicate sensibilities. The fragile body becomes identified with the sensitive soul, implying at the same time that the values associated with the large-scale beauty are accompanied by insensitivity, coarseness, and the absence of those domestic virtues that women should uphold. While a culture never settles upon one ideal, the range of options does change. The process by which ideals of beauty change is governed by the same dialectic that can be made to account for changes in history and language.

I imagine a grid in which any beautiful character can be located. The grid itself is made of words, the connotations of which change over time. It has a synchronic and diachronic axis, and its coordinates are pairs of binary oppositions—conceptual categories that have been historically understood in relation to one another. Oppositions determine where meaning will be discovered because meaning is produced out of the perception of difference.[7] Language organizes the world and creates the spaces for meanings in its codification of antonyms. Thus we learn where to look for meaning as we learn language; we organize our ideas through an inherited system of opposing categories: good, evil; active, passive; present, absent; wild, tame; male, female and so on. But these categories are not fixed, and the connotations of words do not remain stable. In any period of history, the dominant discourse challenges inherited dichotomies as new power relationships challenge inherited wisdom.

In Romantic poetry and criticism, in the discussions of Rousseauism, Evangelicalism, and Darwinism, and in later critical commentary, the qualities associated with art are confused with those of nature, those of birth with those of breeding, and those of strength with those of delicacy. Social, economic, and political phenomena generated changes in discourse which, in turn, influenced the revaluation of beauty. These relationships are multi-levelled and constantly dynamic. I hope that this survey has suggested a complex interaction among language, history, and ideology in the production of beauty, and in so doing has suggested as well the range of idealized types that prevailed in English literature and culture in the nineteenth century.

All of the oppositions that are treated here may be understood as variations on the nature-culture dichotomy, and hence, as variations on each other. At base, a hero's or heroine's beauty is distinguished from the false beauty (value) that everywhere surrounds it because it is a product of nature rather than of culture. These dichotomies are all unstable, however, precisely because the definitions of nature and culture themselves are always changing. That which was once considered a truth of nature comes to be regarded as a product of culture, and a culture's most well-established values/practices come to be regarded as natural. My own investigation, therefore, derives its organization from the very polarities which it labors to problematize: with scrutiny, the beauty of nature becomes indistinguishable from that of art, that of birth from that of breeding, that of strength from that of delicacy. Yet to write about beauty without pretending that this structure exists would be to leave beauty as it wants to be left: alone and shrouded in the privilege of silence.

I have chosen three oppositions (art and nature, birth and breeding, delicacy and strength) not because they are the only or the most fundamental. They are, however, oppositions that nineteenth-century England worried over out loud, and these musings had consequences for the representation of beauty in literature and the treatment of people in nonfictional worlds. These oppositions reflect peculiarly middle-class worries, concerns of the novel-reading population. It is also clear that there is something arbitrary and interchangeable about the literary texts selected to illustrate my arguments. For example, Dorothea Brooke is chosen to demonstrate how, through a revaluation of charm, the beauty of art resolves itself into that of nature; she might as well have been used to demonstrate how, through a revaluation of grace, the beauty of breeding resolves itself into that of birth, or how, through a revaluation of health, the beauty of delicacy resolves itself into strength.

In any linguistic system, each opposition depends intimately on the others that surround it, and the value of one side of an axis is determined by the value assigned to that which opposes it. For example, if, in one context, nature is divine and good, then art is a human corruption and evil; if, however, nature is associated with the wild and beastly, then art will have the positive connotations of human achievement. If femininity is associated with artfulness, then masculinity is likely to have connotations of naturalness and honesty, but if masculinity is associated with brutishness, then femininity can be valorized either as refined domesticity or angelic purity. The words that a writer chooses when he or she describes a character's beauty resonate because they are enriched by an entire system of associations. As a result, though my choice of oppositions is not inevitable, each opposition is an entrance into this more complex system. Once a description is selected to begin the archaeology of a particular opposition, that choice points to particular antecedent texts.

Beauty is everywhere. Each figure of beauty has a history, and any number of characters may share a common ancestry. Thus, if we locate ourselves somewhere between art and nature (or any other opposition) and choose a character (here, Dorothea Brooke), then we have positioned ourselves on a spot in the terrain from which we can begin an excavation. Rich as the ground is with artifacts, ten feet over to the right or left would have served as well. Once the digging starts, however, it would be inefficient to move. But because the ground is so full with images of beauty portrayed in terms of art and nature, it is easy to miss evidence on the way down. I turn up Walter Scott's Rebecca; my reader may certainly turn up other characters and characteristics of beauty which contributed as well to Eliot's construction of her heroine. Just as the evolutionary model is borrowed from Gombrich, the archaeological model is borrowed from Michel Foucault.[8] These models give the illusion of a controlled system.[9]

Punning can cause oppositions to collapse. "Charm," "grace," and "delicacy" all name qualities of beauty that were, in the nineteenth century, ambiguous themselves: a charming woman could be dangerous in her allure; a graceful man could be effeminate; a delicate man or woman could be too weak to be beautiful. These ambiguities derive from the fact that art and nature, birth and breeding, and strength and delicacy need not be presented as contrasting categories. When we play with these words, we can speak of art's nature, of the time when good breeding was itself born, such that the quality of grace could thereafter be learned rather than inherited, and of the flowering of health as a value, such that if delicacy had once been a strength of beauty (and character) it became associated with illness. And illness itself, particularly as embodied in the frail woman, was once beautiful, though it is no longer so. Beauty and health are often described in what I have called a "code of flowers." Pretty as a flower—delicate, fragile—described a Romantic ideal of bodily frailty. Literary transformations generated the "bloom" of youth which championed a quite different style of beauty, one characterized principally by health and vigor. Qualities like charm, grace, and bloom mediate between, challenge, and reconcile competing authorities of beauty.

These changing definitions of beauty accomplish the work of subtly naturalizing social change. As art came to have a nature, the virtuous middle-class woman could safely transform her body into a work of art by wearing charms; when good breeding was born, one need not have been born into the aristocracy to be graced with "natural grace"; and as delicacy became reassociated with undesirable qualities of weakness, the languishing lady and the frail aristocratic man lost their appeal. In the nineteenth century, an array of middle-class beauties were invented. At the same time, literature, art, and advertisements—relying for their models on the literary and artistic tradition—easily made it seem as if these ideals of beauty always existed; current ideals became articulations of truth itself.

While physical description can be even-handed—merely calling forth images of men and women—the role of desire in the production of beauty objectifies the female body while it enforces male subjectivity. The female figure of beauty is a repository of values and a desired possession (an object of art), while the male beauty is the actor, the person we desire to be. In *Ways of Seeing,* John Berger describes how women see themselves and the world through female and male eyes;[10] when women function as readers of fictional worlds, they are also required to read both as women and as men. The gaze of desire, directed at the female character of beauty, is a phenomenon so rooted in our lived experience that we call forth one kind of response when we meet a beautiful heroine in literature and another kind of response when we meet a hero. Thus, in the reestablishment of oppositions, ideal femininity always ends up finally on the side of negativity in relation to the positive attributes of masculinity.

In an essay written for *Vogue* magazine, Susan Sontag regrets the fact that we no longer think like the Greeks for whom beauty was a "virtue: a kind of excellence"; unlike us, the Greeks did not pretend to distinguish between internal and external beauty.[11] Sontag explains that beauty itself enjoys a mixed reputation because it has since become associated with female essence. "Handsome," she argues, is a word that conveys the masculine refusal of female beauty. "In men," she writes, "good looks is a whole, something taken in at a glance." When the gaze is directed at women, however, each part comes under inspection, and the whole is inevitably found lacking. The power of female beauty in literature is as different from the power of male heroism as it is in life. Sontag writes:

> To be sure, beauty is a form of power. And deservedly so. What is lamentable is that it is the only form of power that women are encouraged to seek. This power is always conceived in relation to men; it is not the power to do but the power to attract. It is a power that negates itself. For this power is not one that can be chosen freely—at least, not by women—or renounced without social censure.

Finally, she writes that "one could hardly ask for more important evidence of the dangers of considering persons as split between what is 'inside' and what is 'outside' than that interminable half-comic half-tragic tale, the oppression of women."

How a culture identifies sexual difference governs how its literature will represent ideal figures of masculinity and femininity. As possible figures—bodies and metaphors—for the hero and heroine change, they change in relation to one another: what we value in men determines what we expect of women and vice versa. Because the distinction between the masculine and the feminine underlies our perceptions of beauty, changing ideals of beauty threaten prevailing definitions of gender roles. For example, I looked at how finery empowered heroines in ancient texts and how the commenting tradition changed the connotations of that beauty which had been associated with ornament. Artistry became artfulness, and charm became a mixed blessing. In the nineteenth century, the dark jewelled heroine once again challenged the fair heroine who had exemplified passive duty.

Efforts to recover the woman of art were undercut by the revised ideal of masculinity. With the premium that came to be placed on marketplace ruthlessness, the delicate male aristocrat lost his usefulness as a model figure deserving emulation. Brute strength became a new value, and heroes grew darker and stronger. Machismo was born at the same historical moment that Rousseau valorized man in a state of nature, a time when European society developed its fascination with wild children. But as the ideal man ceased to be the embodiment of well-bred delicacy, the ideal woman was required to be increasingly domestic. Male sexual energy was expressed in the Byronic ideal, but women had to redouble their efforts to preserve the Victorian values of well-restrained energy and Christian virtue that were threatened by the demands of the new economy. The differences between male and female habits of dress and demeanor reflect the shifting definitions of sex roles.

The fragile woman was likely to survive as a reigning ideal only as long as the upper and middle classes could afford to suffer women as burdens. As the middle class rose to power and began to economize on its energies, female pallor came to signify dullness of personality. As this Romantic ideal died, the culture's preoccupation with spirituality faded as well.

Scientific and critical knowledge contributed to definitions of both the sexes and beauty. For example, Wordsworth's and Coleridge's discussions of the relative merits of art and nature in the production of poetry had implications for the value of "ornament" as a feature of personal beauty; the history of the wild man in philosophical and mythical discourses contributed to the phenomenon of Byronism; revisions in scientific knowledge had implications for fashion. Acting in good faith, doctors first prescribed the corset (when the restricted figure was regarded as beautiful), and then later condemned it as a health hazard just as fashion and literature began to have nostalgic feelings for the uncorseted beauty of the peasant girl. By this time, factory conditions had made the lower-class woman weak; accordingly, middle-class women came to regard a healthy body as beautiful. Another of the resurrected ideals of beauty born of these redefinitions of masculinity and femininity was the tomboy: this diminutive female man, like the "new woman," was deprived of masculine freedoms by the imposition of a new set of dichotomies.

In the magic of Arden, Shakespeare's Rosalind can enjoy the freedom to be courted by Orlando while she masquerades as Ganymedes. She is beautiful as a woman and as a boy. Jude admires Sue when, dressed in his clothes, she looks like Ganymedes. The tomboy derives from a tradition that permits women to attractively play the part of young boys, but men who act as women are never represented as desirable. Beauty is a matter of convention, and as issues of beauty are enmeshed in issues of gender, changes in these conventions redefine the sexes.

Beast in the Beauty: *The Picture of Dorian Gray*

By the century's end, Oscar Wilde would produce the classic statement on the relationships between beauty and ugliness and between body and soul in *The Picture of Dorian Gray*. My chapter's epigraph from the preface to the novel suggests that Wilde regarded his story as a critique of Victorian categories of value, particularly as those values found expression in aesthetic criteria. The Victorian novel located beauty in the beast, valorizing male animalism. Female kittens, like Hetty Sorrel and Rosamund Vincy, might be beastly but were no less pretty for that. *Dorian Gray* finds beastliness in male beauty, but the corruption of the man is made legible in the changing character of his portrait rather than on his own face.

Dorian Gray, who, like Joseph, is defined by his beauty, is feminized by the text as Joseph had been feminized by commentary. Insofar as beauty signifies desirability on the one hand and corruption, idleness, and absence of intellect on the other, beauty is decidedly feminine. This hero's cruelty and sexual aggressiveness save him from effeminacy, though his greatest admirers are men. When Lord Henry compares Dorian's portrait with the artist Basil's appearance, the reader discovers the tradition from which Dorian Gray derives:

> "I really can't see any resemblance between you, with your rugged strong face and your coal black hair, and this young Adonis, who looks as if he was made out of ivory and rose-leaves.... he is a Narcissus.... But beauty, real beauty, ends where intellectual expression begins."[12]

Basil, the sensitive artist, looks like Heathcliff or Rochester, and Dorian looks like a youthful Greek God.

While Lord Henry corrupts Dorian by telling him that "the search for beauty is the real secret of life," he will expound a prevalent understanding of women that ironically and powerfully applies to Dorian himself. Henry explains that

> "no woman is a genius. Women are a decorative sex. They have nothing to say, but they say it charmingly. Women represent the triumph of matter over mind, just as men represent the triumph of mind over morals....
> I find that ultimately there are two kinds of women, the plain and the coloured. The plain women are very useful. If you want to gain a reputation for respectability, you have merely to take them down to supper. The other women are very charming. They commit one mistake, however. They paint in order to try to look young. Our grandmothers painted in order to talk brilliantly. *Rouge* and *esprit* used to go together. That is all over now." (p. 52)

Figure 24. Carlo Pellegrini (Ape), *Portrait of Oscar Wilde*
(*Vanity Fair*, 1884)
London, British Museum.
(© *Snark; Photo courtesy Art Resource*)

Henry here sums up the history of the "woman of art," as I have dubbed her, and Dorian responds appropriately with a description of his beloved who ostensibly derives from the opposite code. Ironically, she is an actress. In a textual gesture of reversal and displacement, the dreadful orchestra leader of the production is a young Hebrew at a cracked piano, "a fat Jew manager, with fat jewelled hands." Sibyl Vane (vain) is defined by contrast. She is "hardly seventeen... with a flower-like face, a small Greek head with plaited coils of dark brown hair, eyes that were violet wells of passion, lips that were like the petals of a rose." After Dorian completes this description of delicacy in the code of flowers, he goes on to number her many roles, among them Rosalind, "disguised as a pretty boy." He says, "I have seen her in every age and every costume" (pp. 55–56).

Wilde's narrator continues to write with some distance on nineteenth-century ideas about beauty. Having dissolved the opposition of art and nature, he moves on to dissolve animalism and spiritualism:

> Soul and body, body and soul—how mysterious they were! There was animalism in the soul, and the body had its moments of spirituality.... The separation of spirit from matter was a mystery and the union of spirit with matter was a mystery also. (p. 64)

Dorian's criminality consists in his destruction of women, as Wilde evokes them in the century's various codes. *Adam Bede* finds specific revision in *Dorian Gray,* as Wilde demonstrates that Hetty would have been doomed to misery even had Arthur not gone through with the seduction. Dorian tells Henry that he spared a woman "wonderfully like Sibyl Vane":

> "Hetty was not one of our own class of course. She was simply a girl in a village.... We were to have gone away together this morning at dawn. Suddenly I determined to leave her as flower-like as I had found her.... Hetty's heart is not broken. Of course she cried, and all that. But there is no disgrace upon her. She can live, like Perdita, in her garden of mint and marigold."

Lord Henry cynically reminds us of the time when women of Hetty's beauty were princesses. He finishes Dorian's tale by adding that Hetty will "weep over a faithless Florizel.... I suppose she will be married some day to a rough carter or a grinning ploughman. Well, the fact of having met you, and loved you will teach her to despise her husband, and she will be wretched" (p. 233).

Finally, having come to loathe his own beauty, Dorian Gray shatters the mirror, stabs the picture, and dies heroically, "withered, wrinkled, and loathsome of visage."

Arrowy Nose in Short Tense Flight, Eyes like Drenched Violets: Woolf's *Orlando*

Dorian Gray saw Sibyl Vane as Rosalind, "a pretty boy," and as a beauty "in every age and every costume." Such universal and androgynous beauty mimics Wilde's general challenge to realism in this novel. Virginia Woolf also uses the varieties of beauty to play with the possibility of androgynous figures. She chooses not the figure of Rosalind, but Rosalind's beloved, Orlando.

In *Orlando* Woolf too creates a beauty "in every age and costume," male and female, sexually ambiguous. But as Woolf moves beyond the conventions of realist fiction, she moves beyond the rhetoric of realist description as well. We all remember that Orlando is beautiful, desired, and has good legs. But Woolf's only full description of Orlando is parodic. His/her features contradict one another, s/he sports "an arrowy nose in short tense flight," and his eyes are admittedly "like drenched violets." This description suggests that Woolf recognizes that realistic descriptions of beauty are not remembered in the specificity of their details, but rather are encoded with other meanings:

> Thus, those who like symbols, and have a turn for the deciphering of them, might observe that though the shapely legs, the handsome body and the well-set shoulders were decorated with tints of heraldic lights, Orlando's face, as he threw the window open, was lit solely by the sun itself. A more candid, sullen face it would be impossible to find. Happy the mother who bears, happier still the biographer who records the life of such a one! Never need she vex herself, nor he invoke the help of novelist or poet. From deed to deed, from glory to glory, from office to office he must go, his scribe following after, till they reach whatever seat it may be that is the height of their desire. Orlando, to look at, was cut out precisely for some such career. The red of his cheeks was covered with peach down; the down on the lips was only a little thicker than the down on the cheeks. The lips themselves were short and slightly drawn back over teeth of an exquisite whiteness. Nothing disturbed the arrowy nose in its short, tense flight; the hair was dark, the ears small, and fitted closely to the head. But alas, that these catalogues of youthful beauty cannot end without mentioning the forehead and eyes. Alas, that people are seldom born devoid of all three; for directly we glance at Orlando standing by the window, we must admit that he had eyes like drenched violets, so large that the water seemed to have brimmed in them and widened them; and a brow like the swelling of a marble dome pressed between two medallions which were his temples. Directly do we glance at eyes and forehead, thus do we rhapsodise. Directly do we glance at eyes and forehead, we have to admit a thousand disagreeables which it is the aim of every good biographer to ignore.[13]

Beauty is asserted with confidence. Though eyes and forehead admit of a thousand disagreeables, though traditional metaphors are more than made strange by exaggeration, the reader will forget about the drenched violets. Thus, Orlando's beauty (as Fielding had said of Joseph Andrews) is beyond simile, beyond description. The sexual play too, here, as in *Dorian Gray,* directs our attention to beauty as an encoder of sexuality. Orlando's beauty expresses Woolf's fascination with, love, and ambivalence towards the beauty and wealth of her friend, Vita Sackville-West.

From the relatively spare and generalized physical descriptions of much of earlier narrative literature,[14] over the course of the Victorian Age, physical description in realist fiction became increasingly detailed and deliberate. As writers became sensitive to and suspicious of the conventions of realism, the rhetoric of description also moved beyond realism. Joyce's *Ulysses* is not a brief book, but Molly Bloom is briefly described. Such description as we are given (Spanish eyes, curvy body) is sufficiently encoded with meaning as to satisfy the reader.

Twentieth-century realist fictions that respond to the classic Victorian novel, Jean Rhys' *Wide Sargasso Sea* or John Fowles' *The French Lieutenant's Woman,* for example, challenge Victorian values in their portraits of beauty. Rhys gives us a magnificently beautiful Bertha Mason, née Antoinette Cosway, who, by her very being, betrays the Byronic hero's love for plain Janes as a victimization of her sex. Valuing plain English Jane means oppressing she who is independent and not English. Fowles portrays a beautiful Victorian servant; in idealizing a maid who was not born a princess (which seems perfectly natural today), Fowles moves beyond the Victorian democratization of beauty.

Realism developed descriptions; post-modernism often omits them entirely. Theories of realism have accordingly come to analyze the rhetoric of description. Gombrich finds that beauty's expression is "blank." Roland Barthes calls beauty "empty." But such notions precede realism as well. In anticipation of the realist novel, Laurence Sterne's *Tristram Shandy* often anticipates post-modern conventions of form and structure. Aware that beauty is both meaningful and of subjective value, Sterne makes a peculiarly post-modern gesture when he rejects describing Uncle Toby's beloved and leaves a blank page in his text instead. The reader is offered the following invitation to draw:

> Never did thy eyes behold, or thy concupiscence covet anything in this world more concupiscible than widow Wadman.... To conceive this right,—call for pen and ink—here's paper ready to your hand.—Sit down, Sir, paint her to your own mind—as like your mistress as you can—as unlike your wife as your conscience will let you—it's all one to me—please but your own fancy in it.[15]

Here we please our own fancy, but our fancy has been created in the first place by such images of beauty as we have been taught to admire. Descriptions of beauty, because they conflate competing ideals, are particularly powerful as these ideals are unrealizable. Wilde and Woolf acknowledge as much in their descriptions of Dorian Gray and Orlando. Signs that realistic characterization has given way: beauty beyond belief; beauty beyond description.

Notes

Chapter 1

1. Philippe Hamon observes in "Rhetorical Status of the Descriptive," *Yale French Studies* (no. 61, 1981), 17: "It seems that description begins to reach a 'normal' literary status at the turning point of the eighteenth and nineteenth centuries. This is certainly somewhat delayed, with the importance taken by description in certain different areas of knowledge born in the eighteenth century (natural history, for example)." It seems to me that the practical importance of description in the natural sciences slowly and increasingly led the culture at large to use and value detail as the scientific enterprise became more prestigious.

    Jeanne Fahnestock writes in "The Heroine of Irregular Features: Physiognomy and Conventions of Heroine Description," *Victorian Studies* (Spring, 1981), 325: "In 1816 Scott's brief vague description was typical, and in 1865, Yonge's fuller description was common. In fifty years the heroine came out of the shadows and into focus." While Fahnestock demonstrates that the description of heroines becomes increasingly elaborate over the course of the century, she does not trace the implications of her discovery for characterization. Nor does she notice that the very irregularity of the heroine's features became a feature of her beauty. It will be important to my argument that all heroes and heroines develop into standards of beauty even when such figures are called "plain." A novelist's intention to render a heroine plain will be subverted by the decision to position that character as the heroine.

2. Charles Child Walcutt, in *Man's Changing Mask: Modes and Methods of Characterization in Fiction* (Minneapolis: Univ. of Minnesota Press, 1966), p. 3, writes: "First, I try to show that characterization is a function or product of action (I use this term in the Aristotelian sense of plot and everything that goes with it).... [C]haracterization depends upon action." Walcutt expresses the prevailing view since Aristotle, through Henry James' famous discussion of character and incident, and until the present. See for example, Ian Watt's influential discussion in *The Rise of the Novel: Studies in Defoe, Richardson and Fielding* (London: Chatto and Windus, 1957), pp. 18–27, and on description, p. 30. Like Walcutt, Arnold Weinstein in *Fictions of the Self: 1550–1800* (Princeton: Princeton Univ. Press, 1981) also regards characterizations as prescriptions for living in the world. Most studies of characterization do not focus on techniques of characterizing but are instead character studies; see for example, John Bayley, *The Characters of Love: A Study in the Literature of Personality* (London: Chatto and Windus, 1968); Leo Bersani, *A Future for Astyanax: Character and Desire in Literature* (Boston: Little, Brown, and Co., 1969); William Gass, *Fiction and the Figures of Life* (New York: Knopf, 1970); W. J. Harvey, *Character and the Novel* (London: Chatto and Windus, 1965).

Notes for Chapter 1

While Tzvetan Todorov does focus on characterization in his discussion of "Narrative Men" in *The Poetics of Prose* (Ithaca: Cornell Univ. Press, 1977), pp. 66–67, he distinguishes between characterization by transitive or intransitive action. Still it is verbs and action that are thought to characterize.

The notion of mimesis classically illustrated in Erich Auerbach's *Mimesis: The Representation of Reality in Western Literature* (Princeton Univ. Press, 1953) has been qualified by, among others, Roland Barthes, who writes instead of "the-effect-of-the-real" ("L'Effet de réel," *Communications,* No. 11, 1968). Whether the implication here is that language is nonreferential or that reality cannot really be represented, Barthes' alternative still suggests that description, which produces this "effect," is not integral to narrative meaning; it still suspends the story.

Frederic Jameson in "The Realist Floor-Plan," in *On Signs,* ed. Marshall Blonsky (Baltimore: The Johns Hopkins Univ. Press, 1985), pp. 373–83, makes much of the importance of descriptions of architectural space in realist literature.

3. I think most notably of Svetlana Alpers, *The Art of Describing: Dutch Art in the Seventeenth Century* (Chicago: Univ. of Chicago Press, 1983), which calls the low critical appraisal of descriptive art into question. Jeffrey Kittay introduces the issue of *Yale French Studies* subtitled "Towards a Theory of Description" (no. 61, 1981) by remarking upon the relative critical neglect of description: "We still operate very much within the Aristotelian concept of action, which suggests that description be viewed as secondary, and purely functional, or merely decorative." While the volume addresses the problem of this neglect, with the exception of Michael Riffaterre, the contributors do not analyze description in fiction as a peculiar vehicle for meaning. Riffaterre's essay "Descriptive Imagery," 107–25, concludes: "...the primary function of description is not to make the reader see something.... Description, like all literary discourse, is a verbal detour so contrived that the reader understands something else than the object ostensibly represented.... Its primary purpose is not to offer a representation, but to dictate an interpretation."

4. Norman Bryson, *Word and Image: French Painting of the Ancien Régime* (New York: Cambridge Univ. Press, 1981), p.8.

5. From Plato and Aristotle through Augustine, Shaftesbury, Kant, Schelling, Hegel, Schopenhauer, Nietzsche, and Heidegger, the study of beauty as "aesthetics" has been in the domain of philosophy. Albert Hofstadter and Richard Kuhns, *Philosophies of Art and Beauty: Selected Readings in Aesthetics from Plato to Heidegger* (Chicago: Univ. of Chicago Press, 1964) collects a selection of these materials. Among the philosophers, Hegel has written about physiognomy as well as aesthetics. I have benefited from Alasdair MacIntyre, "Hegel on Faces and Skulls," in *Hegel: A Collection of Critical Essays* (New York: Doubleday, 1972), pp. 219–36.

Beauty has been studied from other perspectives in other disciplines. Anthropologists have compared ideas of beauty across cultures. A portion of Mary Douglas' work, in particular, usefully attends to the symbols connected with the human body.

6. On page 152, Shah introduces "The Algonquin Cinderella" as follows:

> At the end of the last century, Mrs. M. R. Cox collected three hundred years of Cinderella-type stories. They totalled 345 versions: and she added that they could be multiplied. This may be one of the most enduring of all tales—a variety has been noted (by Arthur Waley) in a Chinese book of the ninth century A.D. My father published a Vietnamese variant, claimed to be thousands of years old, in 1960. It has also been observed that the story of Aslaug, daughter of Siegfried and Brunhild in the Volsung Saga, is a striking parallel. Apart from the now popular version of Perrault, published in

the 18th century, there are other intriguing and excellent tales featuring the pathetic Cinders.... But for sheer beauty and delight, this American version, found among the Algonquin Indians, seems hard to beat.

Chapter 2

1. For examples of how analyses of physical description often maintain that authors were conscientiously applying the principles of physiognomy see, Fahnestock, "The Heroine of Irregular Features," and John Graham, *The Development of the Use of Physiognomy in the Novel* (Diss. Johns Hopkins, 1960). See also Hugh Witemeyer, *George Eliot and the Visual Arts* (New Haven: Yale Univ. Press, 1979), who curiously treats Eliot both as a physiognomist and as a novelist who is too sophisticated a judge of character to resort to so naive a strategy of representation.

2. Francis Bacon, "Of Beauty," in *Bacon's Essays* (New York: C. S. Francis and Co., 1857), p. 406.

3. Thomas Aquinas, *Thomas Aquinas Dictionary*, ed. Morris Stockhammer (New York: Philosophical Library, 1965), p. 18.

4. E. H. Gombrich, *Art and Illusion: A Study in the Psychology of Pictorial Representation* (Princeton: Princeton Univ. Press, 1960, 1969), pp. 340-41.

5. Gombrich, *Art and Illusion*, pp. 351-52.

6. E. H. Gombrich, *The Story of Art* (New York: Phaidon, 1950), p. 311. Hals was poor in his lifetime because his work seemed unrealistic; he would be wealthy today because he helped to shape our perception of the real.

7. E. H. Gombrich, "The Mask and the Face: The Perception of Physiognomic Likeness in Life and in Art," in *Art, Perception and Reality* (Baltimore: Johns Hopkins Univ. Press, 1972), p. 22.

8. Gombrich, "The Mask and the Face," p. 21.

9. John Berger, *Ways of Seeing* (New York: Penguin, 1977), p. 61.

10. Roland Barthes, *S/Z: An Essay*, trans. Richard Miller (New York: Hill and Wang, 1974), p. 67.

11. E. M. Forster, *Aspects of the Novel* (New York: Harcourt, Brace, Jovanovich, 1927), p. 43.

12. Berger, *Ways of Seeing*, pp. 45 ff, provides a useful discussion of how women are conditioned to see even themselves from the outside and from a male point of view that corresponds to the dominant cultural perspective. He convincingly describes the female's double seeing self, half of which is always male. For discussion of the related issue of woman's writing voice, see Judith Kegan Gardiner, "On Female Identity and Writing by Women," in *Writing and Sexual Difference*, ed. Elizabeth Abel (Chicago: Univ. of Chicago Press, 1982), pp. 177-91; and the introductory discussion to Sandra M. Gilbert and Susan Gubar, *The Madwoman in the Attic: The Woman Writer and the Nineteenth-Century Literary Imagination* (New Haven: Yale Univ. Press, 1979). See also Laura Mulvey, "Visual Pleasure and Narrative Cinema," *Screen*, Vol. XVI, no. 3 (1975), 6-18, and Kaja Silverman's discussion of "suture and sexual difference" in *The Subject of Semiotics* (New York: Oxford Univ. Press, 1983), pp. 222ff.

13. For a developed history, theory, and application of the principle of *ut pictura poesis*, see Wendy Steiner, *The Colors of Rhetoric: Relations between Modern Painting and Literature* (Chicago: Chicago Univ. Press, 1982). On pictorialism in Eliot's fiction see Witemeyer, *George Eliot and the Visual Arts*.
14. Roland Barthes, *S/Z*, pp. 33-34.
15. Gombrich, *Art and Illusion*, "The Beholder's Share," pp. 181-287.
16. On the triangle of desire, see Tony Tanner, *Adultery in the Novel: Contract and Transgression* (Baltimore: The Johns Hopkins Univ. Press, 1979).

Chapter 3

The first of my chapter's epigraphs is from *Pensées*, trans. William Finlayson Trotter (1904), Dutton; rpt. Monroe C. Beardsley, ed. *The European Philosophers from Descartes to Nietzsche* (New York: Random House, 1960), p. 105.

The second of the epigraphs: *Gottfried Wilhelm Leibniz: Philosophical Papers and Letters*, trans. Leroy E. Loemker, 2 vols., 1956 (Univ. of Chicago Press); rpt. Beardsley, ed. *The European Philosophers*, p. 248.

1. William Hogarth, *The Analysis of Beauty* (Chicago: The Reilly & Lee Co., 1908), pp. 203-7. These comments are part of a digression from Hogarth's discussion of sculpture. The fuller contexts of these two contradictory remarks are as follows: "With regard to character and expression; we have daily many instances which confirm the common received opinion, that the face is the index of the mind; and this maxim is so rooted in us, we can scarce help—if our attention is a little raised—forming some particular conception of the person's mind whose face we are observing, even before we receive information by any other means. How often is it said, on the slightest view, such a one looks like a good-natured man, that he has an open countenance, or looks like a cunning rogue; a man of sense or a fool, etc. And how our eyes are riveted to the aspects of kings and heroes, murderers and saints; and as we contemplate their deeds, seldom fail making application to their looks. It is reasonable to believe that aspect to be a true and legible representation of the mind which gives everyone the same idea at first sight; and is afterwards confirmed in fact: for instance, all concur in the same opinion of a downright idiot."

    Not long afterwards Hogarth reverses himself: "But lest I should be thought to lay too great a stress on outward show, like a physiognomist, take this with you, that it is acknowledged there are so many different causes which produce the same kind of movements and appearances of the features, and so many thwartings by accidental shapes in the make of faces, that the old adage, *fronti nulla fides*, will ever stand its ground on the whole; and for the very wise reasons nature has thought that fit it should."

2. In an early review of *Jane Eyre*, the critic Elizabeth Rigby (1809-1893) writes: "... in these days of extravagant adoration of all that bears the stamp of novelty and originality, sheer rudeness and vulgarity have come in for a most mistaken worship." And of the hero: "Mr. Rochester is a man who deliberately and secretly seeks to violate the laws both of God and man, and yet we will be bound half our lady readers are enchanted with him for a model of generosity and honour. We would have thought that such a hero had had no chance.... He is made as coarse and brutal as can in all conscience be required to keep our sympathies at a distance." The review appeared in *The Quarterly Review*, December, 1848, pp. 162-76; rpt, *Jane Eyre*. Norton Critical Edition, pp. 449-53.

3. E. H. Gombrich, *The Sense of Order: A Study in the Psychology of Decorative Art* (Ithaca: Cornell Univ. Press, 1979), p. 169.

4. E. H. Gombrich, "The Mask and the Face," in *Art, Perception, and Reality* (Baltimore: The Johns Hopkins Univ. Press, 1972), p. 11.

5. Anthony Ashley Cooper, Third Earl of Shaftesbury, *Characteristics;* rpt., *Philosophies of Art and Beauty: Selected Reading in Aesthetics from Plato to Heidegger,* edited by Albert Hofstadter and Richard Kuhns (Chicago: Univ. of Chicago Press, 1964), p. 241.

6. Immanuel Kant, *Critique of Judgment* III, 13; rpt., Hofstadter and Kuhns, p. 296.

7. Georg Wilhelm Friedrich Hegel, *The Philosophy of Fine Art;* rpt., Hofstadter and Kuhns, p. 384.

8. Samuel Taylor Coleridge, *Biographia Literaria,* ed. George Watson (New York: Dutton, 1965), pp. 166–69.

9. M.H. Abrams, *The Mirror and the Lamp: Romantic Theory and the Critical Tradition* (New York: Oxford Univ. Press, 1953), pp. 116–24.

10. Carl Woodring, "Nature and Art in the Nineteenth Century," *PMLA* 92 (March 1977), 193–202.

11. Lois Banner, *American Beauty* (New York: Knopf, 1983), p. 14. This work is a social history of the American ideal of beauty over two centuries. Banner's historical research supports many of my own discoveries about the literature of this period in England. She correlates beauty ideals with other historical phenomena and fully documents nineteenth- and twentieth-century notions of beauty and etiquette, attending to everything from department stores and periodicals to theater and fashion.

12. Comparing the histories of Eastern and Western thought, Maruyama Masao remarks upon this paradox: "It is paradoxical but true that the history of philosophy from Thomas Aquinas, representing the high point of scholasticism, to Descartes, the founder of modern philosophy, is the history of reinforcement of God's absolute, transcendental nature. Of course, in the Christian worldview it is universally recognized that God holds absolute and transcendental authority of the world order that he has created. However, in medieval theology, based on Aristotelian philosophy, the natural and supernatural were seen as continuous. The world order was conceived as an organic body stamped in every part with divine reason and one in which goodness is inherent. In their rational action, all men cooperate with the action of divine grace. There is thus a necessary inner connection between the otherworldly God and the this worldly society. The intellectual currents of later scholasticism and religious reform, however, severed this inner connection between God and the world and ascribed to God absolute freedom." *Studies in the Intellectual History of Tokugawa Japan,* trans., Mikiso Hane (Princeton: Princeton Univ. Press, 1974), p. 234.

13. Norman Cohn, *The Pursuit of the Millennium: Revolutionary Millenarians and Mystical Anarchists of the Middle Ages* (New York: Oxford Univ. Press, 1957; revised 1970), illustration 2, between pp. 161 and 162.

14. Edward Dudley and Maximillian E. Novak, eds., *The Wild Man Within: An Image in Western Thought from the Renaissance to Romanticism* (Pittsburgh: Univ. of Pittsburgh Press, 1972).

15. See, for example, the analysis of Bertha Mason in Sandra M. Gilbert and Susan Gubar, *The Madwoman in the Attic: The Woman Writer and the Nineteenth-Century Literary Imagination* (New Haven: Yale Univ. Press, 1979). The title of this critical work testifies to the importance of the figure of the madwoman, who is made here to represent the woman writer's second self.

16. Of course as natural history developed into a science of importance, accurate description became an important value. And as I mentioned earlier, realism's increasing emphasis on description follows this trend.
17. Keith Thomas, *Man and the Natural World: A History of the Modern Sensibility* (New York: Pantheon, 1983), p. 15.
18. John Berger, *About Looking* (New York: Pantheon, 1980), p. 1.
19. Ovid, *Metamorphoses,* trans. Rolfe Humphries (Bloomington: Indiana Univ. Press, 1955), pp. 241–43.
20. Robert Palfrey Utter and Gwendolyn Bridges Needham, *Pamela's Daughters* (New York: Macmillan, 1936), p. 8.
21. Charles Dickens, *The Old Curiosity Shop* (New York: Penguin, 1972), p. 654.
22. Nina Auerbach, *Woman and the Demon: The Life of a Victorian Myth* (Cambridge: Harvard Univ. Press, 1982), pp. 41–42.
23. Mario Praz, *The Romantic Agony,* trans. Angus Davidson, 2nd edition (New York: Oxford Univ. Press, 1957), p. 31.
24. Sigmund Freud, "Medusa's Head," in *Sexuality and the Psychology of Love,* ed. Philip Rieff (New York: Collier, 1978), pp. 212–213. Freud goes on to say that it is appropriate that the Medusa's Head, this "symbol of horror," is worn upon the dress of the virgin goddess Athena because "thus she becomes a woman who is unapproachable and repels all sexual desires." Freud does not seem to notice the contradiction in his argument that the snakes at once repel desire and, because the spectator stiffens, they arouse desire.
25. Rachel M. Brownstein, *Becoming a Heroine: Reading about Women in Novels* (New York: Viking, 1982), p. 43.
26. Dorothy Van Ghent, *The English Novels: Form and Function* (New York: Harper and Row, 1953), pp. 48–49.
27. Elizabeth MacAndrew and Susan Gorsky, "Why Do They Faint and Die—The Birth of the Delicate Heroine," *Journal of Popular Culture* 8 (1974–75), 735–45.
28. Bruce Haley, *The Healthy Body and Victorian Culture* (Cambridge: Harvard Univ. Press, 1978), p. 19. Haley's work devotes surprisingly little attention to the special medical situation of women in Victorian culture.
29. Sarah Stage, *Female Complaints: Lydia Pinkham and the Business of Women's Medicine* (New York: Norton, 1979), pp. 67–72.
30. Alison Lurie, *The Language of Clothes* (New York: Random House, 1981), pp. 216–20. I am indebted to others who have written about the history of fashion, especially to: the work of James Laver; Quentin Bell, *On Human Finery* (New York: Schocken Books, 1976); and Anne Hollander's comprehensive historical survey of the connections between clothes and art, *Seeing Through Clothes* (New York: Viking, 1975).
31. Peter T. Cominos, "Innocent Femina Sensualis in Unconscious Conflict," in *Suffer and Be Still: Women in the Victorian Age,* ed. Martha Vicinus (Bloomington: Indiana Univ. Press, 1972), pp. 155–72.
32. James Baldwin, *Fairy Stories and Fables: Eclectic School Readings* (New York: American Book Co., 1895), p. 111. The relevant paragraph in the schoolbook reads: "The sisters had laced themselves very tightly for they wanted to look thin and slender; and they had eaten

scarcely anything for two days. It is no wonder, then, that they were more ill-tempered that night than they had been before; and they scolded and fretted and frowned until there was no getting along with them."

While children learn that tight-lacing can make you feel ill, compare this letter on corsets which appeared in *Englishwoman's Domestic Magazine* (July 1870). The author is a brother who has just returned home from school: "When my sisters were, the one sixteen, the other nearly two years younger, our mother considered it was time that their figures, hitherto unrestrained, should be subjected to some control, and accordingly she laced them, rather tightly, in stiff new stays, both day and night. They tried the usual expedients of cutting laces, and so forth, at first, but were entirely frustrated by mamma procuring a steel belt, fitted with a lock and key, to be worn at night outside the corset.... the pressure of the stays, being an equal pressure, they were obliged to allow was not altogether unpleasant (although they could not racket about quite so easily); but the pressure of the belt, being unequal, was very uncomfortable indeed. Mamma was inexorable. I proposed a compromise. The girls should be relieved from their belts, and presented with very tiny-waisted riding habits (they were mad to be allowed to ride), which they should have facilities for using as soon as they could fit them on. They, on their part, should promise that their corsets should always be tightly laced. The compromise was agreed to.... When I supervised their first mount, I can assure you I was very proud of my sisters' figures; and—dare I say—with the charming inconsistency of their sex, I believe they were, and still are, as proud of them themselves. When the subject is mentioned they will laughingly quote *"Qu'il faut souffrir pour être belle"* but they declare that the very slight suffering at first is fully compensated by the delicious sensation of perfect compression when once accustomed to it, and that they would go through it all again for that end alone if appearance were no consideration at all." Quoted in Janet Horowitz Murray, *Strong-Minded Women and Other Lost Voices from Nineteenth-Century England* (New York: Pantheon, 1982), p. 66.

33. Susan Sontag, *Illness as Metaphor* (New York: Random House, 1977).

34. Bernard Rudofsky, *The Unfashionable Human Body* (Garden City: Doubleday, 1971). Elaine Scarry, *The Body in Pain: The Making and Unmaking of the World* (New York: Oxford Univ. Press, 1985). See also Elaine Showalter, *The Female Malady: Women, Madness and English Culture* (New York: Pantheon, 1986).

Chapter 4

1. Jane Austen, *Northanger Abbey and Persuasion,* ed. Mary Lascelles (New York: Dutton, 1906), p. 210. Subsequent references occur in the text and are to this edition.

2. Barbara Johnson, "Melville's Fist: The Execution of *Billy Budd*," in *The Critical Difference: Essays in the Contemporary Rhetoric of Reading* (Baltimore: The Johns Hopkins Univ. Press, 1980), pp. 79–109. While Johnson points to the mixed messages of Budd's character, she does not comment upon Budd's beauty as an integral part of Melville's manipulations. Billy Budd, identified as the "handsome sailor," is handsome in the style of the gentleman, *not* in the style of rugged masculinity that was coming into vogue and was to be (with Melville's help) epitomized in the figure of the sailor. Budd's act of violence confirms his masculinity, when such beauty as his was increasingly devalued as effeminite. In this way, Melville embodies in his hero values on both sides of the current fashion's threshold.

Chapter 5

1. George Eliot, *Middlemarch,* ed. Gordon Haight, Riverside Edition (Boston: Houghton Mifflin, 1956), p. 9. Subsequent references are to this edition.

2. All translations from the Bible and Apocrypha are taken from *The New Oxford Annotated Bible with Apocrypha,* revised standard edition (New York: Oxford Univ. Press, 1977).

3. G. M. Young, *Portrait of an Age: Victorian England* (New York: Oxford Univ. Press, 1936), p. 14. Walter E. Houghton, in *The Victorian Frame of Mind: 1830–1870* (New Haven: Yale Univ. Press, 1957), pp. 394–95, makes a similar point about the Victorian concern about hypocrisy:

> Of all the criticisms brought against them by the Lytton Stracheys of the twentieth century, the Victorians would have pleaded guilty to only one.... they would have confessed to an unfortunate strain of hypocrisy. To understand the charge, it must be broken down into three specific counts. One, they concealed or suppressed their true convictions and their natural tastes. They said the "right" thing or did the "right" thing: they sacrificed sincerity to propriety. Second, and worse, they pretended to be better than they were. They passed themselves off as being incredibly pious and moral; they talked noble sentiments and lived—quite otherwise. Finally, they refused to look at life candidly. They shut their eyes to whatever was ugly or unpleasant and pretended it didn't exist. Conformity, moral pretension, and evasion—these are the hallmarks of Victorian hypocrisy.

4. Gordon Haight, *George Eliot: A Biography* (New York: Oxford Univ. Press, 1968), pp. 448–49.

5. Haight, p. 450.

6. Alison Lurie, *The Language of Clothes* (New York: Random House, 1981), p. 69. In a section entitled "Victorian Women: The Angel in the House and the Queen-Size Beauty," pp. 68–73, Lurie provides us with a context in which to place, and better admire, Dorothea. She writes:

> In the final decades of the nineteenth century, the ideal female continued to become larger and older. Her size was a sign of increased visibility; in growing numbers now women were going to college, working for a living and campaigning for legal and political equality. But even when she remained at home as a showpiece, the late Victorian and Edwardian woman was an impressive creature physically...
>
> We can see the ideal type in photographs of famous beauties like Maud Gonne, Lily Langtry and Jennie Churchill.... She was opulently built, with the figure of a woman in prosperous middle age.... The timid, fairylike child of the early nineteenth century had become the confident Junoesque beauty painted by Sargent and drawn by Charles Dana Gibson.

7. Seeing the snake that walks erect as a phallic symbol is not just a post-Freudian reading of the myth. In some rabbinic commentaries and mystic literature, the snake's seduction of Eve is quite literally sexual. These stories influenced Milton's portrayal of Satan as seducer in *Paradise Lost.*

8. Nathaniel Wander, "Structure, Contradiction and 'Resolution' in Mythology: Father's Brother's Daughter Marriage and the Treatment of Women in Genesis 11–50," *Journal of the Ancient Near East Society,* 13 (1981), 92–99 explains how Rebekah functions as a "condensation of the type of the barren mother." His interest differs from ours, but this observation is relevant: "This matter of multiple wives never emerges in the case of Isaac and Rebekah.... Consequently she herself bears two kinds of sons (acceptable and unacceptable as successor to the patriarch) who are, appropriately enough, twins. Rebekah's siding with Jacob against the interests of his older brother Esau, however, creates a situation as if the latter were the son of another mother. As soon as this 'as if' is posited, the events of the narratives develop as in the cases of Sarah and Rachel...."

Notes for Chapter 5   225

9. Louis Ginzberg, *The Legends of the Jews.* Vol. 4 (Philadelphia: Jewish Publication Society, 1974), p. 37. *Midrash* names a large body of literature, anthologized in numbers of collections, over several hundred years. The remarks that I am quoting from here are taken from texts as widely separated as approximately 500 C.E. to 1300 C. E. Rather than represent this diverse body of literature fairly, my selections are meant to illustrate a procedure and a predominant point of view that developed between the canonization of Hebrew Scriptures and the Renaissance.

10. I. Epstein, trans. *The Babylonian Talmud: Seder Nashim,* Vol. I (London: Soncino, 1936), p. 711.

11. Frank Kermode in *The Genesis of Secrecy: On the Interpretation of Narrative* (Cambridge: Harvard Univ. Press, 1979), p. x, writes of the Gospel of Mark: "There comes a point when interpretation by the invention of new narrative is halted; in the present instance that point was reached with the establishment of the canon of the gospels. Interpretation thereafter usually continues in commentary. These interpretative continuities are illuminated, I have suggested, by the practice of midrash. By midrash the interpreter, either by rewriting the story or explaining it in a more acceptable sense, bridges the gap between an original and a modern audience." Canonization will, of course, affect the status and the nature of interpretation upon any "classic" text.

    See also Gershom Scholem, *The Messianic Idea in Judaism: And Other Essays on Jewish Spirituality,* (New York: Schocken, 1971), p. 284: "In all religions, the acceptance of a divine revelation originally referred to the concrete communication of positive, substantive and expressible content. It never occurred to the bearers of such a revelation to question or limit the specific quality and closely delineated content of the communication they had received.... But inasmuch as such revelation, once set down as Holy Scriptures, takes on an authoritative character, an essential change takes place. For one thing, new historical circumstances require that the communcation, whose authoritativeness has been granted, be applied to ever changing conditions."

12. *The New Oxford Annotated Bible,* p. 87, note to Judith 10:1–5.

13. Germaine Greer, *The Obstacle Race* (New York: Farrar, Straus and Giroux, 1979), p. 189.

14. Bedroom murder divests women of power in public space at the same time that it invests her with supernatural powers in sexual space. The painting *Judith Beheading Holofernes* by the seventeenth-century female painter Artemisia Gentileschi has horrified viewers by making the woman's power and the man's passivity so boldly explicit that the sexes function in reverse roles. Greer, in *The Obstacle Race,* p. 189, describes Gentileschi's portrayal:

    > The painting depicts an atrocity, murder of a naked man in his bed by two young women. They could be two female cutthroats, a prostitute and her maid slaughtering her client whose up-turned face has not had the time to register the change from lust to fear. The strong diagonals of the composition all lead to the focal point, the sword blade hacking at the man's neck from which gouts of blood spray out, mimicking the lines of the strong arms that hold him down, even as far as the rose-white bosom of the murderess.

    Greer goes on to discuss Artemisia's rendering of violence and of Judith: "all the interest centres upon the ferocious energy and application of dark, angry Judith, who plies her sword like a peasant woman slaughtering a calf..." even "the tinkle of blood against Judith's jewelled forearm" is read as an expression of callousness. Greer continues: "The spectator is rendered incapable of pity or outrage before this icon of violence and hatred, while he is delighted by such cunning. The painting was, in its own time, both notorious and inconspicuously exposed."

15. Robert Kellogg and Oliver Steele, eds., Intro. to *The Faerie Queene* by Edmund Spenser (New York: Odyssey Press, 1965), p. 20: "Sansfoy's companion Duessa is the opposite of Una. As one (Una) represents truth, goodness, beauty, order and whatever is perfect and eternal in Platonic thought (Timaeus); so two (Duessa) represents all that is imperfect, chaotic, earthly and evil. Spenser's description of Duessa shows that she is the whore of Babylon 17:3–4."

16. Merritt Hughes. *John Milton: Complete Poems and Major Prose* (Indianapolis: Bobbs-Merrill, 1957), p. 564 note.

17. Edith Hamilton, *Mythology: Timeless Tales of Gods and Heroes* (New York: New American Library, 1942), p. 32.

18. Christopher Hill, *Milton and the English Revolution* (New York: Penguin, 1978), pp. 428–48.

19. Sir Walter Scott, *Ivanhoe: A Romance* (New York: New American Library, 1962), pp. 464–67. Subsequent references appear in the text and are to this edition.

20. See the discussion in Francis R. Hart, *Scott's Novels: The Plotting of Historical Survival* (Charlottesville: The University of Virginia Press, 1966), p. 152.

21. Alexander Welsh, *The Hero of the Waverley Novels* (New Haven: Yale Univ. Press, 1963) pp. 78–80.

22. Compton MacKenzie, Afterword, *Ivanhoe*, p. 496.

23. William Makepeace Thackeray, *Vanity Fair: A Novel without a Hero*, eds., Geoffrey and Kathleen Tillotson (Boston: Houghton Mifflin, 1963), p. 34. Subsequent references are to this edition.

24. This is the thesis of J. Y. T. Greig in *Thackeray: A Reconsideration* (n.p.: Archon Books, 1967).

25. Geoffrey and Kathleen Tillotson, *Vanity Fair*, p. xix.

26. Kellogg and Steele, p. 23: "The lion's protection of Una is also a traditional indictment of man (Red Cross), who falls away from reason and revelation, whereas the lower creatures conform exactly to the same truth as it is manifested in nature."

27. E. M. Forster, *Aspects of the Novel* (New York: Harcourt, Brace, 1927), p. 43.

28. Geoffrey and Kathleen Tillotson, *Vanity Fair*, p. xi.

29. A. E. Dyson, "An Irony Against Heroes," in *Vanity Fair: A Casebook*, ed. Arthur Pollard (New York: Macmillan, 1978), pp. 163–82, presents an interesting discussion of the narrator's ironic perspective on his characters.

30. Roger B. Henkle, *Comedy and Culture: England 1820–1900* (Princeton: Princeton Univ. Press, 1980), p. 91.

31. For a discussion of the power of the woman as mermaid and snake in Victorian literature, see Nina Auerbach, *Woman and the Demon: The Life of a Victorian Myth* (Cambridge: Harvard Univ. Press, 1982).

32. Derek Oldfield, "The Language of the Novel: The Character of Dorothea," in *Middlemarch: Critical Approaches to the Novel*, ed. Barbara Hardy (New York: Oxford Univ. Press, 1967), p. 73.

33. For a discussion of Dorothea's education by Ladislaw in art and the language of art as Ladislaw transforms Dorothea, a woman ignorant of art, into an admirer of art, see Philip Fisher, *Making Up Society: The Novels of George Eliot* (Pittsburgh: Univ. of Pittsburgh Press, 1981), pp. 165-80.

34. Sandra M. Gilbert and Susan Gubar, *The Madwoman in the Attic: The Woman Writer and the Nineteenth-Century Literary Imagination* (New Haven: Yale Univ. Press, 1979), p. 476.

35. Both Trollope and his critics make much of the fact that Lizzie, whose interest lies in her being a charming woman with a jewel box, is modelled on Thackeray's Rebecca. In the novel itself the narrator comments: "the historian begs his readers not to believe that that opulent aristocratic Becky Sharp is to assume the dignity of a heroine" (New York: Penguin, 1969) p. 57. In his *Autobiography* (1883; rpt. New York: Humphrey Milford Oxford Univ. Press, 1924), p. 314, Trollope writes that "the idea constantly presented itself to me that Lizzie Eustace was but a second Becky Sharpe." James R. Kincaid writes in *The Novels of Anthony Trollope* (London: Clarendon Press, Oxford, 1977), p. 205, of Lizzie that: "for her great energy... and for her creative zeal she deserves and is granted our respect, the same sort of respect we grant to other morally deficient but artistically active characters: ... Becky Sharp. There are moments when Lizzie sounds very much like Becky, when she abuses the virtuous heroine for instance" (p. 205). Kincaid points out that Trollope admired Thackeray, though Trollope was "equivocal" about Scott (p. 51), and Kincaid further observes that *The Eustace Diamonds* is "an attack on romance" (p. 209). Thackeray, I would add, wrote both *Rebecca and Rowena* and *Vanity Fair* as attacks on romance. In spite of these attacks, all of these Beckys derive their most engaging qualities from Scott's Rebecca: all of these less-than-heroines are socially marginalized, but upwardly mobile, vital linguists who carry a jewel box.

36. Nancy Nystul, *"Daniel Deronda:* A Family Romance," *Enclitic* 7 (Spring 1983), 45-53.

37. Sigmund Freud, *Dora: An Analysis of a Case of Hysteria* (New York: Collier, 1963), p. 87.

38. The name Rebecca seems to encode exotic and foreign beauty. When Pocahontas was given an English name, she was named Rebecca.

39. Sigmund Freud, *The Future of An Illusion* (Garden City: Doubleday, 1964), pp. 72-85.

40. Earl Miner, "Allusion," in *The Princeton Encyclopedia of Poetry and Poetics,* enlarged edition (Princeton: Princeton Univ. Press, 1974).

41. Frank Kermode, *Continuities,* 1968; rpt. *George Eliot's Middlemarch: A Casebook,* ed. by Patrick Swinden (New York: Macmillan, 1972), p. 137.

42. Arnold Kettle, *An Introduction to the English Novel,* 1951; rpt. *Middlemarch Casebook,* p. 163.

43. Hallett Smith in his introduction to *The Winter's Tale* in *The Riverside Shakespeare,* ed. G. Blakemore Evans (Boston: Houghton Mifflin, 1974), p. 1566, writes:

> The characterization of Perdita is the glory of the fourth act. Her charming modesty and diffidence about her role as the humble sweetheart of a disguised prince make her hold back as the mistress of the feast.... Her bestowal of flowers on the guests involves her in a discussion with the disguised king, Polixenes, on the questions of nature and artifice, a major theme of this portion of the play. She fears and distrusts anything that is not natural, and though Polixenes gives her the standard humanistic answer in defense of art... she nevertheless rejects artificially crossed flowers as she would reject cosmetics.

Though she is, unknown to herself, a princess, yet she is a child of nature. (Ironically, Polixenes in his argument unconsciously undermines his own case against the marriage of a prince with a shepherdess.)

Chapter 6

1. The chapter's epigraph comes from Reid, 1789, *Intell. Powers* VIII, iv (1803), 561, quoted in *OED* entry for "Grace."
2. Raymond Williams, *The Country and the City* (New York: Oxford Univ. Press, 1973), pp. 9–12.
3. Emily Brontë, *Wuthering Heights,* ed. William M. Sale, Jr. (New York: Norton, 1963), pp. 54–55. Further references appear in the text and are to this edition.
4. Longus, *Daphnis and Chloe,* trans. Paul Turner (Baltimore: Penguin, 1968), pp. 29–30. Further references appear in the text and are to this edition.
5. Edgar Rice Burroughs, *Tarzan of the Apes: The Adventures of Lord Greystoke* (New York: Ballantine, 1912) pp. 168–69.
6. Jean-Marc-Gaspard Itard, rpt. in *Wolf Children and the Problem of Human Nature with the Complete Text of the Wild Boy of Aveyron by Jean-Marc-Gaspard Itard,* edited by Lucien Malson (New York: Monthly Review Press, 1972), p. 96.
7. Roger Shattuck, *The Forbidden Experiment: The Story of the Wild Boy of Aveyron* (New York: Washington Square Press, 1981), pp. 53–54. Further references appear in the text.
8. See Ellen Moers, "Female Gothic" in *The Endurance of Frankenstein: Essays on Mary Shelley's Novel,* edited by George Levine and U. C. Knoepflmacher (Los Angeles: Univ. of Calif. Press, 1979) pp. 77–88, on *Frankenstein* as a myth about birth and mothering.
9. Jacques Derrida, *Of Grammatology.* trans. Gayatri Chakravorty Spivak (Baltimore: Johns Hopkins Univ. Press, 1976), pp. 145–46.
10. "But when he told it to his father and to his brothers, his father rebuked him, and said to him 'What is this dream that you have dreamed? Shall I and your mother and brothers indeed come to bow ourselves to the ground before you?'" Genesis 37:10, though the narrator hastens to add that, "Jacob kept the saying in mind."
11. Rabbi Dr. H. Freedman and Maurice Simon, eds., *Midrash Rabbah: Translated into English with Notes, Glossary and Indices* (London: The Soncino Press, 1983), Genesis, II, p. 774. A footnote refers us to a midrash on the story of Cain and Abel in which Abel (not entirely a blameless victim in midrash) is criticized, like Joseph, for "pencilling his eyes, curling his hair and lifting his heel," I, xii. Further references to midrash are to this translation of the Midrash Rabbah.
12. H. St. J. Thackeray et al., eds., *Jewish Antiquities,* Vol. IV of *Josephus with an English Translation* (Cambridge, Ma.: Loeb Classical Library, 1926–1965), p. 173.
13. E. R. Goodenough, *An Introduction to Philo Judaeus* (New Haven: Yale Univ. Press, 1940), p. 77.
14. F. H. Colson et al., eds., *Philo with an English Translation* (Cambridge, Ma.: Loeb Classical Library, 1949–1961).
15. Mohammed Marmaduke Pickthall, trans., *The Meaning of the Glorious Koran* (New York: New American Library, n.d.).

Notes for Chapter 6   229

16. Henry Fielding, *Joseph Andrews* (New York: New American Library, 1960), p. 21. Further references are to this edition.
17. Q. D. Leavis, "A Fresh Approach to *Wuthering Heights*," Norton Critical Edition of *Wuthering Heights*, p. 208.
18. See Terence Eagleton, *Myths of Power: A Marxist Study of the Brontës* (New York: Knopf, 1975).
19. Leo Bersani, *A Future for Astyanax: Character and Desire in Literature* (Boston: Little Brown, & Co., 1969), p. 201, writes,

> The contrast between the Grange and Wuthering Heights is a false, or at least an insignificant, one. Emily Brontë does not oppose a world of civilized moral conventions to one of untamed passions. Edgar and Isabella belong as little as the Earnshaws and Heathcliff do to "society"; they are uninterested in its pleasures (which Lockwood vaguely evokes) and indifferent to its morality (which Nelly tirelessly proposes). When Cathy and Heathcliff first go to the Grange, they come upon a scene worthy of Wuthering Heights.... Edgar and Isabella's parents, the possible representatives of civilized society, practically don't exist in the novel... To go from Wuthering Heights to the Grange is not to go from nature to society; it is to go from the strong children to the weak children, or more precisely, from aggressively selfish children to whiningly selfish children.

> The difference between "strong" and "weak" children is precisely the difference between nature and society. While it is true that the Linton children are as isolated and seemingly ungoverned as the Earnshaw children, Heathcliff wishes that he behaved and spoke as well as Linton; Linton lacks wildness, for good and for ill, because he is trained for company. Brontë makes much of the difference between fair and dark beauty, the homes of the Lintons and Earnshaws, and the presence of overbreeding in the one case (the Linton children are spoiled) and the absence of breeding in the other. *Wuthering Heights* is, at least on one level, about the rights to property and Brontë clearly compares the qualities of the natural and brutal self-made man with the self-confident pride of the man who has inherited his wealth. Bersani's need to state this case, even if to refute it, suggests to me that the novel does indeed encourage us to contrast the Lintons and the Earnshaws.

20. J. Hillis Miller, *Fiction and Repetition: Seven English Novels* (Cambridge: Harvard Univ. Press, 1982), pp. 42-72.
21. Charlotte Brontë, *Jane Eyre*, ed. Richard J. Dunn (New York: Norton, 1971), p. 99. Further references appear in the text and are to this edition.
22. E. C. Gaskell, *The Life of Charlotte Brontë* (London: Smith, Elder, 1857), p. 324.
23. Elizabeth Rigby, "An Anti-Christian Composition," *Jane Eyre*, Norton Critical Edition, pp. 449-53. From *The Quarterly Review*, December, 1848, pp. 162-76.
24. Sandra M. Gilbert and Susan Gubar, *The Madwoman in the Attic: The Woman Writer in the Nineteenth-Century Literary Imagination* (New Haven: Yale Univ. Press, 1979), pp. 337-71.
25. Lord Raglan, *The Hero: A Study in Tradition, Myth and Drama* (London: Methuen, 1936), pp. 145-46.
26. See Patricia Thomson, *The Victorian Heroine: A Changing Ideal, 1837-1873* (New York: Oxford Univ. Press, 1956), pp. 36-56. Thomson entitles this chapter "The Noble Body of Governesses."

27. The best parts of this analysis come from Professor Philip Fisher's lectures on *Jane Eyre*, which I remember imperfectly from my undergraduate days in his classroom at Brandeis University. See also Philip Fisher, *Making Up Society: The Novels of George Eliot* (Pittsburgh: Univ. of Pittsburgh Press, 1981), pp. 155–56.
28. Angus Calder, ed., *Great Expectations* by Charles Dickens (Baltimore: Penguin, 1965), Appendix A, p. 494.

Chapter 7

1. Bruce Haley, *The Healthy Body and Victorian Culture* (Cambridge: Harvard Univ. Press, 1978), p. 196.
2. George Eliot, *Adam Bede*, foreword by F. R. Leavis (New York: New American Library, 1961), pp. 33–34. Further references in the text are to this edition.
3. This scene is part of the nostalgic formula of this novel. By 1859 working conditions for factory needleworkers were most severe, and such workers were notoriously sickly. See George Rosen, "Disease, Debility, and Death," in *The Victorian City: Images and Realities*, vol. II, eds., H. J. Dyos and Michael Wolff (Boston: Routledge and Kegan Paul, 1973), pp. 625–68.
4. Herbert G. May and Bruce M. Metzger, eds., *The New Oxford Annotated Bible with the Apocrypha,* Revised Standard Version (New York: Oxford Univ. Press, 1977), footnote to Genesis 34: 2.
5. H. Freedman and Maurice Simon, eds., *Midrash Rabbah: Genesis,* 2 vols. (New York: The Soncino Press, 1983), p. 63. Further references to the midrash are to this commentary.
6. In modern Hebrew, "Shoshanna"—Susanna—has come to mean rose or lily, a conflation that corresponds to the literary tradition's conflation of the scarlet woman and the pure woman.
7. Nathaniel Hawthorne, *The Scarlet Letter* (New York: Bantam, 1965), p. 46. Further references are to this edition.
8. Dorothy Van Ghent, "On *Adam Bede,*" in *The English Novel: Form and Function* (New York: Harper and Row, 1953), pp. 171–82.
9. Cf. Erich Auerbach, *Mimesis: The Representation of Reality in Western Literature,* trans. Willard Trask (Princeton: Princeton Univ. Press, 1953.)
10. Philip Fisher, *Making Up Society: The Novels of George Eliot* (Pittsburgh: Univ. of Pittsburgh Press, 1981), p. 58. Fisher notes John W. Cross, *The Life and Letters of George Eliot* (New York: Wanamaker, 1910), p. 281.
11. See also Nina Auerbach, *Woman and the Demon: The Life of A Victorian Myth* (Cambridge: Harvard Univ. Press, 1982).
12. Fisher, p. 63.
13. Alison Lurie, commenting on William Holman Hunt's "The Hireling Shepherd," writes that, "In the second half of the nineteenth century female fashions reached extremes of elaborate discomfort from which only the lower strata of the working class were exempt. By Victorian standards, though not our own, this shepherdess's uncorseted figure, loose, simple dress and healthy look would be considered coarse and unattractive," *The Language of Clothes* (New York: Random House, 1981), p. 218.

14. Because the novelist has been forced into positions of compromise, the novel's ending remains unconvincing to some readers. For example, Jenni Calder, in *Women and Marriage in Victorian Fiction* (New York: Oxford Univ. Press, 1976), p. 134, betrays her own preference for Seth over Adam as she regrets the transformations upon Dinah's character that have made her a "devoted, gentle wife" to Adam:

    > I think there is a failure at the novel's close, for George Eliot does not positively characterize the "fuller life" and "higher feelings" that have come to Adam as a result of sorrow, except in showing how he falls in love with Dinah Morris. But he has always understood Dinah's worth, and when they marry she has been deprived of some of her strength and achievement by the fact that she is no longer allowed to preach. The final characterization of Dinah as devoted, gentle wife, accommodating in her household two men who love her—Adam, and his brother Seth who had wanted Dinah as his wife long before the thought occurred to Adam—seems neither convincing nor rewarding. For those aspects of Dinah's personality, her quick and decisive independence, which saved her from an insipid priggishness, have been shorn away.

15. George Gissing, *The Odd Women* (New York: Norton, 1971), p. 3. Further references are to this edition.

16. Fredric Jameson, *The Political Unconscious: Narrative as a Socially Symbolic Act* (Ithaca: Cornell Univ. Press, 1981), p. 285.

17. D. H. Lawrence, *Phoenix: The Posthumous Papers (1936)*, edited by Edward McDonald (New York: Viking, 1936), 488-510.

18. Albert J. Guerard, *Thomas Hardy: The Novels and Stories* (Cambridge: Harvard Univ. Press, 1949); rpt. *Jude the Obscure,* ed. Norman Page (New York: Norton, 1978), p. 447.

19. Robert Gittings, *Young Thomas Hardy* (London: Heinemann, 1975); rpt. *Jude the Obscure,* ed. Norman Page (New York: Norton, 1978), pp. 448-50.

20. Thomas Hardy, *Jude the Obscure,* ed. Norman Page (New York: Norton, 1978), p. 10. Further references are to this edition.

21. See Albert Habegger, "A Well Hidden Hand," *Novel* (Spring, 1981), 197-212.

Chapter 8

1. Gérard Genette, *Figures of Literary Discourse,* trans. Alan Sheridan (New York: Columbia Univ. Press, 1982), p. 68.

2. For a study of how stock conventions of description function as a kind of shorthand in medieval literature, see D. S. Brewer, "The Ideal of Feminine Beauty in Medieval Literature, Especially 'Harley Lyrics,' Chaucer, and Some Elizabethans," *MLR,* 50 (1955), 257-69. And for a comparison of Greek and biblical conventions of physical description see Shaye J. D. Cohen, "The Beauty of Flora and the Beauty of Sarai," *Helios,* 8 (Autumn, 1981), 41-54.

3. Introducing a recent and fascinating study of stereotypes, Sander L. Gilman writes: "We all create images of things we fear or glorify. These images never remain abstractions: we understand them as real-world entities. We assign them labels that serve to set them apart from ourselves." The term stereotype, he explains, was coined "as a technical designation for the casting of multiple papier-maché copies of printing type," and by mid-nineteenth century the term had already achieved a level of abstraction in usage. "For, just as a series of unvarying casts could be made from one mold, so too were commonplaces seen as unchanging." *Difference and Pathology: Stereotypes of Sexuality, Race, and Madness* (Ithaca: Cornell Univ. Press, 1985), p. 15.

4. Cf. Harold Bloom, *The Anxiety of Influence* (New York: Oxford Univ. Press, 1973).
5. E. H. Gombrich, *Art and Illusion*, pp. 22-23.
6. Cf. John Berger, *Ways of Seeing* (New York: Penguin, 1977), pp. 129-54.
7. Ferdinand de Saussure, in his studies of phonology, shows that meaning is connected to the perception of difference. Structural anthropology advanced and extended this claim. Gombrich brings this insight to art and shows that the converse is equally true: we perceive difference as we organize things according to our prearranged system of classification. See also Umberto Eco, *The Role of the Reader: Explorations in the Semiotics of Texts* (Bloomington: Indiana Univ. Press, 1979), especially "On the Possibility of Generating Aesthetic Messages in an Edenic Language," pp. 90-104.
8. Cf. Michael Foucault, *The Archaeology of Knowledge and the Discourse on Language*, trans. A. M. Sheridan Smith (New York: Harper Torchbooks, 1972).
9. Cf. Max Black, *Models and Metaphors* (Ithaca: Cornell Univ. Press, 1962). See also Roger Brown, *Words and Things: An Introduction to Language* (New York: The Free Press, 1958) and Robin Lakoff, "Concepts We Live By" for discussions of how metaphor controls our perception of the real.
10. Berger, *Ways of Seeing*, pp. 45 ff.
11. Susan Sontag, "Beauty," *Vogue* magazine, 1975; rpt. *The Riverside Reader*, Vol. 2, eds., Joseph Trimmer and Maine Hairston (Boston: Houghton Mifflin), pp. 298-301.
12. Oscar Wilde, *The Picture of Dorian Gray* (New York: Modern Library, Random House, 1926), p. 3. Further references are to this edition.
13. Virginia Woolf, *Orlando: A Biography* (New York: Penguin, 1946), p. 2.
14. The blason as a genre, as for example the extravagant descriptions and extended similes in *The Song of Songs*, is a notable exception.
15. Laurence Sterne, *The Life and Opinions of Tristram Shandy, Gentleman* (Boston: Houghton Mifflin, 1965), pp. 356-58.

Bibliography

Abel, Elizabeth, ed. *Writing and Sexual Difference.* Chicago: Univ. of Chicago Press, 1982.
Abel, Elizabeth et al., eds. *The Voyage In: Fictions of Female Development.* Hanover: Univ. Press of New England, 1983.
Abrams, M. H. *The Mirror and the Lamp: Romantic Theory and the Critical Tradition.* New York: Oxford Univ. Press, 1953.
Adam, Ian, ed. *This Particular Web: Essays on Middlemarch.* Buffalo: Univ. of Toronto Press, 1975.
Alpers, Svetlana. *The Art of Describing: Dutch Art in the Seventeenth Century.* Chicago: Univ. of Chicago Press, 1983.
Aquinas, Thomas. *Thomas Aquinas Dictionary.* Ed. Morris Stockhammer. New York: Philosophical Library, 1965.
_____. *Philosophical Texts.* Ed. & Trans. Thomas Gilby. New York: Oxford Univ. Press, 1951.
Auerbach, Erich. *Mimesis: The Representation of Reality in Western Literature.* Trans. Willard Trask. Princeton Univ. Press, 1953.
_____. *Scenes From the Drama of European Literature: Six Essays.* New York: Meridian Books, 1959.
Auerbach, Nina. *Woman and the Demon: The Life of a Victorian Myth.* Cambridge: Harvard Univ. Press, 1982.
Austen, Jane. *Northanger Abbey and Persuasion.* Ed. Mary Lascelles. New York: Dutton, 1906.
Bacon, Francis. "Of Beauty" in *Bacon's Essays.* Ed. Richard Whately, D.D. New York: C.S. Francis and Co., 1857, pp. 406–8.
Bakhtin, Mikhail. *Problems of Dostoevsky's Poetics.* Trans. R.W. Rotsel. Ann Arbor: Ardis, 1973.
Baldwin, James. *Fairy Stories and Fables: Eclectic School Readings.* New York: American Book Co., 1895.
Balmary, Marie. *Psychoanalyzing Psychoanalysis: Freud and the Hidden Fault of the Father.* Trans. Ned Lukacher. Baltimore: Johns Hopkins Univ. Press, 1982.
Banner, Lois. *American Beauty.* New York: Knopf, 1983.
Barthes, Roland. *Image Music Text.* Trans. Stephen Heath. New York: Hill & Wang, 1977.
_____. *Roland Barthes by Roland Barthes.* Trans. Richard Howard. New York: Hill & Wang, 1977.
_____. *S/Z: An Essay.* Trans. Richard Miller. New York: Hill & Wang, 1974.
Bayley, John. *The Characters of Love: A Study in the Literature of Personality.* London: Chatto & Windus, 1968.
Beardsley, Monroe C., ed. *The European Philosophers from Descartes to Nietzsche.* New York: Random House, 1960.

Bell, Alan, ed. *Scott Bicentenary Essays: Selected Papers Read at the Sir Walter Scott Bicentenary Conference.* London: Scottish Academic Press, 1973.
Bell, Quentin. *On Human Finery.* New York: Schocken Books, 1976.
Berger, John. *About Looking.* New York: Pantheon, 1980.
──────. *Ways of Seeing.* New York: Penguin, 1977.
Berger, Peter L. *The Sacred Canopy: Elements of a Sociological Theory of Religion.* Garden City: Doubleday, 1969.
Bersani, Leo. *A Future for Astyanax: Character and Desire in Literature.* Boston: Little, Brown & Co., 1969.
Black, Max. *Models and Metaphors.* Ithaca: Cornell Univ. Press, 1962.
Bloom, Harold. *The Anxiety of Influence.* New York: Oxford Univ. Press, 1973.
Booth, Wayne C. *The Rhetoric of Fiction.* Chicago: Univ. of Chicago Press, 1961.
Breton, André. *L'Amour Fou.* Gallimard, 1937.
Brewer, D. S. "The Ideal of Feminine Beauty in Medieval Literature, Especially 'Harley Lyrics,' Chaucer and Some Elizabethans." *MLR* 50 (1955), 257-69.
Brontë, Charlotte. *Jane Eyre.* Ed. Richard J. Dunn. New York: Norton, 1971.
Brontë, Emily. *Wuthering Heights.* Ed. William M. Sale, Jr. New York: Norton, 1963.
Brown, Roger. *Words and Things: An Introduction to Language.* New York: The Free Press, 1958.
Brownstein, Rachel. *Becoming a Heroine: Reading about Women in Novels.* New York: Viking, 1982.
Bryson, Norman. *Word and Image: French Painting of the Ancien Régime.* New York: Cambridge Univ. Press, 1981.
Buckley, Jerome, ed. *The World of Victorian Fiction.* Cambridge: Harvard Univ. Press, 1975.
Burroughs, Edgar Rice. *Tarzan of the Apes: The Adventures of Lord Greystoke.* New York: Ballantine Books, 1912.
Cain, Thomas H. *Praise in The Faerie Queene.* Lincoln: Univ. of Nebraska Press, 1978.
Calder, Jenni. *Women and Marriage in Victorian Fiction.* New York: Oxford Univ. Press, 1976.
Campbell, Joseph. *The Hero with a Thousand Faces.* Princeton: Princeton Univ. Press, 1949.
Cecil, David. *Victorian Novelists: Essays in Revaluation.* Chicago: Univ. of Chicago Press, 1958.
Clark, Kenneth. *Feminine Beauty.* New York: Rizzoli, 1980.
Cohen, Shaye J. D. "The Beauty of Flora and the Beauty of Sarai." *Helios,* 8 (Autumn, 1981), 41-54.
Cohn, Norman. *The Pursuit of the Millennium: Revolutionary Millenarians and Mystical Anarchists of the Middle Ages.* New York: Oxford Univ. Press, 1957; revised 1970.
Coleridge, Samuel Taylor. *Biographia Literaria.* Ed. George Watson. New York: Dutton, 1965.
Coveney, Peter. *Poor Monkey: The Child In Literature.* rpt. *The Image of Childhood.* Baltimore: Penguin, 1967.
Coward, Rosalind and John Ellis. *Language and Materialism: Developments in Semiology and the Theory of the Subject.* Boston: Routledge & Kegan Paul, 1977.
Cox, Don Richard. *Sexuality and Victorian Literature.* Knoxville: The Univ. of Tennessee Press, 1984.
Crompton, Louis. *Byron and Greek Love: Homophobia in 19th-Century England.* Univ. of California Press, 1985.
Culler, Jonathan. *Structuralist Poetics: Structuralism, Linguistics and the Study of Literature.* Ithaca: Cornell Univ. Press, 1975.
Davies, John. *Phrenology, Fad and Science: A Nineteenth-Century American Crusade.* New Haven: Yale Univ. Press, 1955.
Derrida, Jacques. *Of Grammatology.* Trans. Gayatri Spivak. Baltimore: Johns Hopkins Univ. Press, 1976.

Dickens, Charles. *Great Expectations.* Ed. Angus Calder. Baltimore: Penguin, 1965.
———. *The Old Curiosity Shop.* Baltimore: Penguin, 1972.
Dudley, Edward and Maxmillian E. Novak. *The Wild Man Within: An Image in Western Thought from the Renaissance to Romanticism.* Pittsburgh: Univ. of Pittsburgh Press, 1972.
Dyos, H.J. and Michael Wolff. *The Victorian City: Images and Realities.* 2 vols. Boston: Routledge and Kegan Paul, 1973.
Eagleton, Terence. *Myths of Power: A Marxist Study of the Brontes.* New York: Knopf, 1975.
Eco, Umberto. *The Role of the Reader: Explorations in the Semiotics of Texts.* Bloomington: Indiana Univ. Press, 1979.
Eliot, George. *Adam Bede.* New York: New American Library, 1961.
———. *Daniel Deronda.* Ed. Barbara Hardy. Great Britian: Penguin, 1967.
———. *Middlemarch.* Ed. Gordon S. Haight. Boston: Houghton Mifflin, 1956.
Evans, G. Blakemore, ed. *The Riverside Shakespeare.* Boston: Houghton Mifflin, 1974.
Fahnestock, Jeanne. "The Heroine of Irregular Features: Physiognomy and Conventions of Heroine Description." *Victorian Studies,* 24 (Spring 1981), 325–51.
Fielding, Henry. *Joseph Andrews.* New York: New American Library, 1960.
Fisher, Philip. *Making Up Society: The Novels of George Eliot.* Pittsburgh: Univ. of Pittsburgh Press, 1981.
Flynn, Elizabeth A. and Patrocinio P. Schweickart. *Gender and Reading: Essays on Readers, Texts, and Contexts.* Baltimore: Johns Hopkins Univ. Press, 1986.
Forster, E. M. *Aspects of the Novel.* New York: Harcourt, Brace, 1927.
Foucault, Michel. *The Archaeology of Knowledge and the Discourse on Language.* Trans. A. M. Sheridan Smith. New York: Harper & Row, 1972.
Freedman, H. and Maurice Simon, eds. *Midrash Rabbah.* 10 vols. London: Soncino Press, 1983.
Freud, Sigmund. *Dora: An Analysis of a Case of Hysteria.* Ed. Philip Rieff. New York: Collier, 1963.
———. *The Future of an Illusion.* Trans. W. D. Robson-Scott. Garden City: Doubleday, 1964.
———. *Sexuality and the Psychology of Love.* Ed. Philip Rieff. New York: Collier, 1978.
Friedman, Alan. *The Turn of the Novel: The Transition to Modern Fiction.* New York: Oxford Univ. Press, 1966.
Gaskell, E. C. *The Life of Charlotte Brontë.* Edinburgh: John Grant, 1911.
Gass, William H. *Fiction and the Figures of Life.* New York: Alfred Knopf, 1970.
Genette, Gérard. *Figures of Literary Discourse.* Trans. Alan Sheridan. New York: Columbia Univ. Press, 1982.
———. *Narrative Discourse: An Essay in Method.* Trans. Jane E. Lewin. 1972; rpt. Ithaca: Cornell Univ. Press, 1980.
Gilbert Sandra M. and Susan Gubar. *The Madwoman in the Attic: The Woman Writer and the Nineteenth-Century Literary Imagination.* New Haven: Yale Univ. Press, 1979.
Gilman, Sander L. *Difference and Pathology: Stereotypes of Sexuality, Race, and Madness.* Ithaca: Cornell Univ. Press, 1985.
Ginzberg, Louis. *The Legends of the Jews.* 7 vols. Philadelphia: Jewish Publication Society, 1974.
Gissing, George. *The Odd Women.* New York: Norton, 1971.
Gittings, Robert. *Young Thomas Hardy.* London: Heinemann, 1975.
Gombrich, E. H. *Art and Illusion: A Study in the Psychology of Pictorial Representation.* Princeton: Princeton Univ. Press, 1969.
———. *Ideals and Idols: Essays on Values in History and in Art.* Oxford: Phaidon, 1979.
———. *The Sense of Order: A Study in the Psychology of Decorative Art.* Ithaca: Cornell Univ. Press, 1979.
———. *The Story of Art.* New York: Phaidon, 1950.

Gombrich, E. H., Julian Hochberg and Max Black. *Art, Perception, and Reality*. Baltimore: Johns Hopkins Univ. Press, 1972.

Goodenough, E. R. *An Introduction to Philo Judeaus*. New Haven: Yale Univ. Press, 1940.

Graham, John. *The Development of the Use of Physiognomy in the Novel*. Diss. Johns Hopkins, 1960.

Graver, Suzanne. *George Eliot and Community: A Study in Social Theory and Fictional Form*. Berkeley: Univ. of Calif. Press, 1984.

Greer, Germaine. *The Obstacle Race*. New York: Farrar, Straus and Giroux, 1979.

Greig, J. Y. T. *Thackeray: A Reconsideration*. n.p.: Archon Books, 1967.

Griffin, Susan. *Pornography and Silence: Culture's Revenge Against Nature*. New York: Harper and Row, 1981.

Guerard, Albert J. *Thomas Hardy: The Novels and Stories*. Cambridge: Harvard Univ. Press, 1949.

Habegger, Albert. "A Well Hidden Hand." *Novel* (Spring 1981), 197-212.

Haight, Gordon. *George Eliot: A Biography*. New York: Oxford Univ. Press, 1968.

Haley, Bruce. *The Healthy Body and Victorian Culture*. Cambridge: Harvard Univ. Press, 1978.

Halperin, John, ed. *The Theory of the Novel: New Essays*. New York: Oxford Univ. Press, 1974.

Hamilton, Edith. *Mythology: Timeless Tales of Gods and Heroes*. New York: New American Library, 1942.

Handke, Peter. *Kaspar and Other Plays*. Trans. Michael Roloff. New York: Farrar, Straus and Giroux, 1969.

Hardy, Barbara, ed. *Middlemarch: Critical Approaches to the Novel*. New York: Oxford Univ. Press, 1967.

Hardy, Thomas. *Jude the Obscure*. Ed. Norman Page. New York: Norton, 1978.

Harrison, Fraser. *The Dark Angel: Aspects of Victorian Sexuality*. London: Sheldon Press, 1977.

Hart, Francis. *Scott's Novels: The Plotting of Historical Survival*. Charlottesville: Univ. of Virginia Press, 1966.

Harvey, Geoffery. *The Art of Anthony Trollope*. London: Chatto & Windus, 1980.

Harvey, W. J. *Character and the Novel*. Ithaca: Cornell Univ. Press, 1965.

Hawthorne, Nathaniel. *The Scarlet Letter*. New York: Bantam, 1965.

Heath, Stephen. *The Nouveau Roman*. London: Elek, 1972.

Hegel, G. W. F. *The Phenomenology of Spirit*. Trans. A. V. Miller. New York: Oxford Univ. Press, 1979.

Henkle, Roger. *Comedy and Culture: England 1820-1900*. Princeton: Princeton Univ. Press, 1980.

Hill, Christopher. *Milton and the English Revolution*. New York: Penguin, 1978.

Hofstadter, Albert and Richard Kuhns, eds. *Philosophies of Art and Beauty: Selected Readings in Aesthetics from Plato to Heidegger*. Chicago: Chicago Univ. Press, 1964.

Hogarth, William. *The Analysis of Beauty*. Chicago: The Reilly & Lee Co., 1908.

Hollander, Anne. *Seeing through Clothes*. New York: Viking, 1975.

Houghton, Walter E. *The Victorian Frame of Mind: 1830-1870*. New Haven: Yale Univ. Press, 1957.

Howells, William Dean. *Heroines of Fiction*. 2 vols. New York: Harper Bros., 1901.

Irwin, Michael. *Picturing: Description and Illusion in the Nineteenth-Century Novel*. Boston: George Allen & Unwin, 1979.

Jameson, Fredric. *Marxism and Form*. Princeton: Princeton Univ. Press, 1971.

_____. *The Political Unconscious: Narrative as a Socially Symbolic Act*. Ithaca: Cornell Univ. Press, 1981.

_____. "The Realist Floor-Plan." In *On Signs*. Ed. Marshall Blonsky. Baltimore: Johns Hopkins Univ. Press, 1985, pp. 373-83.

Janson, H. W. *History of Art: A Survey of the Major Visual Arts from the Dawn of History to the Present Day.* Englewood Cliffs: Prentice-Hall, 1962.
Johnson, Barbara. *The Critical Difference: Essays in the Contemporary Rhetoric of Reading.* Baltimore: Johns Hopkins Univ. Press, 1980.
Kahler, Erich. *The Inward Turn of Narrative.* Trans. Richard and Clara Winston. Princeton: Princeton Univ. Press, 1973.
Keohane, Nannerl O. et al., eds. *Feminist Theory: A Critique of Ideology.* Chicago: Univ. of Chicago Press, 1981.
Kermode, Frank. *The Genesis of Secrecy: On the Interpretation of Narrative.* Cambridge: Harvard Univ. Press, 1979.
Kincaid, James R. *The Novels of Anthony Trollope.* London: Clarendon Press, Oxford, 1977.
Kittay, Jeffrey, ed. *Yale French Studies: Towards a Theory of Description.* No. 61, 1981.
Kris, Ernst. *Psychoanalytic Explorations of Art.* New York: International Universities Press, 1952.
Kristeva, Julia. *About Chinese Women.* Trans. Anita Barrows. New York: Urizen Books, 1977.
———. *Desire in Language: A Semiotic Approach to Literature and Art.* Ed. Leon S. Roudiez. New York: Columbia Univ. Press, 1980.
———. *Powers of Horror: An Essay on Abjection.* New York: Columbia Univ. Press, 1982.
———. "The Subject in Signifying Practice." *Semiotext(e),* 1975.
Lacan, Jacques. *The Language of the Self: The Function of Language in Psychoanalysis.* Trans. Anthony Wilden. Baltimore: Johns Hopkins Press, 1968.
Lakoff, Robin Tolmach and Raquel L. Scherr. *Face Value: The Politics of Beauty.* Boston: Routledge & Kegan Paul, 1984.
Langland, Elizabeth. *Society in the Novel.* Chapel Hill: Univ. of North Carolina Press, 1984.
Leavis, F. R. *The Great Tradition.* New York: New York Univ. Press, 1960.
Levine, George and U. C. Knoepflmacher, eds. *The Endurance of Frankenstein: Essays on Mary Shelley's Novel.* Berkeley: Univ. of California Press, 1979.
Longus. *Daphnis and Chloe.* Trans. Paul Turner. Baltimore: Penguin, 1968.
Lowe, Donald M. *History of Bourgeois Perception.* Chicago: Univ. of Chicago Press, 1982.
Lubbock, Percy. *The Craft of Fiction.* New York: Viking, 1957.
Lucie-Smith, Edward. *The Art of Caricature.* Ithaca: Cornell Univ. Press, 1982.
Lukacs, Georg. *The Historical Novel.* Intro. Frederic Jameson. Lincoln: University of Nebraska Press, 1983.
———. *The Theory of the Novel.* Cambridge: The MIT Press, 1971.
Lurie, Alison. *The Language of Clothes.* New York: Random House, 1981.
MacAndrew, Elizabeth and Susan Gorsky. "Why Do They Faint and Die—The Birth of the Delicate Heroine." *Journal of Popular Culture* 8 (1974–75), 735–45.
MacIntyre, Alasdair. "Hegel on Faces and Skulls" in *Hegel: A Collection of Critical Essays.* Garden City: Doubleday, 1972.
MacLean, Charles. *The Wolf Children.* New York: Hill & Wang, 1977.
Malouf, David. *An Imaginary Life: A Novel.* New York: George Braziller, 1978.
Malson, Lucien. *Wolf Children and the Problem of Human Nature: With the Complete Text of the Wild Boy of Aveyron by Jean-Marc-Gaspard Itard.* New York: Monthly Review Press, 1972.
Marcus, Steven. *The Other Victorians.* London, 1966.
Marks, Elaine and Isabelle de Courtivron, eds. *New French Feminisms.* New York: Schocken Books, 1981.
Masao, Maruyama. *Studies in the Intellectual History of Tokugawa Japan.* Trans. Mikiso Hane. Princeton: Princeton Univ. Press and Univ. of Tokyo Press, 1974.
May, Herbert G. and Bruce M. Metzger, eds. *The New Oxford Annotated Bible with the Apocrypha.* revised standard ed. New York: Oxford Univ. Press, 1977.

May, Keith M. *Characters of Women in Narrative Literature.* New York: Macmillan, 1981.
Miller, J. Hillis. *Fiction and Repetition: Seven English Novels.* Cambridge: Harvard Univ. Press, 1982.
_____. *The Form of Victorian Fiction.* Notre Dame: Univ. of Notre Dame Press, 1968.
Milton, John. *Complete Poems and Major Prose.* Ed. Merritt Y. Hughes. Indianapolis: Bobbs-Merrill, 1957.
Moers, Ellen. *Literary Women.* New York: Doubleday, 1976.
Murray, Janet Horowitz. *Strong-Minded Women and Other Lost Voices from Nineteenth-Century England.* New York: Pantheon, 1982.
Nystul, Nancy. "*Daniel Deronda:* A Family Romance." *Enclitic* 7 (Spring, 1983), 45–53.
Ovid. *Metamorphoses.* Trans. Rolfe Humphries. Bloomington: Indiana Univ. Press, 1955.
Pearsall, Ronald. *The Worm in the Bud: The World of Victorian Sexuality.* New York: Penguin, 1983.
Pickthall, Mohammed Marmaduke, trans. *The Meaning of the Glorious Koran.* New York: New American Library, n.d.
Pollard, Arthur, ed. *Vanity Fair: A Casebook.* New York: Macmillan, 1978.
Poovey, Mary. *The Proper Lady and the Woman Writer: Ideology as Style in the Works of Mary Wollstonecraft, Mary Shelley, and Jane Austen.* Chicago: Univ. of Chicago Press, 1984.
Praz, Mario. *The Romantic Agony.* Trans. Angus Davidson. 2nd edition. New York: Oxford Univ. Press, 1971.
Preminger, Alex et al., eds. *Princeton Encyclopedia of Poetry and Poetics.* Enlarged Edition. Princeton: Princeton Univ. Press, 1974.
Propp, Vladimir. *Morphology of the Folktale.* Rpt. in *International Journal of American Linguistics,* XXIV, 4 (October 1958). Trans. Laurence Scott.
Quayle, Eric. *The Ruin of Sir Walter Scott.* London: Rupert Hart-Davis, 1968.
Raglan, Lord F. *The Hero: A Study in Tradition, Myth, and Drama.* London: Methuen, 1936.
Reingold, Nathan, ed. *Science in Nineteenth-Century America: A Documentary History.* Chicago: Univ. of Chicago Press, 1964.
Riffaterre, Michael. *The Semiotics of Poetry.* London, 1980.
Rimbault, Edward, ed. *The Miscellaneous Works in Prose and Verse of Sir Thomas Overbury, knt.* London: John Russell Smith, 1856.
Roberts, Helene. "The Exquisite Slave: The Role of Clothes in Making of Victorian Women." *Signs.* Vol. 2 (1977) 554–69.
Rose, Phyllis. *Parallel Lives: Five Victorian Marriages.* New York: Vintage Books, 1984.
Rousseau, Jean-Jacques. *On the Origin of Language.* Intro. Alexander Gode. Chicago: Univ. of Chicago Press, 1966.
Rudofsky, Bernard. *The Unfashionable Human Body.* Garden City: Doubleday, 1971.
Said, Edward. *Beginnings: Intention and Method.* New York: Basic Books, 1975.
Scarry, Elaine. *The Body in Pain: The Making and Unmaking of the World.* New York: Oxford Univ, Press, 1985.
Scholem, Gershom. *The Messianic Idea in Judaism: And Other Essays on Jewish Spirituality.* New York: Schocken, 1971.
Scholes, Robert. *Semiotics and Interpretation.* New Haven: Yale Univ. Press, 1982.
_____, ed. *Approaches to the Novel: Materials for a Poetics.* San Francisco: Chandler, 1961.
Scholes, Robert and Robert Kellogg. *The Nature of Narrative.* New York: Oxford Univ. Press, 1966.
Scott, Sir Walter. *Ivanhoe: A Romance.* New York: New American Library, 1962.
Shah, Idries, ed. *World Tales.* New York: Harcourt Brace Jovanovich, 1979.
Shattuck, Roger. *The Forbidden Experiment: The Story of the Wild Boy of Aveyron.* New York: Washington Square Press, 1981.

Shelley, Mary. *Frankenstein.* New York: Signet, 1965.

Showalter, Elaine. *A Literature of Their Own: British Women Novelists from Brontë to Lessing.* Princeton: Princeton Univ. Press, 1977.

———. *The Female Malady: Women, Madness and English Culture.* New York: Pantheon, 1986.

———, ed. *The New Feminist Criticism: Essays on Women, Literature and Theory.* New York: Pantheon, 1985.

Silverman, Kaja. *The Subject of Semiotics.* New York: Oxford Univ. Press, 1983.

Snitow, Ann et al., eds. *Powers of Desire: The Politics of Sexuality.* New York: Monthly Review Press, 1983.

Sontag, Susan. "Beauty." *Vogue* 1975; rpt. *The Riverside Reader,* Vol. 2, eds., Joseph Trimmer and Maine Hairston. Boston: Houghton Mifflin, 1981.

———. *Illness as Metaphor.* New York: Random House, 1977.

Spacks, Patricia Meyer. *The Adolescent Idea: Myths of Youth and The Adult Imagination.* New York: Basic Books, 1981.

———. *The Female Imagination.* New York: Knopf, 1975.

Spenser, Edmund. *The Faerie Queene.* Books I-III. Ed. J. C. Smith. Oxford: Clarendon Press, 1909.

Spilka, Mark, "On the Enrichment of Poor Monkeys by Myth and Dream; or, How Dickens Rousseauisticized and Pre-Freudianized Victorian Views of Childhood." *TLS* 1984; 27: 161-79.

———, ed. *Towards a Poetics of Fiction.* Bloomington: Indiana Univ. Press, 1977.

Stage, Sarah. *Female Complaints: Lydia Pinkham and the Business of Women's Medicine.* New York: Norton, 1979.

Stang, Richard. *The Theory of the Novel in England, 1850-1870.* New York: Columbia Univ. Press, 1959.

Steiner, Wendy. *The Colors of Rhetoric: Relations between Modern Painting and Literature.* Chicago: Chicago Univ. Press, 1982.

Stern, J. P. *On Realism.* Boston: Routledge Kegan Paul, 1973.

Stern, James, ed. *The Complete Grimm's Fairy Tales.* Trans. Margaret Hunt. New York: Random House, 1972.

Sterne, Laurence. *The Life and Opinions of Tristram Shandy, Gentlemen.* Boston: Houghton Mifflin, 1965.

Stevick, Philip, ed. *The Theory of the Novel.* New York: The Free Press, 1967.

Suleiman, Susan Rubin. *The Female Body in Western Culture.* Cambridge: Harvard Univ. Press, 1985.

Sundell, M. G., ed. *Twentieth Century Interpretations of Vanity Fair.* Englewood Cliffs: Prentice Hall, 1969.

Swinden, Patrick. *George Eliot's Middlemarch: A Casebook.* New York: Macmillan, 1972.

Tanner, Tony. *Adultery in the Novel: Contract and Transgression.* Baltimore: Johns Hopkins Univ. Press, 1979.

Taylor, Barbara. *Eve and the New Jerusalem: Socialism and Feminism in the Nineteenth Century.* New York: Pantheon, 1983.

Thackeray, William Makepeace. *Burlesques,* Vol. XVIII in *The Works of William Makepeace Thackeray.* Cornhill Edition. New York: Scribner's Sons, 1911.

———. *Vanity Fair: A Novel without a Hero.* Eds. Geoffrey and Kathleen Tillotson. Boston: Houghton Mifflin, 1963.

Theophrastus. *The Character Sketches.* Trans. Warren Anderson. Kent State Univ. Press, 1970.

Thomas, Keith. *Man and the Natural World: A History of the Modern Sensibility.* New York: Pantheon, 1983.

Thomson, Patricia. *The Victorian Heroine: A Changing Ideal, 1837-1873.* London: Oxford Univ. Press, 1956.
Todorov, Tzvetan. *The Poetics of Prose.* Trans. Richard Howard. Ithaca: Cornell Univ. Press, 1977.
Trollope, Anthony. *An Autobiography.* 1883; rpt. Intro. Michael Sadleir. New York: Humphrey Milford Oxford Univ. Press, 1924.
———. *The Eustace Diamonds.* Eds. Stephen Gill and John Sutherland. New York: Penguin, 1969.
Uspensky, Boris. *A Poetics of Composition: The Structure of the Artistic Text and Typology of a Compositional Form.* Trans. Valentina Zavarin and Susan Wittag. Berkeley: Univ. of California Press, 1970; rpt. 1973.
Utter, Robert Palfrey and Gwendolyn Bridges Needham. *Pamela's Daughters.* New York: Macmillan, 1936.
Van Ghent, Dorothy. *The English Novel: Form and Function.* New York: Harper and Row, 1953.
Vicinus, Martha, ed. *Suffer and Be Still: Women in the Victorian Age.* Bloomington: Indiana Univ. Press, 1972.
Walcutt, Charles Child. *Man's Changing Mask: Modes and Methods of Characterization in*
Walkowitz, Judith R. *Prostitution and Victorian Society: Women, Class, and the State.* New York: Cambridge Univ. Press, 1980.
Fiction. Minneapolis: Univ. of Minnesota Press, 1966.
Wander, Nathaniel. "Structure, Contradiction and 'Resolution' in Mythology: Father's Brother's Daughter Marriage and the Treatment of Women in Genesis 11-50." *Journal of the Ancient Near East Society.* 13 (1981), 75-99.
Watt, Ian. *The Rise of the Novel: Studies in Defoe, Richardson and Fielding.* London: Chatto & Windus, 1957.
Weinstein, Arnold. *Fictions of the Self: 1550-1800.* Princeton: Princeton Univ. Press, 1981.
Welsh, Alexander. *The Hero of the Waverley Novels.* New Haven: Yale Univ. Press, 1963.
Wilde, Oscar. *The Picture of Dorian Gray.* New York: Random House, 1926.
Williams, Raymond. *The Country and the City.* New York: Oxford Univ. Press, 1973.
———. *The English Novel: From Dickens to Lawrence.* London; Hogarth Press, 1984.
Wilt, Judith. *Secret Leaves: The Novels of Walter Scott.* Chicago: Univ. of Chicago Press, 1985.
Witemeyer, Hugh. *George Eliot and the Visual Arts.* New Haven: Yale Univ. Press, 1979.
Woodring, Carl. "Nature and Art in the Nineteenth Century." *PMLA,* 92 (March 1977), 193-202.
Woolf, Virginia. *Orlando: A Biography.* New York: Penguin, 1946.
Xenophon. *An Ephesian Tale in Three Greek Romances.* Trans. Moses Hadas. Garden City: Doubleday, 1953.
Young, G. M. *Portrait of an Age: Victorian England.* New York: Oxford Univ. Press, 1936.
Zabel, Morton Dauwen. *Craft and Character: Texts, Method and Vocation in Modern Fiction.* New York, 1957.

Index

Abrams, M.H., 27
Adam Bede (Eliot), 160–64, 167–68, 175–86, 213
"Algonquin Cinderella, The," 2–8
Allegorical Interpretation (Philo), 130
Allegory, beauty versus art, 74; cf. caricature, 14; transparency of characters, 20
Allusion, etymology, 108
Animal code (language), 118
Art, separate from beauty, 74
Art and Illusion: A Study in the Psychology of Pictorial Representation (Gombrich), 11, 13, 203
Aspects of the Novel (Forster), 13
Auerbach, Nina, 36
Austen, Jane, 23, 25, 27, 39, 43–57

Bacon, Francis, 10
Baroque Era, 26
Barrenness, redemption from, 68
Barthes, Roland, 17, 18, 208
Beauty, ambiguity in descriptions, 170–75; ambiguity in features, 25; appreciation of, 21; in the beast, 121–27, 138–45, 151, 211–14; and chastity, 128–36; and Christianity, 87, 94–101; character of, 3, 9; in contradictory features, 15; cosmic sanction of, 5; in delicacy, 157–200; descriptions of, 1, 23–24; equated with humanity, 31; equated with virtue, 13; equated with work, 6; faults of beholders, 179–80; as a feature, 8; for *femme fatale*, 36–40; and grace, 115–155; and health, 33; hidden, 105; ideal of, 41; as illusion, 109–13; and innocence, 172; in jewels, 79–86; language of description, 7; as measure of character, 11; as mystery, 117–18; as nature, 25–30, 60, 148; nature versus art codes, 79, 101; passivity, 35; perception of, 18; pet as metaphor, 33; in realist novels, 9; as relation of body and spirit, 21; as reward, 6; self-effacing, 65; separate from art, 74; spiritual versus sexual, 120; symbols of, 107; traditional types, 162–63; value of, 21; and witchcraft, 59
Beauty and the Beast, 138
Beerbohm, Max, 28
Berger, John, 17, 32, 208
Bleak House (Dickens), 10
Bloom, Harold, 109
Body in Pain, The (Scarry), 41
Breeding, 115–55
Brontë, Charlotte, 30, 146–52
Brontë, Emily, 116–27, 138–45, 150–52
Brownstein, Rachel M., 37
Bryson, Norman, 2
Burroughs, Edgar Rice, 119

Caricature, 14, 17
Character, ambiguity in, 141; and beauty, 9, 35, 191; economy of production, 19; settings assessment, 62; sex differences, 13; "slippery quality" of, 8; as trait, 11
Characterization, descriptions as strategy, 1; flat versus round, 17
Charm, feature of beauty, 25, 26, 27, 59–113
Christianity, essential to beauty, 87; versus Hebrew beauty, 111–12
Cinderella myth, 2–8, 43–57, 152
Clarissa (Richardson), 167
Codes of fashion, 59
Codes of flowers, 31, 47–49, 157–200, 208
Code of sailor, 48
Code of spirituality, 177–78
Codification of descriptions, 6, 79, 118
Cohn, Norman, 30
Coleridge, Samuel Taylor, 27, 60, 84, 210
Cominos, Peter T., 40
Cosmetics, 25, 28
Cosmic sanctions of beauty, 5
Cosmos, etymology, 25

Cozens, Alexander, 11
Cultural codes in descriptions, 18
Culture defines beauty, 202

Darwin, Charles, 127, 184
David Deronda (Eliot), 107
Delicacy, beauty in, 25, 34; cf. weakness, 34; defined, 158; as health, 157–200; as strength, 38
Derrida, Jacques, 126
Descriptions, in allegory, 14–15; "beauty defies," 202; in caricature, 14; changes upon redemption, 24; codified, 6; lack of, 69; in realist works, 9; translate values, 1; as vehicles for meaning, 1; weighted language of, 10
Dickens, Charles, 10, 18, 23, 35, 153–55

Education of Emile, The (Rousseau), 126
Eliot, George, 13, 17, 62–67, 101–8, 112, 160–64, 167–68, 169, 175–86, 213
Elizabethan Era, 26
Eustace Diamonds, The (Trollope), 106–8

Facial expression, as standard of beauty, 11
Faerie Queene, The (Spenser), 151
Fair, etymology, 36
Fashion as code, 59
Femme fatale, 19, 36, 39, 76, 110, 181, 194
Femme mourante, 37, 41, 181
Fielding, Henry, 127, 132–36
Figure, etymology, 10
Flower code, 31, 47–49, 113, 118, 157–200
The Forbidden Experiment: The Story of The Wild Boy of Aveyron (Shattuck), 120–27
Forster, E.M., 13, 17, 94
Fowles, John, 215
Frailty as beauty, 38, 40
French Lieutenant's Woman (Fowles), 215
Freud, Sigmund, 73, 127; on jewelry, 107; on illusion, 108

Gaskell, E.C., 23
Gilbert, Sandra M., 105, 146, 151, 152
Gissing, George, 186–93
Gombrich, E.H., 11–14, 25, 215
Gorsky, Susan, 38
Grace, feature of beauty, 25, 115–55
Great Expectations (Dickens), 153–55
Grose, Francis, 11
Gubar, Susan, 105, 146, 151, 152

Hardy, Thomas, 23, 193–200
Hawthorne, Nathaniel, 169–175
Health as beauty, 33, 186–93
Hegel, G.W.F., 27, 109
Henkle, Roger B., 95

Hero as beauty, 147–50
Hidden Hand, The (Southworth), 197

Ideals of beauty, 41; changing over time, 24; reflection of culture, 24
Illness as Metaphor (Sontag), 41
Illusion of beauty, 109–13, etymology, 108
Innocence and beauty, 172
Itard, Jean-Marc-Gaspard, 120–27
Ivanhoe: A Romance (Scott), 66, 79–87, 112

Jameson, Fredric, 192
Jane Eyre (C. Brontë), 23, 30, 146–52
Jewels: in *Ivanhoe*, 79–86; in *Jane Eyre*, 150
Joseph Andrews (Fielding), 127, 132–36
Jude the Obscure (Hardy), 23, 193–200

Language of Clothes, The (Lurie), 66
Language of description, 1, 7, 10; ambiguity in, 170; caricature versus allegory, 14; code of fashion, 59; code of flowers, 31, 47, 48, 49; code of sailor, 48; lack of, 69; as pun, 9, 208; in realist works, 9; uses of, 205
Lawrence, D.H., 193
Leibniz, Gottfried Wilhelm, 21
Les Liaisons Dangereuses (Laclos), 10
Leviathan, The (Hobbes), 29
Lurie, Alison, 39, 66
Lyrical Ballads (Wordsworth), 27

MacAndrew, Elizabeth, 38
Madwoman in the Attic, The (Gilbert and Gubar), 105, 146
McKenzie, Compton, 87
Middlemarch (Eliot), 17, 62–76, 101–9, 186
Milton, John, 74–79, 110
Miner, Earl, 109
Mirror and the Lamp, The (Abrams), 27
Mirrors, 150–51
Moderation as beauty, 65
Modesty, 31, 64
Mother, 107
Mother/harlot dichotomy, 67–79

Nature, as "unitary principle," 28; untamed, 30; versus art, 27–29, 32; versus nurture, 113

Odd Women, The (Gissing), 186–93
Of Grammatology (Derrida), 126
On the Origin of Species (Darwin), 127, 184
Orlando (Woolf), 214–15

Paradise Lost (Milton), 74–79
Parody (*see also* Caricature), 14; characterizations in, 13
Pascal, Blaise, 21

Passivity as beauty, 36–38
Persuasion (Austen), 43
Physiognomy, 177; comments on, 11; defined, 10; in life and in art, 14
Picture of Dorian Gray, The (Wilde), 202, 211–14
Political Unconscious, The (Jameson), 192
Portraiture, in *Middlemarch*, 101; pictorial versus verbal, 14; psychology of, 13
Praz, Mario, 37
Psyche, 34
Pursuit of the Millennium (Cohn), 30
Pygmalian myth, 18, 33–36

Raglan, Lord F., 148
Realism, use of description in, 9
Rebecca and Rowena: A Romance upon Romance (Thackeray), 87–101
Redemption: from barrenness, 68; to Christianity and beauty, 87–101; in *Jane Eyre*, 149; in physical recovery, 52; sexual awakening, 176; underlies change in description, 24
Rhys, Jean, 215
Riffaterre, Michael, 109
Romantic period, 27
Rousseau, Jean-Jacques, 60, 119
Rudofsky, Bernard, 41
Rules for Drawing Caricatures (Grose), 11

S/Z: An Essay (Barthes), 18, 110
Sailor code, 48
Satire, characterizations in, 13
Savagery versus beauty, 30, 119
Scarlet Letter, The (Hawthorne), 169–75
Scarry, Elaine, 41
Scott, Sir Walter, 66, 112
Selflessness as beauty, 65
Sexual Enlightenment of Children, The (Freud), 127
Sexuality, 74; and ambiguity, 214–15; as beauty, 73, 176; versus spirituality, 118–20
Shah, Idries, 2
Shakespeare, William, 29, 59, 118–19, 157, 210

Shattuck, Roger, 121–27
Shaw, George Bernard, 154
Sontag, Susan, 41, 209
Spencer, Herbert, 38
Spenser, Edmund, 110
Stage, Sarah, 39
Sterne, Laurence, 215
Story of Art, The (Gombrich), 13
Study of Thomas Hardy (Lawrence), 193–94

Tarzan of the Apes (Burroughs), 119
Tempest, The (Shakespeare), 119
Thackeray, William Makepeace, 66, 87–101
Thomas, Keith, 31, 32
Tristram Shandy (Sterne), 215
Trollope, Anthony, 106–8

Unfashionable Human Body, The (Rudofsky), 41
Utilitarian Age, 32

Van Ghent, Dorothy, 37
Vanity Fair (Thackeray), 66
Virtue, equated with beauty, 13

Ways of Seeing (Berger), 17, 208
Weakness of character (*see also* Delicacy), 45; idealized, 36
Whore, as metaphor, 64
Wide Sargasso Sea (Rhys), 215
Wilde, Oscar, 201, 211–14, 215
Winter's Tale, The (Shakespeare), 118
Witchcraft, and beauty, 59
Woodring, Carl, 28
Woolf, Virginia, 214–15
Word and Image: French Painting of the Ancien Régime (Bryson), 2
Wordsworth, William, 27, 60, 210
Worth, and beauty, 6
Wuthering Heights (E. Brontë), 116–27, 138, 150–52, 160

Young, G.M., 65